THE EARLY YEARS FOUNDATION STAGE

THEORY AND PRACTICE

THE EARLY YEARS FOUNDATION STAGE

THEORY AND PRACTICE

Edited by

IOANNA PALAIOLOGOU

⑤SAGE

Los Angeles | London | New Delhi
Singapore | Washington DC

First published 2010. Reprinted 2010, 2011

SAGE Publications Ltd
l Oliver's Yard
55 City Road
London EC1Y 1SP

SAGE Publications Inc.
2455 Teller Road
Thousand Oaks, California 91320

SAGE Publications India Pvt Ltd
B1/11 Mohan Cooperative Industrial Area
Mathura Road
New Delhi 110 044

SAGE Publications Asia-Pacific Pte Ltd
33 Pekin Street #02-01
Far East Square
Singapore 048763

Library of Congress Control Number: 2009927111

British Library Cataloguing in Publication data

A catalogue record for this book is available from the British Library

ISBN 978–1–84860–126–0
ISBN 978–1–84860–127–7 (pbk)

Typeset by C&M Digitals (P) Ltd., Chennai, India
Printed in Great Britain by the MPG Books Group
Printed on paper from sustainable resources

Mixed Sources
Product group from well-managed
forests and other controlled sources
www.fsc.org Cert no. SGS-COC-2482
© 1996 Forest Stewardship Council
FSC

CONTENTS

LIST OF FIGURES AND TABLES

Figures

Tables

ACKNOWLEDGEMENTS

This book would have never been completed without the help of the people who gave us permission to use observations of their children or material from their settings. We would like to thank the following people:

Anastasia, David, George and Harry Hollings;
Aspire Trust, Merseyside;
Creative Parterships Hull;
Croxteth Children's Centre, Liverpool;
Jude Bird;
Andrew Shimmin and the staff in McMillan Nursery, Hull;
Melvin King Childminders, Liverpool;
Ruth Spencer Nursery School, Hull.

CONTRIBUTORS

About the Editor

Ioanna Palaiologou

Ioanna Palaiologou is coordinating the Early Years provision at the University of Hull. She is also currently Programme Director for BA (Hons) Education and Early Years, Programme Director for Early Years Professional Studies and Masters in Early Years, and Co-Director for Interprofessional Services Centre for Children, Young People and Families. Prior to this she has worked as Programme Director for Educational Studies at the University of Hull. She is an Executive member of the British Educational Studies Association (BESA), and a member of the British Educational Research Association (BERA) and of Training and Advancement Co-operation in Teaching Young Children (TACTYC). She is also a member of the Editorial Board and reviewer for *Educationalfutures*.

About the Authors

Maura Bangs

Maura Bangs has a BA (Hons) in English and History from London University, and initially worked in business administration, before leaving to spend ten years as a full-time mother. Maura gained her PGCE with the Open University in 1996, and has worked in the same large Primary school in the London Borough of Sutton ever since, teaching across the infant age range. Teaching a Reception class is currently combined with responsibilities as Art & Design and Design & Technology Co-ordinator. She recently took part in the two-year Wallington High School for Girls/Kings' College Engineering Project, researching ways of promoting the uptake of Engineering as an option in Higher Education. In her spare time she has studied City & Guilds textile design, and has written articles for craft magazines on computer-aided design, patchwork and quilting. Maura is married to a Secondary School teacher, and has two grown-up children.

Gary Beauchamp

Gary Beauchamp is a Reader in Education working as Programme Director for Educational Studies at the University of Wales Institute, Cardiff (UWIC). He has also been Programme Director for a primary PGCE course and, prior to working in Higher Education, was a primary school teacher. His research interests currently focus on interactive teaching and ICT (especially the interactive whiteboard), and he has also published articles on science and music in the primary school. He has worked for *Estyn* (Office of Her Majesty's Chief Inspector of Education and Training in Wales) on a full-time secondment and as team inspector.

David Coates

David Coates has taught children between the ages of 5 and 18 in a variety of schools. He has been involved in teacher education and associated research for a number of years, teaching on undergraduate and postgraduate programmes. David's most recent research has focused on the education of gifted and talented pupils and supporting teachers to meet the needs of these pupils.

Ally Dunhill

Ally Dunhill has 15 years' experience in Early Years education and care. A significant part of this career has been spent teaching, and leading and managing Early Years settings. Her experience ranges from teaching 0–4 years in the private sector, 5–18 years in main-stream schools and 16–65 years in further and higher education. She has always had a passion for the principles of Early Years education and is a staunch supporter of play in the outdoor environment, principally for the role it plays in contributing to children's learning, knowledge and skills, self-esteem and motivation. Presently, Ally is course leader for the innovative BA Children's Inter-professional Studies degree at the University of Hull. Her current research interests are learning contexts particular to the outdoor environment.

Elizabeth Dunphy

Liz Dunphy is Lecturer in Early Childhood Education, St Patrick's College of Education, a College of Dublin City University. She worked as a primary school teacher for almost two decades. For the past decade she taught on, and co-ordinated, a number of early childhood courses at both pre-service and in-service levels, and also at postgraduate levels. Liz's research is mainly in the area of early childhood mathematics teaching and learning. Other research interests include children's perspectives, early childhood pedagogy, and the assessment of early learning.

Liz has been closely involved at management level with the Centre for Early Childhood Development and Education (CECDE). This is a Department of Education and Science initiative, jointly managed by St Patrick's College and the Dublin Institute of Technology. The main focus of the Centre to date has been the Development of *Síolta,* the National Quality Framework for Early Childhood Education (CECDE, 2004). She has also worked closely with the National Council for Curriculum and Assessment (NCCA) on a number of projects leading to the development of *The Framework for Early Learning* (NCCA, forthcoming), a framework curriculum to support the learning of all children from birth to 6 years of age.

Alex Hallowes

Alex Hallowes is a practising artist who has worked in schools for over 20 years. Her varied career has included training in mask-making, puppetry and in theatre improvisation, although her original degree is as a silversmith. In 2002 she started working as a visual artist in Early Years settings, funded by Creative Partnerships, and her previous experience in theatre skills has enabled her to respond in an organic and lateral sense to children, informing her specific interests in the power of storytelling. In 2005 she gained her MA in Arts Education and recently she has been involved in a project specifically looking at taking the ethos of the Early Years from a Nursery School setting into Reception and Key Stage 1.

Sally Howard

Sally Howard is currently a Senior Lecturer at Nottingham Trent University and an Independent Educational Consultant, having been a Primary Head Teacher and Ofsted inspector across England in a range of settings. She works closely with Dr Christine Harrison and Professor Paul Black from King's College London on the development of Assessment for Learning strategies. She has also recently co-authored 'Primary Inside the Black Box', which covers AFL from the Early Years to the end of Primary stage in England, Scotland and Wales. She is the author of a booklet on the development of thinking in the Early Years. Prior to becoming a teacher she was an experienced nurse and midwife, which has given her a good understanding of issues relating to education from 'womb to tomb'.

Sue Lyle

Sue Lyle has been a class teacher, teacher adviser and teacher educator for almost a quarter of a century. She is currently Head of Continuing Professional Development at Swansea Metropolitan University's School of Education where she also leads the part-time MA programme for teachers. Her research interests have focused on how children make meaning through talk, in particular the role of imagination and role-play in children's learning and the impact of professional development on teachers. She works closely with LAs to provide professional development for teachers and strongly believes in Action Research as the key tool for promoting critical reflection and change. Most recently she has led a large professional development project to train over 900 teachers in South Wales to introduce Philosophy for Children for the 3-19 age range. Her current research is concerned with investigating the impact of P4C on teacher attitudes towards young children.

Nick Owen

Nick Owen has worked as producer, director and educator in Leeds, London and Liverpool. He was the first Head of Community Arts at the Liverpool Institute of Performing Arts (LIPA) between 1994 and 2002, where he led the BA (Hons) in Community Arts. In 2004 he was awarded a unique scholarship by Creative Partnerships to undertake a three-year PhD research programme at the University of Hull. His thesis examined what constitutes a 'creative' 'partnership', derived from an ethnographic study of a Nursery School and artists and educators working within Creative Partnerships programmes in Hull. He is currently Director of the Aspire Trust, an Arts and Creative Industries Development Agency based in Liverpool and the Wirral. This has been working, since 2002, in the field of creative and innovative support for schools and communities in Merseyside, specialising in the field of Early Years arts and creativity.

David Needham

David Needham travels as a teacher within the education system, and this has taken him to three schools, one FE College and two universities. He currently works at Nottingham Trent University. David has written numerous curriculum-based texts for schools as well as a number of pedagogy-based books for the development of teachers. Although his research has mainly focused upon how children learn in the classroom, in recent years he has analysed the reflexive influences upon professionals within an educational workplace. He has written articles for national and international journals and is the Managing Editor of the *International Journal of Quality and Standards*.

Junnine Thomas-Williams

Junnine Thomas-Williams taught in the Early Years and Key Stage 1 classroom for ten years and completed her MA dissertation on young children's understanding of learning. She currently lectures in the School of Education at Swansea Metropolitan University, where she leads Special Educational Needs. She teaches the Foundation Phase at MA level and teaches SEN to BA and PGCE primary students as well as leading the MA provision. Her current research is to investigate the impact of Philosophy for Children on the behaviour of children in the Foundation Phase in Wales; she is part of the team involved in training teachers to introduce P4C in their schools.

Wendy Thompson

Wendy Thompson is a Programme Director for the Early Years at the University of Hull. She has led the PGCE Early Years (3–7 age phase) for a number of years and has a great deal of experience in preparing students for qualified teacher status (QTS). She is currently developing programmes for (CWDC) Early Years Professional Status training (0–5 age phase) and has a research interest in child development and child pedagogy.

Glenda Walsh

Glenda Walsh, BEd (Hons), PhD and ALCM, is a Principal Lecturer in Early Childhood Education at Stranmillis University College, a college of Queen's University Belfast. Her research interests fall particularly into the field of quality issues and the Early Years curriculum. Over the past nine years she has been involved in the longitudinal evaluation of the Early Years Enriched Curriculum Project that is guiding the course of the Foundation Stage of the revised Northern Ireland Curriculum. She is currently heading a project on examining pedagogy for the Department of Education in the Republic of Ireland. Her doctoral thesis concentrated on the 'play versus formal learning' debate in Northern Ireland and Denmark. The observation instrument, known as the Quality Learning Instrument, she devised for the purposes of her thesis has been used as one of the main assessment instruments in the Early Years Evaluation Project and is currently being developed as a self-evaluative tool for use in Early Years settings.

PREFACE

The Early Years Foundation Stage was implemented in all Early Years settings in England in September 2008. In the past few years there have been a number of changes and improvements in the provision for children from birth to 5. Policies such as *Every Child Matters: Change for Children*; *Choice for Parents, The Best Start for Children: A Ten-Year Strategy for Childcare*, the *Childcare Act* and *The Children's Plan: Building Brighter Futures* have brought a number of significant changes in the Early Years sector in terms of curriculum, workforce and legislation. Similar changes, initiatives and reforms have been introduced in Northern Ireland, Scotland and Wales.

A clear vision of all these documents is an improvement in the quality of children's provision, care and education. There is a demand for a highly qualified, well trained and well educated Early Years workforce. Roles and responsibilities are changing, and new roles and qualifications have been introduced. Much has changed, and it has changed very rapidly, in recent years. At the same time, a vast number of research projects demonstrates the complexity of young children's development and learning, as well as the complexities of the implementation of new policies and pieces of legislation. This suggests very strongly that we will see much more research in future.

More than ever students decide either to study early childhood, to be trained in the early years practitioner profession, or in the new Early Years Professional Status programme, and to seek a career in the field of the early years. Thus this book aims to explore theoretical and practical issues around curriculum implementation linked with the new Early Years Foundation Stage. The book does not aim to be a comprehensive guide to how the new EYFS ought to be implemented. A number of contributing authors share their experiences and views of EYFS, in an attempt to raise issues around its implementation.

As EYFS is new to the early years sector it cannot be claimed that each chapter suggests a way towards effective pedagogy and practice. Instead, what we claim is that each chapter helps students to further their understanding around key issues of EYFS and its implementation in order to reflect on their own pedagogy. The book reasserts throughout that the early years workforce needs to be knowledgeable, with a set of skills to develop pedagogy and the implementation of curricula.

The book discusses issues around EYFS, drawing upon its key elements such as planning, play, assessment, and partnerships with parents and others. A number of authors have been brought together to share their experiences, knowledge, and thoughts about the new Early Years Foundation Stage. The tone of the book reflects the variation of these experiences around key themes to celebrate the long distance that early years has travelled in recent years in terms of research, legislation, policy, pedagogy and practice.

The first chapter discusses the policy context that led to the Early Years Foundation Stage in England, in an attempt to help the reader to understand the principles and key themes of the implementation of EYFS. Chapter 2 looks at Northern Ireland, Scotland, Wales, and the Republic of Ireland to investigate the situation in these other countries. While the chapter presents the facts, it does not claim to offer a strict comparison between these three countries. Individual readers can make comparisons via their own further research and reflections.

Chapter 3 deals with the central questions of existing concerns about effective early years practice. It looks at influential psychological theories, which give us insights into children's development and learning, and tries, by investigating the role of play, to understand the key elements of an effective pedagogy.

Central to EYFS is assessment, and one early years practitioner shares her experiences of assessment within EYFS in Chapter 4. Chapter 5 extends the concept of assessment and offers a practical view of assessment in the early years classroom.

In Chapter 6 the new concept of partnership is discussed, with a focus on how an early years workforce creates partnerships and collaborates with parents to further children's learning.

Chapter 7 deals with the important issues of transition in and out of EYFS. Chapter 8 extends the implementation of EYFS in out-of-classroom or settings-based environments: through a discussion of the learning goals of EYFS, and how they can be met outside the classroom or setting, it aims to help the reader to appreciate the local community and what it has to offer for children's development and learning.

The remaining chapters aim to provide essential knowledge underpinning the effective implementation of EYFS. They aim to explore a number of pedagogical innovations around the six areas of development and learning of EYFS. The purpose of each chapter is to use examples, and each places the implementation of EYFS around the learning goals of the EYFS. These are:

Chapter 9 Personal, Social and Emotional Development
Chapter 10 Communication, Language and Literacy
Chapter 11 Problem Solving, Reasoning and Numeracy
Chapter 12 Knowledge and Understanding of the World
Chapter 13 Physical Development
Chapter 14 Creative Development

It was decided to interfere only minimally with the personal style of each author. As the implementation of EYFS is in its embryonic phase, it was considered very important for the voices of each author to be heard and thus for their own personal perspectives to be reflected. The EYFS is detailed and prescriptive enough for the early years workforce. Thus, in order to develop an understanding of the implementation of EYFS, it is important to hear and absorb how others perceive and experience it.

Ioanna Palaiologou

Part 1
POLICY, PEDAGOGY AND KEY ISSUES IN PRACTICE

CHAPTER 1

POLICY CONTEXT IN ENGLAND AND THE IMPLEMENTATION OF THE EARLY YEARS FOUNDATION STAGE

Ioanna Palaiologou

Chapter Aims

The field of early childhood education and care has been transformed over the past decade. As of September 2008, the Early Years Foundation Stage (EYFS) was implemented for all children aged 0 5 in England. It is recognised 'that a child's experience in the Early Years has a major impact on their future life chances' (DCSF, 2008: *Statutory Framework*, p. 7). It is also now recognised that 'families [of children] will be at the centre', in terms of helping them to meet their responsibilities and support them in their involvement in their children's education and care, emphasising the important role of families within Early Years (DCSF, 2007). The field of Early Years has welcomed these developments as the recognition of the significance of Early Years education and care. At the policy level, the Early Years field is now receiving positive attention and appreciates the government's commitment to Early Years becoming a policy priority, after experiencing many years of either low status care for young children or a lack of coherent policies and legislation.

This chapter aims to help you to develop an understanding of:

- the development in Early Years policy and curriculum

- the main principles and learning goals of EYFS

- issues relating to the children's workforce, how roles and responsibilities have been changed, and what challenges are now faced by the Early Years worker.

Historical developments

Conservative initiatives

The field of Early Years has not always received this degree of attention. The study by Bertman and Pascal (2002) revealed that early childhood Education and Care policies in England were dominated by the short-term priorities of government and local authorities. It has taken many years to reach this level of recognition of the importance of early childhood education and care.

Earlier research had emphasised the key role of the Early Years in children's and their families' lives, yet a successful synergy between policy developments and research findings was not then established: it was in the 1990s that the situation began to change. The introduction of Early Childhood studies or Early Childhood education degrees as university subjects in their own right led to the qualification of graduates outside traditional teacher training. Students on these courses found themselves studying a number of child-related subjects, such as psychology, the history of childhood, sociology and pedagogy, while their career intentions remained unclear. At the same time there was a boost in academic research within the field of Early Years. A number of academics started looking at the Early Years provision and services of other countries (Hennessy et al., 1992; David, 1993; Goldschmied and Jackson, 1994; Smith and Vernon, 1994; Pugh, 1996; Penn, 1997; Anning, 2009). This was in addition to looking at the international context of the United Nations Convention on the Rights of the Child (1989) (Nutbrown, 1999), and comparing Early Years education and care in England with those of other European countries. There was an attempt to compare systems and services (Penn, 1997, 2000; Moss, 2000, 2001; Moss and Pence, 2004) then to reflect on the current practices in this country.

There was also a vast quantity of research on the impact of Early Years education and care on children's development and learning (Moyles, 1989, 2007; Athey, 1990; Alexander et al., 1992; Nutbrown, 1999; Moyles et al., 2001; Sylva et al., 2001; Devereux and Miller, 2003; Penn, 2008). All of these findings strongly argued in favour of improvement in the Early Years sector, raising the need for further policy and curriculum development.

Changes in the field of Early Years education and care began as a way to reduce levels of poverty, and to help children to have better prospects in life. The impact of the research by Mortimore et al. (1998) showed that the quality of teaching and management of schools play a central role in children's quality of learning; it was not, as then thought, the socio-economic and educational background of children that brought about changes. The Conservative government took on board the findings of this research and introduced the notion of Effective Schools and School Improvement. A number of developments followed within the school context, including curriculum changes, as well as alterations regarding inspections. However, these changes were not implemented in the Early Years.

It was the attempt to analyse poverty and deprivation that motivated the Conservative government to turn its attention to early childhood care and education. In the early 1990s the Conservative government aimed to provide a better start in life for deprived children, using education as a tool. Pre-school education was seen as a key aspect of helping children to break the 'cycle of deprivation' (Baldock et al., 2009). This resulted in the introduction of practical measures, such as the Children Act 1989, to improve quality in Early Years education and care. However, this attempt was not translated into a long-term 'coherent policy except in so far as practitioners and local politicians made something of any opportunities they offered' (Baldock et al., 2009: 20).

Cohen et al. (2004), in their studies of early childhood care and the educational systems of national governments in three countries – England, Scotland and Sweden – and on the types of children's services found there, summarised the key features of the post-1997 period regarding children's services as: 'Split departmental responsibility between welfare (DoH), responsible for day-care/childcare services, and education (DfEE) responsible for nursery and compulsory schooling' (Cohen et al., 2004: 55) This dichotomy of responsibilities between childcare services and formal schooling had an impact on funding, the structuring of provisions, and, of course, upon different levels of the workforce. As a result this led to a 'fragmented body of services ... low levels of publicly funded childcare and early education ... a growing marketisation of all services ... and an increasing role for central ... controlling government' (Cohen ct al., 2004: 55–6).

Labour initiatives

In 1997, and after nearly 20 years of Conservative government, there was a change in political power. The Labour government brought radical changes in the field of Early Years education and care. It was high on the Labour government's agenda to minimise poverty and increase quality in early childhood education and care by modernising the services. Tony Blair (1998) demonstrated the commitment of the new government to raising quality in the Early Years by investing money in the sector, as well as in research. There was an attempt to keep governmental control over children's services and provision with the introduction of targets, measurements and inspections, with localised responsibilities of decision making, planning and delivering government targets.

As soon as the Labour government commenced its administration, childcare provision became the responsibility of the (then) Department for Education and Employment (since 2007 the Department for Children, Schools and Families; the DfEE introduced the first Childcare Unit in 1998).

The government's commitment to improving Early Years provision was shown immediately by the launch of the Excellence in Schools programme (DfEE, 1997). In this White Paper the targets within early childhood education for the year 2002 were set out. There was an emphasis on improving quality in Early Years for all children from the age of 4, to meet the local needs of childcare and education, and to improve good practice in Early Years. It was evident that the government attempted the decentralisation of children's services by delegating the concomitant responsibilities and implementation to local authorities. However, it was clear that the government was to remain in control by setting targets with specific measurements, and the focal point for measurement was the assessment of all children.

Although the Labour government wanted overall control of children's services, the decentralisation of childcare and education began with the requirement of all local authorities to set up an Early Years Development and Childcare Partnership (EYDCP) (DfES, 2001). The aim of EYDCP was to operate independently of local authorities to expand childcare provision. This service was later replaced by Children's Trusts in 2004. The National Childcare Strategy (DfEE, 1998) stated clearly that childcare would become a top priority for the government in the policy context.

Sure Start: A new start

The commitment to 'lift families out of poverty' and improve educational outcomes for all children was translated into an ambitious and well-funded intervention programme, Sure Start, which commenced in 1998. Sure Start was designed to be a 10-year programme for children under 4 and for families living in deprived and disadvantaged conditions. Norman Glass (1999), influenced by the Head Start intervention programme in the USA, founded Sure Start as an intervention programme to help tackle poverty and offer a good start in life to disadvantaged and deprived children.

The Labour government invested a flow of money to improve services for children, alongside investing money for research and for the evaluation of its projects. This can be seen as a positive attempt to bring synergy between research and policy developments. It occurred at a time when there was an urgent need for the government not only to improve practice but also to investigate in depth, through research findings, the effectiveness of its initiatives and policies.

The impact of research

The most influential study has been the Effective Provision of Pre-School Education (EPPE) Project (Sylva et al., 2001). This government-funded research programme, which lasted for nearly seven years (1997–2003), was further extended until 2008 and followed these children into secondary school, looking at what effect the Early Years education and care had on young children's lives. The project had some interesting findings in terms of the quality of training of people in the Early Years sector, as it was clear from the results that adult and child interactions had a decisive impact on children's development and learning. Also, there was an emphasis on creating relationships with parents and the key role that parent involvement can play within the Early Years.

It was encouraging that it seemed, at the time, that the government was taking into account research findings in the context of policy. Research continued to raise issues about the quality of provision and training in early childhood education and care.

Alongside the EPPE project, research by Anning and Edwards (2006) into what constitutes quality in preschool education offered important evidence regarding the quality of experiences for young children before they start school. They added to the EPPE project and emphasised the effectiveness of Early Years provision. They found that to raise quality in Early Years required a partnership between parents and staff in educational settings. They also proposed an expansion of services for young children to meet the changing needs and lifestyles of modern families and employers. One of the key findings in their research was that preschool children's experiences are determined by the commitment demonstrated by Early Years staff. These, in turn, determine the quality of the relationships and interactions with children and parents. The research by Anning and Edwards further showed that children attending preschool education benefited in many ways, most importantly in their cognitive, social, and emotional development, and were thus better prepared for the demands of formal schooling. However, they also argued that their findings demonstrated that poor quality of day care could result in high levels of aggression and poorer social skills when children come to enter formal schooling. Finally, and equally importantly, they found that children from less privileged backgrounds achieve better results during formal schooling if the Early Years preschool education they have experienced is of a high standard and is delivered by well-trained day carers.

Key findings to both research projects and additional independent research strongly suggested that to improve quality in Early Years education and care, a careful consideration of policy, funding, structuring, staffing and delivering services for young children – and the inclusion of parents – were integral.

In the reforms that followed, these findings appeared to have been embraced to a certain degree by new government policy, and there was a commitment to translating this into practice.

From Sure Start to Children's Centres

In their first term of office the Labour government demonstrated a positive attitude towards improving quality in Early Years. However, the policy and implementation in this first term of power was characterised by haste. For example, the government, despite funding the EPPE project, did not wait for the full report of the Sure Start evaluation, and moved into creating Children's Centres, leaving Sure Start staff uncertain of what was to follow and the new roles and responsibilities that would subsequently emerge. To some extent this haste continued in their second term, after 2001. It appeared that the government was determined to implement changes. This was translated into the creation of policies, and in changes to services and structures for children and young people. A number of reforms followed with important changes in policy, and sometimes these changes were deemed to be too hasty. Local authorities felt they were unable to apply these in practice, as it left professionals with an uncertainty as to how best to proceed. Decentralisation and division of responsibilities continued in the second term of the Labour government.

Local authorities were given the responsibility to develop the Children and Young People's Plan by 2006, establish the Children's Trust, and appoint Directors of Children's Services. They were also responsible for the unification of inspection systems across all children's services. A ten year strategy for childcare (DfES, 2004b) was developed which aimed to provide out-of-school childcare for all children aged between 3 and 14 years. Sure Start Local Programmes were transferred into Children's Centres in 2006, and new changes in professional training and qualifications were introduced. This period can be characterised as a time when Early Years professionals and practitioners, as well as local authorities, were trying to incorporate these restructuring and reshaping issues within the children's services.

Integrated services and The Children's Plan: Building Brighter Futures

Central to all these changes to improve quality of life for children and families, and to promote a welfare concept, was the creation of the 'joined up' thinking of the integration of services. In a commitment to modernise public services, the government aimed to restructure and reshape services so that they would become flexible, immediate and proactive in their responses, and would meet local needs.

At a time when the government was advocating these changes and supporting the ways in which the new integrating services would improve the life of children, a young girl – Victoria Climbié – was killed. This was a shocking case as the child had been abused over a period of time; it seemed that all children's services had an awareness that this was happening, but they failed to communicate information effectively, and none of the services wanted to take the necessary responsibility to act. The inquiry that followed (the Laming Inquiry) revealed problems regarding the structure and management of these services.

The government then appeared to act decisively. More radical policies needed to be implemented; there was no time for delay as children's wellbeing might be at risk. The Laming Inquiry led to new Green Papers. The principles of joined-up thinking and working in a multi-agency, multi-professional and multi-departmental mentality were reflected by two Green Papers: *Every Child Matters* (DfES, 2003) and *Every Child Matters: Change for Children* (DfES, 2004a). These led to the Children Act of 2004.

Children's services now had to respond to five outcomes for all children from birth to 18: being healthy, being protected from harm and neglect, being enabled to enjoy and achieve, making a positive contribution to society, and contributing to economic well-being (DfES, 2004a). Central to the ECM agenda is the protection of children's well-being.

Every Child Matters was followed by *Choice for Parents, The Best Start for Children: A Ten Year Strategy for Childcare* (DfES, 2004b) and the Childcare Act of 2006 identified the need for high-quality, well-trained and educated professionals to work with the youngest child groups.

In December 2007 *The Children's Plan: Building Brighter Futures* (DCSF, 2007) was published. The document emerged in response to the urgent need of the government to demonstrate that they planned for children and families, and that their plans were long term in order to produce effective outcomes. The Children's Plan strategy suggested that it 'strengthen support for all children and for all families during the formative Early Years' (DCSF, 2007). The government's vision to create world class schools, an excellent education for every child, to create partnerships with parents, help young people to enhance their interests, find interesting activities outside the school, and the creation of safe areas for children to play were all incorporated.

There was a clear emphasis on the role of integrated services as facilitators for families and children's needs, and it is suggested that 'traditional institutional and professional structures' would be challenged and reshaped to accommodate these needs. One of the first targets was the creation of new leadership roles for the Children's Trust in every area; in new roles for schools as part of communities, and effective links between schools, the NHS and other children's services, to achieve the engagement of parents in order to tackle problems with children's learning, and the health and happiness of every child. Such a method of services working together is viewed as the beginning of integration, not only to meet government targets, but also to demonstrate to the world how England is meeting the United Nations Children's Rights Convention (see Annex B, DCSF, 2007: 159–61).

The Children's Plan is a principled approach to children's services. There are five key principles:

- supporting parents to bring up their children
- all children to have the potential to achieve and succeed in life if they are given the right opportunities
- children and young people need to enjoy their childhood whilst at the same time becoming prepared for adult life
- services need to be shared and responsive to children
- professional boundaries have to become flexible and adopt a proactive and preventative role. (DCSF, 2007).

Within this document the new targets for 'lifting children and families from poverty' were announced: 'Poverty blights children's lives, which is why we have committed to halve child poverty by 2010 and eradicate it by 2020' (DCSF, 2007). The new joint Department for Children, Schools and Families, and the Department for Work and Pensions Child Poverty Unit will coordinate work across government to break the cycle of poverty from generation to generation.

The government also went ahead with the commitment to children's safety by introducing the Staying Safe Action Plan, 2008, and the Staying Safe consultation. As part of this plan the government intended to continue the flow of money to improve services for children. The government announced that £225m – with a potential increase to £235m – would be invested in creating playgrounds nationally, and make accessible play areas for children with disabilities. In July 2008 a national Play Strategy was published: 'Fair Play'. It stated that research findings had been taken on board, as well as consultation with parents, play experts and children, for transforming the quality of children's play.

Curriculum context in England

These wide changes to policy had an impact in terms of quality in provision, and were reflected in the shape of alterations to the curriculum. In September 2000 the Qualifications and Curriculum Authority (QCA) introduced the Foundation Phase, which aimed to become the 'recognised stage of education relating to children from 3 years old to the end of reception year in primary school'. The 'desirable outcomes' introduced by the Conservative government in the 1990s were replaced with the early learning goals, and all providers of Early Years education followed the Curriculum Guidance for the Foundation Phase (QCA/DfEE, 2000). In 2002, in an attempt to include provision for children under the age of 3, the *Birth to Three Matters* paper was published by the DfES (Sure Start Unit, 2002). However, concerns were raised as to how Birth to Three Matters connected with the Foundation Phase and the transition to the National Curriculum. Young children attending informal (Birth to Three Matters) and formal (Foundation Phase) education were progressing to formal schooling at the age of 6 and were working under the National Curriculum. This presented transitional problems, as well as problems in the continuity of assessment.

The continuity desired appeared not to be implemented. Moreover, in 2003 there was the publication of the National Standards for Under Eights Day Care and Childminding. This set out requirements for all children attending sessional childcare, and formed part of the Ofsted inspection.

As mentioned earlier, Every Child Matters was implemented as a law, and consequently all children's services and settings – including Early Years settings – had to demonstrate that they met the five outcomes of the ECM agenda. In Birth to Three Matters, as well as in the Foundation Phase, it was not clear how the Early Years workforce could meet the ECM outcomes. Moreover, as previously mentioned, the Children's Plan was setting new targets and principles for children's services.

At a time when practitioners, Early Years teachers and professionals in Early Years were trying to adapt to these changes and translate policy into practice, the government moved into introducing the Early Years Foundation Stage in 2007, to be implemented in all Early Years settings from September 2008. The statutory document aimed to ensure a 'coherent and flexible approach to care and learning so that whatever setting parents choose, they can be confident that they will receive a quality experience that supports their development and learning' (DfES, 2007: 7).

The implementation of the Early Years Foundation Stage

The Early Years Foundation Stage (EYFS) was introduced by the government to bring together and replace the existing documents *Every Child Matters, Curriculum Guidance for the Foundation Stage* and the *Full Day Care National Standards for Under 8s Day Care and Child Minders.* It is a cohesive framework for Early Years with a statutory nature. This means that from September 2008 the implementation of EYFS was a legal requirement for all government-funded Early Years settings for children from birth to 5 years old.

The EYFS (DCSF, 2008) comprises the *Statutory Framework for the Early Years Foundation Stage*, which explains the purposes and aims of EYFS, the learning requirements and assessment processes, and *Practice Guidance for the Early Years Foundation Stage,* which describes in detail how EYFS is implemented. There are also supportive resources for providers and Early Years practitioners in the form of CD-ROMs, posters and 'Principles into Practice' Cards.

The central aim of EYFS is to help all in the Early Years sector to meet the outcomes of the Every Child Matters imperative, i.e., for children to be healthy, stay safe, to enjoy and achieve, to make a positive contribution, and to achieve economic wellbeing (DCSF, 2008). Five key procedures are central in achieving these aims. Firstly, EYFS aims to set the standards for children's learning and development, and these standards are to be met by all children. Secondly, it shows a commitment to cultural diversity and anti-discriminatory practice, and thirdly, it places emphasis on bridging the gap between parents and childhood settings. Commitment to such integration is a step towards creating a framework for the 'working together' practice, and parents constitute its focus.

Fourthly, it is stated clearly that there would not be a distinction between 'care' and 'education' in the Early Years, and the Early Years sector would work towards improving quality and consistency with a universal set of standards (DCSF, 2008). As discussed earlier, childcare and education were separated under the respective responsibilities of two different departments, i.e., childcare under the Department for Health, and also under the Department for Education and Employment. Although in early 1998 departmental responsibility for childcare was transferred to Education, the distinction between childcare and education was evident across the Early Years sector. A variation of childcare and Early Years education, as well as Early Years workforce training and qualifications, failed to bridge the gap between childcare and Early Years education. EYFS set an ambitious and positive standard as it now eliminated at policy level the division between childcare and education. It is recognised as an important aspect of providing quality in Early Years that care and education are synonymous, to reflect more accurately the distinct nature of provisions in the Early Years for young children's care and learning. In the Early Years these two should happen together and be indivisible (DCSF, 2008), but in practice it might take a while to change the attitudes towards these two concepts, as variations in training, standards and wages are still obstacles to be overcome.

Finally, the fifth important procedure within EYFS is the observation and assessment of children. Through ongoing observation and assessment the Early Years workforce is asked to plan children's learning and development, in order that individual needs and interests will be met. Based on observations and assessments, the Early Years workforce will provide a diverse range of play-based activities designed to support children's development.

The principles of EYFS

Similarly to the Children's Plan (published in 2007), EYFS is a principled approach to young children's care and education. There are four key principles that illustrate the commitment to the government's emphasis on integration and parental involvement:

- **A Unique Child** recognises that every child is a competent learner from birth who can be resilient, capable, confident and self-assured. The commitments are focused around development, inclusion, safety, health and wellbeing.
- **Positive Relationships** describes how children learn to be strong and independent from a base of loving and secure relationships with parents and/or a key person. The commitments are focused around respect, partnership with parents, supporting learning and the role of the key person.
- **Enabling Environments** explains that the environment plays a key role in supporting and extending children's development and learning. The commitments are focused around observation, assessment and planning, support for every child, the learning environment, and the wider context, i.e., transitions, continuity, and multi-agency working.
- **Learning and Development** recognises that children develop and learn in different ways and at different rates, and that all areas of learning and development are equally important and are inter-connected. (DCSF, 2008: *Statutory Framework*, p. 9)

These principles reflect the commitment of the government to viewing Early Years education as an important part of the community; it recognises the individuality of each child and the diversity of Early Years learning, and the importance of partnerships with parents and other services for better Early Years provision.

First came the early learning goals, which are developmentally driven: personal, social and emotional development; communication, language and literacy; problem solving, reasoning and numeracy; knowledge and understanding of the world; physical development; and creative development. All of these goals need to be covered across the Early Years sector and become part of the overall educational programme, the second element for an effective implementation of EYFS. To support the Early Years workforce in meeting these six areas, EYFS provides a number of guidelines concerning how an educational programme needs to be created, in the *Practice Guidance for the Early Years Foundation Stage* (DCSF, 2008). This document provides detailed examples of what constitutes effective practice, with suggested activities according to the developmental age and abilities of each child.

The role of assessment in EYFS

Of great importance within EYFS are the assessment processes. Considerable emphasis is placed upon the ongoing assessment of children, and this is viewed as an integral part of the learning and development process. Providers must ensure that practitioners are observing children and responding appropriately to help them to make progress from birth towards the early learning goals. It is expected that all adults who interact with the child should contribute to that process, thus information provided from parents would be taken into account. An essential feature in EYFS in terms of parental involvement is an ongoing dialogue, based on observations and the assessment of children. The ongoing dialogue takes the form of a formal, formative assessment, used as evidence to identify learning priorities for children, and to plan relevant and motivating learning experiences for each child. It is also required that for each child an EYFS profile is completed. Formulating a profile is a way of summing up each child's development and learning achievements at the end of the Early Years Foundation Stage; there are 13 assessment scales derived from the Early Years learning goals, and an e-portfolio to be completed for each child.

The important role played by observation and assessment in the Early Years in improving practice constantly and in monitoring children's progress cannot be overestimated. However, a concern exists that the EYFS assessment scales will overtake practice, and the Early Years workforce may feel the need to tick boxes rather than to create the innovative practice so important for the Early Years.

Inspection in EYFS

EYFS providers will be inspected by Ofsted. All settings are now required to register with Ofsted, in respect of all provisions for children from birth to 5. August 2008 saw the publication of *Early Years Leading to Excellence*, a two-part report on how providers should promote the Every Child Matters outcomes for children. Part One reviews childcare and Early Years provision at the end of the three-year cycle of inspections. Part Two describes how providers organise, lead and manage their settings in partnerships, and sets the standards of how providers should develop and improve the quality of their work with children (www.ofsted.gov.uk/ofsted-home/Leading-to-excellence/).

Although EYFS is a detailed and descriptive practical guide to play-based activities for young children, it is clear that the government does not want it to be seen as part of the National Curriculum (DCSF, 2007). This creates a contradiction between policy and practice; perhaps in name EYFS is not a curriculum, yet in practice it is a detailed description of what should be done in each Early Years setting. Moreover, there is also an emphasis on meeting standards and goals. Ofsted, the same body that inspects schools, is responsible for its implementation.

The role of local authorities

Crucial to the implementation of EYFS are the role and responsibilities of the local authorities. As was demonstrated earlier, there is a clear attempt by the government to delegate the responsibilities of the implementation of Early Years provision to local authorities. However, the government maintains overall control, with the inspection reports serving as a measurement tool for effective practice. The local authorities have responsibilities for assessment, training, staff support, and collecting the documentation from all Early Years providers; they are also required to play a key role in meeting the needs of EYFS, as well as the individual needs of each child, in a proactive and protective way, so that cases such as that of Victoria Climbié can be prevented in the future. Although all these policies were introduced to protect children the most recent events such as the Baby P and the Doncaster Children cases have shown that there is still an inability to protect children at risk. Among their main duties is to visit the settings regularly in order to make sure that each provider is completing an effective Early Years self-evaluation form to ensure that local needs are met (Ofsted, 2008).

To summarise, from a period where the Early Years sector was left with no coherent policy, practices or legislation, and there were boundaries between childcare and education, the situation has now moved to the implementation of EYFS, which is focusing on children's development, with clear age ranges, stages and goals 'in an attempt to make clear that there are no clear boundaries, and to value the unique progress made by every child' (Devereux and Miller, 2003: 2).

As EYFS is still in its embryonic phase, questions arise regarding its effective implementation, i.e., meeting the learning goals and the Every Child Matters outcomes, meeting local needs, and the diversity of training among the Early Years workforce. The development of a common understanding of EYFS is to be investigated.

Early Years workforce in England

Dealing with the volume of change, the Early Years workforce has faced a new and challenging period. Recent years have seen changes at policy level as well as at a practical level. In the field of Early Years there is at last recognition of its importance, and there are also regulations that attempt to unify standards and improve quality across the sector. As was shown above, the Early Years services have changed radically; the changes are mirrored in the Early Years workforce and the emerging new roles and responsibilities within the sector. Traditionally, teachers were the main workers in a class. However, there are currently a great number of other professionals alongside teachers, for example, teachers' assistants, practitioners, support staff (with a whole range of different titles), volunteers, students, parents, caretakers, and learning support assistants (National Statistics, 2007). A variety of children's services now exist, such as Children's Centres, Sure Start Children's Trusts, Extended Schools, neighbourhood nurseries, and playgroups implemented from September 2008 by the Early Years Foundation Stage .

The implementation of the Every Child Matters outcomes, alongside the requirement for integration of services and the implementation of EYFS, led the government to introduce, in 2005, a new strategic organisation: the Children's Workforce Development Council (CWDC). Its function was to prepare staff for the delivery of large sections of the government's national children's workforce strategy Action Plan (CWDC, 2007). The CWDC has published the Common Core Skills and Standards that need to be met by all in the Early Years workforce. However, teachers, health visitors and social workers remain excluded from CWDC, whose aim is to reform a 'new workforce' in order to meet the joined-up working philosophy.

A new concept was introduced by the CWDC and has now been implemented across England: Early Years Professional Status. The professional is trained in the CWDC standards to work across the Early Years sector in care, learning and in health. By 2010 the government wants an EYP in all Sure Start Children's Centres, and by 2015 in every Foundation Stage setting. The CWDC has announced the government's vision to have a graduate-led Early Years workforce for the delivery of a high quality Early Years Foundation Stage, in order to improve outcomes for all children. It states: 'If all children are to benefit from a high quality Early Years Foundation Stage, the Early Years workforce must be professional, well qualified and dedicated' (CWDC, 2007). To improve outcomes for children the government is committed to raising the proportion of the Early Years workforce with relevant and appropriate qualifications, in order to work with babies, toddlers and young children in any setting (such as full day care, sessional day care, crèches, out of school care and childminding where EYFS is implemented).

Children Workforce Network's vision is of a workforce that:

- supports integrated and coherent services for children, young people and families
- remains stable and appropriately staffed, whilst exhibiting flexibility and responsiveness
- is trusted and accountable, and is thereby valued
- demonstrates high levels of skills, productivity and effectiveness
- exhibits strong leadership, management and supervision.
  (www.cwdcouncil.org.uk/early-years)

Services for young children were restructured and reshaped, and new roles and responsibilities have emerged to meet the integration of these services. In terms of management, these strategic changes needed to be implemented and be able to demonstrate, through measurement, their effectiveness. Once again, research argued for further training (Aubrey, 2007) as there was a complexity in managing these changes. Important structural changes in services for young children were put in place. The government responded by introducing a new qualification at graduate level for all managers of children's centres: the National Professional Qualification in Integrated Centre Leadership (NPQICL), managed by the National College of School Leadership (www.ncsl.org.uk).

The Children's Plan (DCSF, 2007) clearly states: 'the children's workforce comprises everyone who works with young children, young people and their families. This includes people working in settings like schools, Sure Start children's centres and youth clubs, as well as people working in health services, in social care and youth justice' (2007: 151). It is evident that the Early Years workforce includes a number of professionals and practitioners with different training or education – and who certainly do not enjoy the same scale of pay. Those such as teachers, health visitors, social workers and EYPs are qualified by an official provider, while other practitioners are also qualified and trained, but are not members of such long-established regulatory bodies (Anning and Ball, 2008).

These recent developments have brought challenges for the Early Years workforce. The introduction of new qualifications and levels of status were not always welcomed. Bloom (2006), in an article in *The Times Higher Educational Supplement*, expressed fears that 'the new qualification [Early Years Professional Status] may squeeze teachers out of nursery schools'. There is hesitation in the acceptance of the newly skilled Early Years workforce, as the introduction of new qualifications and levels of status have led to the creation of a number of professionals and practitioners working alongside non-professionals, such as volunteers. Variations in training and standards exist, despite the introduction of common core skills and knowledge goals. Different professionals work at different standards and competencies, as well as earning different salaries. These factors combine to produce a lack of clarity within their roles, a situation that might jeopardise the effective implementation of the 'joined up' philosophy that the government wishes to have implemented across all children's services.

This raises issues around the strategic vision of high quality and high excellence in the Early Years sector. However, on a positive note, the government's emphasis on developing skills among the Early Years workforce has raised the profile of those individuals working in the sector, bringing them recognition as valued and important workers. Issues around different roles, responsibilities and divisions are yet to be fully resolved, and it is believed that in the years to come further changes in the Early Years workforce are to be expected.

Key points to remember

- The field of Early Years has experienced radical changes since the Labour government came to power in 1997. The most important policies are Every Child Matters, the Children's Plan and the Early Years Foundation Stage.
- Key to all government policies is the integration of services, the development of a skilful Early Years workforce, parental involvement, and excellence in provision.
- All the Early Years settings were required to implement the Early Years Foundation Stage from September 2008.
- The Early Years workforce is changing since new roles and responsibilities – as well as new standards – have been introduced by the Children's Workforce Development Council.

 ### Points for discussion

- Try to list in chronological order all the policy changes in the past 20 years. Can you identify any similarities and differences among them?
- How do you think the changes in the policy and curriculum context will affect your practice?
- Try to identify the key roles and responsibilities of Early Years professionals.

Further reading

Baldock, P., Fitzgerald, D. and Kay, J. (2009) *Understanding Early Years Policy,* 2nd edn. London: Paul Chapman Publishing.

Clark, M. and Waller, T. (2007) *Early Childhood Education and Care: Policy and Practice.* London: Sage.

Cohen, B., Moss, P., Petrie, P. and Wallace, J. (2004) *A New Deal for Children? Re-forming Education and Care in England, Scotland and Sweden.* Bristol: The Policy Press.

Useful websites

The Early Years Foundation Stage Standards
www.standards.dfes.gov.uk/eyfs

There is a link that allows you to download as pdfs the booklets for the Statutory Framework and the Practice Guidance and also further resources, including the Principles into Practice Cards.

Every Child Matters:
www.everychildmatters.gov.uk/

Government policies:
www.dcsf.gov.uk/index.htm

Development in the skills and workforce of Early Years:
www.cwdcouncil.org.uk/early-years

CHAPTER 2

THE NATIONAL PICTURE

Ioanna Palaiologou, Glenda Walsh, Elizabeth Dunphy, Sue Lyle and Junnine Thomas-Williams

Chapter Aims

This chapter examines the Early Years provision in Northern Ireland, Scotland, Wales and the Republic of Ireland in an attempt to investigate the Early Years developments in these neighbouring countries.

This chapter aims to help:

- develop an understanding of the implementation of different curricula
- develop an understanding of the role of policy in curricula implementation
- make comparisons via your own reflections.

Early Years in Northern Ireland

Ioanna Palaiologou and Glenda Walsh

Historical perspective

Northern Ireland's history has for many years been dominated by uncertainty due to conflict and violence. In 1998, and after long political negotiations, the Belfast Agreement aimed to halt violence and conflict and to give Northern Ireland its own devolved government in an optimistic attempt to establish peace. This agreement was, for Northern Ireland, the path towards a peaceful society that will lead to economic development, cultural respect and the inclusion of all people, regardless of their ethnicity, religious or political differences (Walsh, 2007), overall a better society for children's growth and development.

A number of initiatives followed the 1998 Belfast Agreement, demonstrating an emphasis on increasing the quantity and improving the quality of provision for young children across Northern Ireland. Towards that aim the publication of two reports – *Investing in Early Learning* (Department of Education Northern Ireland (DENI) and Department for Health, Social Services and Public Safety (DHSS PS), 1998) and *Children First* (DENI, Training and Employment Agency (TEA) and DHSS, 1999) – led to the Preschool Expansion Programme (PEEP) and the Northern Ireland Childcare Strategy. The main aim of *Investing in Early Learning* (DENI and DHSS, 1998) was to provide one year of preschool education for all children whose parents wanted it; while the underpinning objective of the Northern Ireland Childcare Strategy was 'to integrate early education and care within a wider supportive framework of services for children and parents' (DENI, TEA and DHSS, 1999: 10). Prior to 1998 only the statutory sector, through nursery schools, nursery classes or reception classes, provided funded preschool places. The voluntary or private sector had previously been funded principally through parental fees, with some financial support from the Department of Health and Social Services (DHSS). The new Childcare Strategy involved government funding for settings in both sectors.

With the subsequent publication of a Ten Year Strategy for Children and Young People entitled *Our Children and Young People – Our Pledge* (OFMDFM, 2006) and the establishment of the Children's Commission Office, it could be argued that steps are being made towards the development of a more coherent Early Years policy and the establishment of a society where young children are more highly valued and their health and well-being more widely recognised.

Curricular guidance for preschool education

Earlier, in 1997, the Curricular Guidance for Preschool Education (DHSS, CCEA and DENI, 1997) had been issued by Northern Ireland's Council for the Curriculum,

Examination and Assessment (CCEA), representing a shared view of what constitutes good quality preschool provision in the education and care sectors in Northern Ireland (DENI, TEA and DHSS, 1999). All preschool settings from both the statutory and voluntary sectors, funded by the government, were required to follow this guidance. Non-funded settings were not, which fact may, to some extent, limit the intended coherence in good practice throughout the preschool sector as a whole.

This guidance aimed to help meet children's needs: physical, social, emotional and cognitive. It claimed to provide a child-centred approach, with greater emphasis on play and children's opportunities for exploration and less on what children have achieved.

The revised curricular guidance for preschool education

A revised version of the Curricular Guidance for Preschool Education was issued in 2006 (DHSS PS, CCEA and DENI, 2006), in the light of changes taking place in the primary sector, regarding the Foundation Stage for 4–6-year-old children. As is the traditional preschool guidance, this revised version is firmly embedded in a child-centred and play-based approach. It recognises that children develop in different ways, but that 'all children should have the opportunity to follow a curriculum that enables them to make appropriate progress in learning and to achieve in their full potential' (p. 3). In contrast to the Early Years Foundation Stage (DCSF, 2008), it is less prescriptive and takes the form of guidelines. The guidance develops around children's needs such as safety, opportunities for investigation, exploration, play-based activities, and the role of adults in children's well-being.

There are six themes suggested as 'discrete headings ... children should experience in a holistic way through play and other relevant experiences [such as ICT resources] which will motivate them, enhance and extend their learning, and give them opportunities to engage in self-directed learning' (p. 19).

These are:

- the arts
- language development
- early mathematical experiences
- personal, social and emotional development
- physical development
- exploration of both the indoor and outdoor worlds.

Within the Revised Curricular Guidance for Preschool Education, a flexible planning process with which all the staff are involved, and which is informed by the on-going observation of children, is suggested as good practice. Such planning can lead to effective assessment that will be shared with parents. Finally, reflection on and evaluation of the practice are recommended as tools towards making improvements to the learning and the teaching of young children.

Other preschool developments

In June 2004, after a period of consultation, the Review of Preschool Education in Northern Ireland (DENI, 2004) revealed that 95% of children in their preschool year were enjoying funded preschool places (part-time or full-time), exceeding the target of 90%. The review also revealed a 60% decline in reception classes. Reception classes in Northern Ireland are provided in a primary school context and have been described by writers such as Pinkerton (1990) as a less suitable form of preschool provision. In fact the document *Outcomes from the Review of Preschool Education in Northern Ireland* (DENI, 2006) indicated the Department's intention to discontinue primary school reception classes in the main. Walsh (2007) points out such a decision reflects the Department's commitment to a more play-based and practical curriculum for preschool-aged children.

In addition, the Review document revealed a certain amount of progress towards providing a more co-ordinated preschool service. In the past the statutory preschool settings were under the remit of the Department of Education, while the Department of Health and Social Services was responsible for the voluntary settings. The Review document (DENI, 2004) announced that responsibility for Early Years services such as Sure Start would be moved from the Department of Health, Social Services and Public Safety to the Department of Education, thus creating a 'lead department' for Early Years services, a step towards ensuring a more centralised and coherent policy approach.

The Department of Education is currently in the process of creating an Early Years Strategy for 0–6-year-olds, due for publication late 2009. This strategy will replace the Childcare Strategy of 1999 and may provide greater cohesion within issues relating to Early Years education and care, including training, qualifications, salaries, ratios and curriculum matters.

The Foundation Stage curriculum

While the ten years since 1998 have certainly brought developments within the Northern Ireland preschool sector, some progress regarding an appropriate curriculum for young children in the Early Years of primary schooling is also being made. Northern Ireland has the youngest statutory school starting age of all the devolved nations. Since the Education Reform Order (Great Britain, 1989), children are obliged to commence formal schooling in the September after their fourth birthday. With the cut-off point being the first of July, some children begin primary school in Northern Ireland as young as four years and two months. Up until September 2007, these children were required to follow the demands of a curriculum that appeared not to be meeting their needs (Sheehy et al., 2000; Walsh et al., 2006). Since early 1999, CCEA has been involved in revising the existing primary curriculum (DENI, 1996) and from September 2007 have introduced a

Foundation Stage curriculum (CCEA, 2007) that is more play-based and practical in approach for 4- to 6-year-old children in Years 1 and 2 of primary school. This curricular change has been described by Walsh (2007) as 'a huge landmark in the education system of Northern Ireland' and it 'paves the way for an exciting but challenging future for Early Years education in general' (p. 68).

Early Years in Scotland

Ioanna Palaiologou

Historical perspective

In 1999 the Scottish Parliament was re-established through devolution, where the geographical power was transferred to an elected regional assembly based in Edinburgh. This was characterised as a time for the Scottish people when 'all things seemed possible' (Cohen et al., 2004: 237). The re-establishment of the Scottish Parliament was clearly defined by central government yet had an impact upon the education system in Scotland. A number of initiatives and developments in education followed, including in early childhood education, in an attempt to improve quality in Early Years. These changes in the Scottish Early Years system reflect parallels to what was also happening in England. For example, the Sure Start programme for children 0–3 years was established in Scotland.

In 1997 a Curriculum Framework for children in their preschool years was published; it was to provide equality of opportunity for children aged 3–5 years. It outlined five main areas of learning:

- Emotional, Personal and Social Development
- Communication and Language
- Knowledge and Understanding of the World
- Expressive and Aesthetic Development
- Physical Development and Movement.
  (http://www.hmie.gov.uk/documents/publication/sqpse-05.htm)

This was similar in content to the six areas of learning and development in the Early Years Foundation Stage in England, and was followed in 1998 by the New Community School programme. This pilot programme aimed to become an integrated approach to education, health and family support, with a child-centred ideology.

The 1997 Curriculum Framework for children in preschool was followed by *National Guidance: A Curriculum Framework for Children 3 to 5 Years* (Scottish Office, 1997). In 2000 the publication of *The Child At the Centre* aimed to provide a self-evaluation document for Early Years settings (Scottish Executive, 2000), and soon afterwards the *National Care Standards: Early Education and Childcare up to the Age of 16* (Scottish Executive, 2002) was published.

There was a commitment from the Scottish Parliament to raise the standards of children's services and provision. Towards this end a flow of money was invested in a variety of programmes and initiatives. In Scotland the emphasis on children was illustrated by the appointment of a Children's Commissioner in 2004.

As the preschool education in Scotland was undergoing major changes and developments it was felt that younger children, below the age of 3 years, were being ignored. In an attempt to include younger children in the provision the Scottish Executive of Learning and Teaching published, in 2005, *Birth to Three: Supporting our Youngest Children* (Scottish Executive, 2005). This document offers guidelines for all those providing care for very young children, such as Early Years workers, social carers and health practitioners, and included all students preparing to work in Early Years settings.

Birth to Three: Supporting Our Youngest Children recognised the variety of Early Years care and education. Thus it sets out three key elements of what it characterises as an effective practice: relationships, responsive care and respect (instead of setting standards or goals), and offered examples of effective practice. What is interesting in the Scottish *Birth to Three* document is its flexibility towards the implementation of these key elements. It is clearly stated that effective practice should be built around these three elements, and that settings need to create their own practice to meet their own needs. There is an emphasis on the promotion of both Gaelic and English languages, and the document is available in both.

A Curriculum for Excellence

In 2002 there was an extensive consultation exercise, the 'National Debate on Education', which aimed to review the curriculum; it then led to the publication of the report *Educating for Excellence*. The main outcome was the vision of creating a 'single coherent curriculum' for children from the age of three to eighteen. In November 2004 *A Curriculum for Excellence* was published, setting the values and purposes for education of children from 3–18. The Curriculum for Excellence report aims to replace the existing curricula (the 3–5 curriculum, 5–14 curriculum, and the post-14 curriculum) (http://www.scotland.gov.uk/Topics/Education/Schools/curriculum/ACE).

The Curriculum for Excellence contains a commitment to attempt to provide structures to support all children's learning. This is not *per se* a curriculum but, as in all Scottish educational systems, guidance towards what constitutes effective practice. First, it suggests four key elements within this curricular approach: children as effective contributors, responsible citizens, successful learners and confident individuals.

Secondly, seven key principles are suggested for the design of an effective curriculum:

1. Challenge and enjoyment
   Young people should find their learning challenging, engaging and motivating. The curriculum should encourage high aspirations and ambitions for all. At all stages, learners of all aptitudes and abilities should experience an appropriate level of challenge, to enable each individual to achieve his or her potential. They should be active in their learning and have opportunities to develop and demonstrate their creativity. There should be support to enable young people to sustain their efforts.

2. Breadth
   All young people should have opportunities for a broad, suitably weighted range of experiences. The curriculum should be organised so that they will learn and develop through a variety of contexts within both the classroom and in other aspects of school life.

3. Progression
   Young people should experience continuous progression in their learning from 3 to 18 within a single curriculum framework. Each stage should build upon earlier knowledge and achievements. Young people should be able to progress at a rate that meets their needs and aptitudes, and keep options open so that routes are not closed off too early.

4. Depth
   There should be opportunities for young people to develop their full capacity for different types of thinking and learning. As they progress, they should develop and apply increasing intellectual rigour, drawing different strands of learning together, and explore and achieve more advanced levels of understanding.

5. Personalisation and choice
   The curriculum should respond to individual needs and support particular aptitudes and talents. It should give each young person increasing opportunities for exercising responsible personal choice as they move through their school career. Once they have achieved suitable levels of attainment across a wide range of areas of learning their choices should become as open as possible. There should be safeguards to ensure that choices are soundly based and lead to successful outcomes.

6. Coherence
   Taken as a whole, children's learning activities should combine to form a coherent experience. There should be clear links between the different aspects of young people's learning, including opportunities for extended activities that draw different strands of learning together.

7. Relevance
   Young people should understand the purposes of their activities. They should see the value of what they are learning and its relevance to their lives, both present and future.
   (http://www.scotland.gov.uk/Publications/2004/11/20178/45862#6)

These significant changes in Scottish Early Years education were followed by changes in the Early Years workforce. In 2006, the *National Review of the Early Years Childcare Workforce Report* was published (Scottish Executive, 2006a). This led to the 2006 publication of *Response to the Report of the Education Committee on the Early Years Inquiry* (Scottish Executive, 2006b) with an introduction to the Early Years educator. Overall, a number of changes are taking place in Scotland in relation to Early Years practice and education. However, there is no move similar to that in England for a curriculum from birth to 5 (Carmichael and Hancock, 2007). Instead, the Scottish government is moving towards curriculum guidance for children from 3 to 18.

To summarise, in Scotland there is a single curriculum covering children's learning from the age of 3 to 18. The Curriculum for Excellence emphasises that the transition of children from nursery to primary is utterly critical for children's learning; the experiences for children across this transition need to be consistent, thus it needs regularly to be reviewed for standardisation. Consequently, the Scottish government is reviewing the approaches to teaching and learning so that children's learning through nursery school (3–5) is continued in similar ways in primary school. The government has introduced the term 'active learning' to describe the desired continuation of pedagogy from nursery to primary school.

In 2009, the Scottish Government launched The Early Years Framework (www.scotland.gov.uk, accessed April 2009). As with all aspects of Scottish education, the new framework covers the interests of children from pre-conception to the age of 8, and it aims to become a ten-year strategy for related developments. It will consist of guidelines and not of a set curriculum. The aim of the framework is to enable carers to develop a child's social and interactive skills, in order to help the child to achieve its full potential within the context of best possible care and nutritional strategies. Key elements in this framework are emphasis on children's play, active and experiential learning (as well as a holistic approach to learning), and children's progression and transitions.

Early Years in Wales

Sue Lyle and Junnine Thomas-Williams

Historical perspective

Following a referendum in 1997, the people of Wales voted by a very small margin to devolve power from central government in Westminster to a Welsh Assembly. Since 1999 the Welsh Assembly Government (WAG) has devolved law-making powers in a number of key areas of children's lives, including education and training, social welfare and health services. However, some areas, such as defence, police, youth justice, the courts, asylum and immigration, and the benefits system, are retained by Westminster. These arrangements are unsatisfactory; the Commissioner for Children in Wales has urged the government in Westminster to confer upon the Assembly the powers it needs to promote and protect all of the rights of children in Wales, regardless of the area of life.

Wales is a small country yet its infrastructure means that it is not easy to travel within the country. A journey by train from North to South Wales can take over eight hours, while the journey to London rarely takes more than three hours from most parts of Wales. There is no major motorway linking the North to the South; in many respects the different parts of Wales are indeed very different. The economy of Wales has changed considerably in the past 50 years. Once a noted producer of primary raw materials in the form of coal, slate and copper, with agriculture as the second economic activity, it now has little industrial activity, and tourism has become a major part of the economy. This presents considerable challenges to the government as regards the creation of sufficient jobs for the population. Education is therefore seen as a key tool in the future well-being of the nation.

The population of Wales in 2004 was 2.94 million, including 651,800 children and young people under 18 years of age; in fact, children are a declining proportion of the population. Education is provided through 22 local education authorities (LEAs), while in contrast, Birmingham, for example, with a population of 1 million has only one LEA. This factor makes it difficult for local authorities, especially small ones, to provide a coherent service to its schools, and leads to different interpretations of government recommendations.

The state of children in Wales

In its report to the UN Committee on the Rights of the Child (2008), the UK Children's Commissioners list some positive and negative aspects of being a child in Wales as follows:

Positive factors:
- No school league tables or statutory assessment tests at ages 7, 11 and 14
- The adoption of the UNCRC by the Welsh Assembly Government as the guiding principle for policy development for children and young people
- The Welsh language and culture have status and recognition
- The environment
- The participation of children and young people at both local and national levels, for example, through Funky Dragon and through school councils, a statutory require-ment in schools
- Advocacy for children in need has been placed on a statutory footing and a new strategic direction for advocacy services has been announced
- School-based counselling services are to be provided to pupils over the age of 11.

Negative factors:
- Many policies are not implemented fully and consistently across Wales
- Child poverty is still very high in Wales (28%)
- Child and adolescent mental health services are struggling to cope with demand for their services
- Children's health services are not as well funded as are adult services

- Children are still not offered equal protection from violence despite commitment to change from the Welsh Assembly Government and the National Assembly for Wales
- Outcomes for children looked after away from home are still poor
- Only 8% of children know about their rights as defined by the UNCRC
- Disabled children's experiences are worse than those of their peers.

Despite the list of positive aspects of childhood provision in Wales, the list containing negative items is long; this has clear implications for the provision for children in Wales.

Policy and provision

The Learning Country (WAG, 2001) and subsequently *The Learning Country: Vision into Action* (WAG, 2002a) set out the aims and objectives of the Welsh Assembly Government for the future of education in Wales. The cornerstone of the aims is to promote inclusive practices and the well-being of the child.

The Welsh Assembly Government's policies for children and young people have their basis in the UN Convention on the Rights of the Child (UNCRC, 1992), which includes the right to have a comprehensive range of education and learning opportunities. The rights-based approach is set out in seven core aims for children and young people. The *Rights to Action* (WAG, 2002b) document outlines these aims as follows:

Aim 1: A Flying Start in Life: looks at Sure Start; Parenting Support; Early Years Education and development of language and literacy skills.
Aim 2: A Comprehensive Range of Education, Training and Learning Opportunities: includes an examination of The Learning Country, Assessment and Testing; Listening to Learners; Bullying; Exclusion; Inclusive education and School breakfasts.
Aim 3: The Best Possible Health Free from Abuse, Victimisation and Exploitation: looks at children in need, safeguarding children, and the health of children and young people.
Aim 4: Play, Leisure, Sporting and Cultural Activities.
Aim 5: Treated with Respect, and have race and cultural identity recognised.
Aim 6: A Safe Home and Community: looks at preventing homelessness, youth offending; safe routes to school and substance misuse.
Aim 7: Children and Young People not disadvantaged by poverty.

The Assembly Government's programme requires collaboration across services for young people, with a clear focus on the citizen, in order to deliver holistic outcomes. Accordingly, schools are essential partners with other service providers in working together to meet the needs of children and young people, as required by the Children Act, 2004. Similar to the situation in England, the well-being of the child is at the heart of this programme; as part of this work, local authorities are required to publish a Children and Young People's Plan.

Foundation Phase

The vision for the future of education in Wales is set out in *The Learning Country* (WAG, 2001), and *The Learning Country: Vision into Action* (WAG, 2002a). A major difference between England and Wales is the Welsh language. Although only 15% of the country is Welsh-speaking, since devolution all children learn Welsh in school. The number of parents choosing Welsh-medium schools for their children has grown and continues to grow. A key aim for the Welsh Assembly Government is the development of Wales as a bilingual country, thus since 1999 many aspects of the National Curriculum have changed to reflect the Curriculum Cymreig (the Welsh cultural dimension).

A number of other key changes that signal significant differences from the situation in England have taken place. The first major break came when the Welsh Assembly Government abolished the SATs (standard assessment tests) for 7-, 11- and 13-year-olds. The introduction of Curriculum 2008 indicates major differences between England and Wales. Of these, the most significant in Wales is the Foundation Phase in school, which will cover the period between 3 and 7 years (in England, the Foundation Stage covers 0–5 years) and combines the Early Years and Key Stage 1.

Pilot settings have been implementing the Foundation Phase since 2006. In 2008 it was introduced into all nursery and reception classes so that by 2010 all children in the current Early Years and Key Stage 1 will be incorporated.

The Foundation Phase curriculum (WAG, 2008a) has been designed following extensive research into the ways in which our European partners organise the curriculum. The Government has drawn on the experiences of Reggio Emilia in Italy, Forest Schools in Sweden and the Early Years curriculum of Belgium, Denmark and others. As a result the curriculum in Wales will be formed under areas of learning rather than under subjects, and will have a list of experiences and objectives for children's learning rather than subject content.

Seven areas of learning have been identified as follows:

- Personal and Social Development, Well-Being and Cultural Diversity
- Language, Literacy and Communication Skills
- Mathematical Development
- Bilingualism (key WAG aim in learning)
- Knowledge and Understanding of the World
- Physical Development
- Creative Development.

Each area of learning is not to be approached in isolation. Emphasis is placed on developing children's skills across the seven areas of learning, to provide a suitable and integrated approach for young children's learning. Greater emphasis is laid on celebrating differences and on developing children's knowledge and understanding of racial, cultural and religious diversity.

Planning for all aspects of education in Wales, including the Foundation Phase, is to be informed by a Skills Framework 3–19 (WAG 2008b), which includes: thinking skills, communication skills (incorporating oracy, reading and writing), ICT and numeracy.

The Skills Framework provides for continuity and development across the 3–19 age range and links the Foundation Phase with Key Stages 2 and 3.

The key aim of the Foundation Phase is to raise standards of achievement, enhance pupils' positive attitudes to learning, and to address their developing needs. The role of the community is emphasised and a key focus is to help the children become active citizens within their respective communities. Emphasis is also placed on helping children learn *how* to learn and to become independent learners. Teachers in the Foundation Phase are charged with supporting children's curiosity, or what Laevers (2005) describes as 'the exploratory drive'. He suggests that in schools curiosity and the exploratory drive do not get the attention they deserve. Laevers (2005) believes that it is the exploratory attitude and alertness to surroundings, and the stimuli within these surroundings, which will bring a person to 'intense forms of concentration and involvement.' He goes further by suggesting that keeping this motivation alive is a major challenge for education. This has implications for the organisation and management of the classroom, pedagogy, and the role of adults and assessment, each of which will be considered below.

Organisation and management of the classroom

If children are to become independent learners then they need to make choices about when, what and with whom they work. Resources need to be made readily available to encourage independence and to enable children to explore, practise and refine their skills. Central to the new curriculum is the creation of an atmosphere where risk-taking and making mistakes are encouraged. Learning opportunities are expected to encourage children to engage in a wide range of social interactions with their peers and with adults. There should be greater use of the outdoor environment for solving real-life problems and an emphasis on experiential learning. As a result all schools are seeking to develop outdoor classrooms and to use the school grounds to provide rich learning opportunities.

Pedagogy

The key pedagogic emphasis is learning through play and active involvement with a balance between child-initiated and adult-led activities (WAG, 2008c). Movement is seen as essential to the young child's learning as is the provision of active, multi-sensory experiences and opportunities for play of all kinds (both planned and free play); both indoor and outdoor activity are seen as the key to successful implementation. The Foundation Phase documents assert that 'movement is essential to learning'; the importance of children obtaining learning 'in the muscle' is widely recognised and cannot be over-emphasised.

The importance of pupil engagement, such that they enjoy learning, emphasises the affective as well as the cognitive aspects if learning is to be pleasurable. In contrast to the pressure of content coverage in the National Curriculum, the Foundation Phase acknowledges that children need time and plenty of space to become absorbed in activities; this has implications for assessment, as is discussed below.

The active engagement of pupils is emphasised through the requirement to involve them in planning and reviewing their work. An important aspect of this is helping children learn *how* to learn, to develop their thinking skills and positive dispositions to learning. Oracy is seen as particularly important and essential to providing solid foundations for reading and writing. It has received even more emphasis in an attempt to become proactive when children upon starting school are identified as having speech and language difficulties.

In summary, the emphasis on play/active learning is justified by the claim that such an approach:

- motivates
- stimulates
- supports
- develops skills
- develops concepts
- develops language/communication skills
- develops positive attitudes
- demonstrates awareness/use of recent learning and skills
- consolidates learning.
  (WAG, 2008a)

Implications for staffing

All staff working in the Foundation Phase are expected to be well trained and qualified. New teachers should have an appropriate degree for teaching in the Phase. The ratios of staff and children should reflect the standard set by the Care Standards Inspectorate for Wales; that is, one adult to eight children for 3–5-year-olds, and one adult to 15 children for 5–7-year-olds.

Adult interactions with the children should aim to promote 'sustained shared thinking' through effective questioning (WAG, 2008d). Activities should aim to develop children's observation, creative and expressive skills.

Assessment

The importance of having the support of an interested adult to encourage 'sustained shared thinking' has been prioritised; with no standardised tests to measure progress the means of assessment will be based on the close observation of children, and separate guidance has been produced for teachers and other para-professionals. Following Laever (2005), observations should be able to judge the two major indicators of the quality of the educational process, i.e., well-being and involvement, in order to answer two essential questions:

- How is each child doing?
- Are the efforts we make sufficient to secure the emotional health and real development in all important areas and for each of the children?

In addition, teacher assessment must be related to an assessment continuum linking at 7 years with the National Curriculum. This has enormous implications for staff training.

It follows that staff should be trained to:

- observe and assess children accurately
- know when and where to intervene
- to use open questioning techniques
- to evaluate children's performance and make decisions to move them forward
- support children's learning
- to deliver quality talk and key vocabulary.

In summing up the aims of the Foundation Phase, the Welsh Government claims that the most valuable tools we can give children are the ability:

- to choose
- to think for themselves
- to negotiate
- to work collaboratively
- to persevere.

These abilities are seen as essential to giving children a sound basis for lifelong learning and enquiry.

Of course, the raison d'être of all changes in the curriculum is to raise standards. The rationale behind the Foundation Phase is the expectation that standards will rise because the Foundation Phase has placed the child at the centre, a positive attitude to learning is fostered, the planned curriculum addresses developing needs, the child is involved in his/her learning, there is a balance between teacher- and child-initiated learning through well-planned and well-resourced activities, and there will be increased adult involvement with considerable emphasis on outdoor play.

Early Years in the Republic of Ireland

Elizabeth Dunphy

Historical perspective

The Republic of Ireland, one of the smallest countries in Europe (approximately 300 miles from north to south and 170 miles east to west), has a population of about 4.5 million. The Republic comprises 26 of the 32 counties of Ireland; the remaining six counties comprise Northern Ireland, which forms part of the United Kingdom. The country has enjoyed a decade of unprecedented economic boom that lasted from the mid-1990s until recently. Rapid social, cultural and demographic changes have taken place. Due to increases in women's participation in the workforce there is a strong demand for out-of-home care for children in the age range of birth to 6 years.

Policy and provision of Early Childhood Education and Care in the Republic of Ireland

The *White Paper on Early Childhood Education* (Government of Ireland, 1999a) presents the statement of Government policy in relation to early childhood education. The *National Children's Strategy* (Government of Ireland, 2000) proposes a holistic view of childhood. A clear agenda for the development of aspects of early childhood education and care was set out in the Organisation for Economic Co-operation and Development's (OECD) *Thematic Review of Early Childhood Education and Care Policy in Ireland* (2004). The National Economic and Social Forum Report on *Early Childhood Care and Education* (2005) reviewed progress made on implementing ECEC policy. The report concluded that there had been very little policy implementation and that very inadequate financial investment had been forthcoming in the five-year period under review.

The term 'early childhood education and care' (ECEC) is now one generally promoted in describing the arrangements for the care and education of children from birth to 6 years in Ireland. This reflects a concerted effort by those who influence policy to change the generally held perception (in both the public mind, and also by policy makers) that care and education are separate processes. The establishment of the Office of the Minister for Children and Youth Affairs, established as the Office of the Minister for Children in 2005, is significant since it seeks to integrate the work of various key government departments (Health and Children; Education and Science (DES); and Justice, Equality and Law Reform) for the benefit of children.

Statutory school starting age in Ireland is 6 years although in practice about half of all 4-year-old children and almost all 5-year-old children attend primary school. There is no universal provision of ECEC for children under 4 years of age. Preschool education and care is to a large extent provided by community and voluntary agents and agencies. The DES provides targeted provision for some 1,600 children identified as at risk because of economic and social disadvantage. The DES also provides various targeted forms of support for young children with special educational needs. In 2005 additional resources were provided to enhance the educational dimension of existing childcare provision in areas of economic and social disadvantage. This arose as a result of the initiation of a Social Inclusion Programme, Delivering Equality of Opportunity in Schools (DEIS). The programme extends additional support for schools in areas of economic and social disadvantage; it also seeks to contribute to existing childcare programmes in these communities by supporting the enhancement of the educational value of such services. It is clear, then, that various governments over the years have favoured targeted, rather than universal, support of ECEC. Current policy in terms of investment in childcare is to support families to buy childcare through receipt of an Early Years Supplement rather than to fund services.

Key legislation

The *Child Care Act* (Government of Ireland, 1991) provides for the notification and inspection of preschools, which is carried out by the Health Service Executive. The *Education Act* (Government of Ireland, 1998) sets out the requirements on schools and teachers in relation to the education and care of young children attending primary schools. More recently, the *Education for Persons with Special Educational Needs Act* (Government of Ireland, 2004) sets out the statutory requirements for the educational planning for children with special educational needs.

Developing ECEC in Ireland

The *National Childcare Strategy 2006–2010* (Government of Ireland, 2006a) has as a key objective the further development of the childcare infrastructure. It seeks to do so by investing in creating up to 50,000 new childcare places and by providing capital grants for the development of childcare facilities by both private and community sector childcare providers. The strategy encompasses a government commitment to the importance of a trained workforce for the future development of childcare services. A National Childcare Training Strategy is currently being developed and the new training programme, when implemented, will increase by the end of 2010 the number of trained childcare personnel by 17,000. Details regarding the extent and nature of the training to be offered to individuals as yet remain unclear.

The Centre for Early Childhood Development and Education (CECDE) was established in 2002. In 2006 it published *Síolta: The National Quality Framework for Early Childhood Education*. ('Síolta' is the Irish word for seed.) This quality framework presents 12 principles related to quality (see www.cecde.ie). They include the value of early childhood; children's rights and needs; the importance of relations; the centrality of play; and the role of adults. The principles are articulated in a set of 16 standards towards which all settings within which young children learn and develop are encouraged to aspire. Unfortunately, in a retrograde step, the Department of Education and Science has withdrawn all funding from the CECDE Autumn 2008 and its work has now ceased.

A national framework to support all children's learning from birth to 6 years is currently being developed by the National Council for Curriculum and Assessment (2004) (see www.ncca.ie). It is anticipated that the *Framework for Early Learning* will be published in 2009 after a period of extensive consultation with the Early Years sector in Ireland. It sets out advice on early learning goals and advises on key aspects of pedagogy. The curriculum framework will use the four themes of Well-being, Identity and Belonging, Communicating and Exploring, and Thinking to express the goals of the curriculum. The Framework will be accompanied by a number of guideline documents that will support practitioners in implementing the framework. For instance, there will be guidelines on Interactions and on Assessment. There will be no requirement for any specific content, programme or philosophy with the framework. Rather, the intention is that practitioners will judge how best to work with the themes to enable children to achieve the goals of the curriculum. It is anticipated that the curriculum will be widely welcomed. It is also anticipated that its implementation will assist settings in meeting a number of the standards set out in the Síolta framework. However, serious questions remain regarding the capacity of the sector to adopt this new framework curriculum, given the relatively low level of training and qualifications available to most practitioners.

Summary

It is apparent that there is a considerable lack of coherence within the ECEC policy framework for Ireland. While government policy seems to articulate the need to consider childhood and children in a holistic way, and to view education and care as one integrated process, the piecemeal manner in which various pieces of legislation and strategic plans have been enacted appears contradictory. The *National Childcare Strategy 2006–2010* (Government of Ireland, 2006) represents a major programme of investment by government in ECEC. The strategy is limited, however, since it focuses very closely on the mechanisms of providing childcare. There has been almost no visible indication that policy makers are engaging with issues around the purposes and potential of ECEC, of quality, and the centrality of the child's perspective in relation to ECEC.

In Ireland advisory arrangements relating to learning and development are laid down, as are principles for high-quality provision of ECEC. However, unlike the situation in Great Britain, these are not legally enforceable. Legislation covering all aspects of the operation of preschool settings is set out in the *Childcare (Pre-School Services) (No. 2) Regulations* (Government of Ireland, 2006b). The *Primary School Curriculum* (Government of Ireland, 1999b), which lays down the educational requirements for children aged 4–12, is statutory. There is an ad hoc quality to those aspects of ECEC to be legislated, and this appears to be directly related to government policy of targeted provision rather than universal provision. There is also the potential for considerable tension, in the eyes of the general education community in particular, in terms of the status of the Framework for Early Learning and Síolta versus the Primary Curriculum. It also raises questions of continuity and progression in terms of ethos and principles across ECEC settings, and of coherence between the early childhood and primary curricula.

The overall picture, then, is one of a limited vision of what constitutes quality provision of ECEC at national level. There appears to be no understanding, at policy level, of the importance and potential of ECEC for all children. There is discontinuity between the vision, as portrayed in policy documents and strategic plans, and the reality. Deeply significant investment is needed, well beyond recent commitments, if Ireland is to develop the high-quality provision that its young citizens deserve. The recent closing of the CECDE is certainly a serious retrograde step in relation to the development of early childhood education in Ireland, and does not bode well for the immediate future.

Key points to remember

- Attitudes towards improving Early Years provision can be indentified in all countries of the British Isles. A common element is that these changes resulted from political changes.
- Key themes to all the curricular approaches are an emphasis on play and play-based activities, bridging the gap between parents and Early Years settings, with observations as a tool to inform planning, inform assessment, and to open communication with families and to other services. Integration is the new concept that all curricula try to embody.
- However, integration hides its problems, as there are complex issues to be overcome, such as the professional and financial boundaries, variations in training, the creation of a common work culture, and a lack of clarity in roles and responsibilities. The Early Years workforce is asked to overcome these problems in order to meet the individual children's needs and to promote children's development and learning.
- The emerging role of the Early Years workforce across all curricula appears to be more complex than ever. Meeting standards or competencies is not the only challenge they face. The role of the Early Years workforce in curricular imple-mentation is becoming multidimensional. The Early Years workforce requires a very good understanding of the theoretical aspects of children's development, as well as its pedagogical aspects. It is also necessary to develop a very good understanding of the curriculum.
- It is argued that it is equally important for members of the Early Years workforce to voice their own opinions about curricular implementation. These voices need to be informed not only by a knowledgeable, theoretically grounded Early Years workforce, but also by effective practice. The Early Years workforce is required to develop a range of skills in order to be able to promote a pedagogy based on flexible planning, driven by children's interests, and informed by on-going observation of children and an on-going evaluation of practice. An on-going dialogue requiring listening to children's interests and needs will become the starting point, in order to communicate with parents, staff and other necessary, related services.
- The other important aspect is recognition that in early childhood education an effective practice cannot be seen in isolation from the community and the family environment. Considerable emphasis is placed on the role of parents in children's activities, assessment and observation.

Points for discussion

- Compare the Early Years provision among these countries and try to indentify the similarities and differences in their curriculum practices.
- What are your personal thoughts on curriculum developments in Early Years in the region you are studying/working?
- What do you think about the role of play in curriculum implementation in early years?

Further reading

Anning, A., Cullen, J. and Fleer, M. (2004) *Early Childhood Education: Society and Culture,* 2nd edn. London: Sage.

Clark, M. and Waller, T. (2007) *Early Childhood Education and Care: Policy and Practice*. London: Sage.

Nutbrown, C. (2006) *Key Concepts in Early Childhood Education and Care*. London: Sage.

Useful websites

Northern Ireland curriculum:
www.deni.gov.uk/index/pre-school-education_pg/

Scottish curriculum:
www.ltscotland.org.uk/earlyyears/index.asp

Welsh curriculum:
http://wales.gov.uk/topics/educationandskills/policy_strategy_and_planning/early-wales/foundation_phase/?lang=en

Republic of Ireland curriculum:
www.cecde.ie
www.ncca.ie

CHAPTER 3

*[handwritten: * can refer to holistic development. work/assignment.]*

PEDAGOGY IN CONTEXT

Sally Howard

Chapter Aims

The opening statement of the *Statutory Framework for the Early Years Foundation Stage* declares that: 'Every child deserves the best possible start in life and support to fulfil their potential' (DCSF, 2008: 7). It highlights an acceptance that children's experiences during their early years at the physical, emotional, social and cognitive levels have a long-term impact on their lives.

For the Early Years workforce to manage effective learning opportunities, they need to reflect on their own beliefs about how children develop and learn, as well as consider the underlying theories inherent in new educational policies. By articulating the beliefs that underpin practice, professionals and practitioners can engage in purposeful self-reflection. From this they can hone and refine their current practice to create a suitable pedagogy based on relevant theorists and a sound taxonomy for the development of the individuals' physical, emotional and cognitive progress.

'Pedagogy' in this instance means the selection and use of the best strategies to engage and extend learning in both indoor and outdoor environments, as well as knowing how and when to engage in direct instruction or when to stand back.

'Taxonomy', on the other hand, refers to the classification and ordering of how learners acquire specific skills or concepts such as speaking, reading and number acquisition, as well as the way in which motor skills develop.

This chapter aims to help you:

- develop an understanding of the key psychological child developmental theories that have influenced Early Years practice

- discuss pedagogy in relation to child developmental theories

- clarify what constitutes effective Early Years practice

- develop critical thinking on pedagogical practices.

An overview from key theories of child development

Ecological theory of child development

The most important aspect of the ecological model is its child-centred focus across settings, with the family environment exerting the greatest emotional influence on the individual (Bronfenbrenner, 1977). Urie Bronfenbrenner's ecological theory is premised on the fact that humans develop not in isolation, but in a complex inter-relationship among them and their family, the school, and the wider community, including global factors where environmental systems each influence one another in an itera-tive and dynamic way throughout life, where nature and nurture both matter.

Child development starts off with the individual child and their specific biological make-up. This helps to create their personality and is influenced by nurturing from, most often, the mother. This inner circle of influence comprises 'the microsystem' and corresponds in approximate terms to the Piagetian stages of cognitive development around the age of 0–2 years (see Table 3.1, pp. 45–6) (Benson, 2003; Howard, 2006; Piaget, [1950] 2001).

The next environment to influence the infant is the 'mesosystem', where the family starts to exert a greater influence on cognitive and physical development; the mesosystem is determined by the collaborative experiences the child enjoys with the respective people, objects and activities in a variety of settings. The later stages of influence are the complex interactions among the wider communities, such as religious and cultural beliefs, economic and political practice, and the broader physical aspects of the environment, such as inner city life or rural isolation, all of which are referred to as the 'exosystem'.

Finally, the 'macrosystem' acknowledges the influences of the wider world, including global factors such as world events and cultural differences (Palaiologou, 2008). This developmental model holds aspects of humanist and behaviourist models of learning, as there is great emphasis placed on the influence of the various environments upon the development of the individual, with language and dialogic communication also key features in the process of interaction.

According to Bronfenbrenner's ecological theory, positive relationships are crucial to successful development. If, for example, there are deficiencies in the immediate family environment sustained mutual interaction with significant adults is inhibited, the child is less well able to explore other aspects of his or her mesosytem and make the appropriate developmental gains. This may manifest itself as inappropriate and antisocial behaviour in school, as an attempt to gain the attention the child otherwise lacks. With the face of 'family life' rapidly changing through situations such as divorce and a higher incidence of stress within the family because of employment or poverty, the Early Years workforce needs to be ever-alert to environmental factors outside of their own setting; practitioners need to respond by fostering an environment that not only welcomes and nurtures the children, but which also recognises that parents, guardians, foster parents, and care home workers are highly influential in the development of the child. Parents, too, need to be given support for application within the home. Studies have shown that where a special relationship between the parents and the setting has been nurtured, positive development outcomes in the numeracy, literacy and self-esteem of the child have been achieved (PEEP, 2003).

A special relationship such as this may include the sharing of the educational aims of the setting with the parents, training them in how to support their child at home, especially where there may be social disadvantage or where English is an additional language and is under-represented in the home. Practitioners might have to be pro-active in influencing and supporting the role of parents, such as creating a toy library, book bags or organising outings with parental instruction as to how to interact and create opportunities for dialogue (PEEP, 2003).

The Early Years Foundation Stage attempts to consider the different environments where children develop and learn. It can be argued that the principles of EYFS, i.e., setting the standards, providing for equality of opportunity, creating the framework for partnership working between parents and professionals, improving quality and consistency in the Early Years sector and laying the foundation for future learning, reflect the ecological approach suggested by Bronfenbrenner. As the Early Years settings are children's 'mesosytem', EYFS attempts to make links between the children's microsystem and mesosystem, preparing them to move to the 'macrosystem' by creating enabling environments. This means considering children's needs, listening to them and observing them through observations, which are essential elements of EYFS, and crucial aspects for successful transition from one system to another.

Behavioural child development

A behaviourist model of child development, as first proposed by John B. Watson (Benson, 2003), focused on observable responses to changes in the environment as it was deemed impossible to observe the child's internal processes. It is based on the belief that learning is about acquiring the right behaviours; this occurs through a process of observation and imitation (Pennington, 2002). They may be accidental, such as a baby's babbling 'mmmma' – which happens to occur when the mother is around. The baby is rewarded by a smile from her, thus over time the infant associates 'mother' with 'mama', otherwise the sound may be elicited deliberately, as the early work of Pavlov demonstrated. Pavlov noted that responses could be conditioned by using a previously neutral stimulus alongside a response. His famous experiment (of showing dogs some food which made them salivate while simultaneously ringing a bell) resulted eventually in their salivating in response only to the ringing of the bell (Benson, 2003: 62). This stimulus-and-response model of learning was further developed by authors such as Thorndike (Benson, 2003) and Skinner (Benson, 2003), who proposed that the educator's role was to arrange the environment to provide a series of experiences in order to help the child to acquire knowledge, where positive reinforcement is used when the child's repeated response is required, and ignoring or giving negative reinforcement to train the child out of acting inappropriately. The behavioural strategy was termed 'operant conditioning'. An example of operant conditioning is when the child makes an association between behaviour and a consequence, e.g., completing a task obtains a reward, therefore the promise or possibility of the reward causes an increase in the desired behaviour. A child might exhibit a certain behaviour after direct observation, such as mimicking a parent carrying out an action and at the same moment receiving praise and encouragement; alternatively, by observing others gaining praise or rewards then later mimicking that behaviour in the anticipation of reward and acknowledgment.

Routines can assist in creating a secure environment when EYFS is implemented, where the young child can anticipate practice and procedures. These will smooth the child's way into the process of socialisation and conformity with Early Years settings. Physical repetition helps to fix behaviour in the mind, making rapid recall easier, along with the reinforcement given by adults through their positive body language and praise. It could also be likened to a social or situational orientation to learning, one recognising the fact that observing the actions and behaviours of others allows the learner to see the consequence of others' behaviour; from this, their learning evolves from a participation at the periphery towards a more central role of social participation (Benson, 2003: 91).

Adaptations of a behaviourist approach to learning in EYFS can be seen in many approaches and systems used in Early Years settings, from the creation of the right environment to reinforcing 'good' behaviours. This might include asking parents to bring and leave special toys and comforters at the setting so that the young child associates this external stimulus with internal feelings of security. Another example of a behaviourist approach might be seen in a parent's attempts at early toilet training; it often involves classical conditioning, where the uncontrolled reflex action of urinating is accidentally caught in the 'potty' and the child is rewarded with smiles and verbal praise. During repeated experiences the desired response of urinating only in the 'potty' is achieved and rewarded, from which circumstance the potty is the stimulus to urinate on demand in an appropriate place. Within EYFS, its practitioners may use operant conditioning techniques to manage group behaviour, such as tapping a tambourine a few times to indicate a change in routines or the playing of specific music to indicate 'story time' or 'carpet time'. Individual behaviour may also be managed through visual rewards such as stars and stickers or the opportunity to self-select 'golden time'. Some teachers may use a predominantly behaviourist approach for the development of reading, such as 'flash cards', to develop sight recognition of key vocabulary. Negative reinforcement could be used with older children, such as 'time out' or the child's name being moved from the 'smiley face' poster when inappropriate behaviours are being exhibited.

Humanist approach to development

The humanist approach focuses on the human's unique and individual capability to change, to develop and to achieve self-actualisation, as advocated by researchers such as Rogers (1970) and Maslow (1987). From this psychological tradition Gardner's theories of Multiple Intelligences evolved (Gardner, 1993, 1999), where he challenged the notion that the IQ was a single concept known as 'g'. He made a powerful case that intelligence exists in several forms, stating that much intelligence had largely been ignored since it was not measured easily through the then traditional testing systems favouring linguistic and mathematical prowess. Gardner concluded that human intelligence is a combination and blend of a range of abilities, talents and mental skills possessed by all individuals in the varying degrees and combinations that afford uniqueness. While he challenged Piaget's view of a rigid 'stage theory' – Gardner claimed that a child at any one time can be at different stages of development – he simultaneously concurred with the view that children are capable of cognitive growth in all areas of intelligence given the appropriate stimuli, encouragement and support.

As a result of his Multiple Intelligence theory Gardner has encouraged Early Years practitioners to look beyond academic achievement as defined by narrow tests and to create supportive learning environments developing each of the multiple intelligences in every child. Within EYFS the broadening of teaching approaches to support diverse learning opportunities and promote collaboration is suggested. EYFS promotes a distinct shift towards the creative curriculum; greater emphasis has been placed on interpersonal and intrapersonal skills development.

More recently, Gardner (2007) indicates that to thrive in the coming era, education needs to focus less on a content-driven curriculum and more on developing 'five minds', namely: a disciplined mind to address knowledge and skills associated with the curriculum; a synthesising mind to decide on what is important and useful and what is superfluous to the situation in hand; the creative mind to think 'outside of the box' and explore new ideas; the respectful mind to welcome human diversity and, lastly, the ethical mind to consider the notion of citizenship and community both within the child's direct environment and world wide.

Cognitive theory of development

A constructivist view of learning, as advocated by Piaget, Vygotsky and Bruner, is that knowledge is not an entity imparted or one we are born with, but is constructed slowly over many years through experiences and interaction with others (Vygotsky, 1978); however, each believed that infants are born with some basic 'hard wiring'. Piaget focused on the motor reflexes and sensory abilities, while Vygotsky highlighted the elementary mental functioning, such as attention, sensation, perception and memory. He also emphasised the role of socio-cultural interaction in developing these into higher mental functions. In the following paragraphs the work of two theorists will be examined in an attempt to understand their main ideas and their applicability to the Early Years environment.

Jean Piaget

Piaget's earlier work emphasised the most important source of cognition as the children themselves, and this influenced practitioners' ideas of self-directed learning and self-discovery. In his later works with Barbel Inhelder, he focused more closely on pitching work at an appropriate stage of cognition including challenge, as through the process of assimilation and accommodation new learning is acquired.

Piaget is best known for his view that young children think differently from older children, as cognition develops through a series of stages (Burman, 1994). The 'stage' theory consists of four developmental stages from the sensory motor stage in babies through to the pre-operational stage of cognition at around the age of 2 years. The third stage occurs around the ages of 5–6, into the concrete operational stage of thinking. The final stage occurs around adolescence and is termed 'formal operational thinking', which continues into adulthood. Each stage of development has recognisable attributes. Children in a foundation stage setting are highly likely to be somewhere along the continuum of 'pre-operational' thinking and are therefore not yet thinking logically or using language symbolically.

Pre-operational thinking exhibits the following attributes and is recognisable by the words and actions of young thinkers:

- **Egocentrism**: This is the inability to comprehend another person's perspective or point of view, an example being that a young child will think that because he likes peanut butter with jam on toast, everyone else will, too.
- **Animism**: This is attributing life and thinking to inanimate objects, so a child might explain that a shadow follows her because it likes her and wants to be with her.
- **Irreversibility**: This is the inability mentally to reverse a sequence of events, such as being unable to grasp that if you add 1 to 3 you get 4, and therefore if you take 3 away from 4 you must be left with 1.
- **Centration**: This is the tendency to focus or centre on only one aspect of a situation and to ignore other important aspects. If a young child is presented with a situation where there are four green sweets and two yellow sweets, and is asked, 'Are

there more green sweets or more sweets?', he would answer, 'More green sweets', failing to recognise that a subset can never be larger than the whole set.

- **Conservation:** This is a key difference between a pre-operational thinker and a concrete operational thinker; it concerns understanding that two equal physical quantities remain equal even if the appearance of one is changed, as long as nothing is added or subtracted. For example, when two rows of cubes in parallel are confirmed by the child as having the same number of cubes in each row (by virtue of her having counted each cube) then one of the rows is elongated by the adult's spacing out the cubes, the pre-operational thinking child is likely to say – unless they re-count each row – the longer row has more cubes. In contrast, the concrete operational thinking child will recognise without having to re-count that nothing has been added or removed. Conservation has a hierarchy starting with the ability to understand numbers, then length, and by the phase of late concrete-operational thinking children can comprehend mass and finally liquid. Children develop their ability to understand through a combination of maturation and experience, by engaging in early play activities and problem-solving situations that address these aspects in a social setting. Examples are counting out biscuits for a tea party, or pouring drinks into beakers of different sizes while making sure everyone has an equal share.

While some critics of Piaget comment that his studies were methodologically flawed and underestimated the capability of young children because the tasks were confusing and culturally biased (Donaldson, [1978] 2006), Piaget's work and that of Inhelder remain highly influential in child education, especially when linked with the work of Vygotsky.

Lev Vygotsky

Vygotsky was developing his theories of the socio-cultural approach to cognitive development around the same time as Piaget, yet was unaware of the latter's work because of the political situation in Russia, then the Soviet Union. While there are similarities between the two there are also differences, especially in relation to the roles both of language as a tool for thought (Vygotsky, 1978) and the emphasis placed by Vygotsky on that of cultural settings in shaping cognitive development (Burman, 1994).

Vygotsky suggested that learning first takes place through social settings of person-to-person interactions, and then at an individual personal level through an internalisation process (Vygotsky, 1978). A Vygotskian view is that the development of language is similar in structure to the development of thought, yet these are separate, especially in the earlier stages of development (see Table 3.1, pp. 46–47). He emphasised that through collaborative dialogue the child first observes the modelled thinking process and then internalises it for independent use; furthermore, by working with a more knowledgeable other on a task which would be just beyond what a child could achieve on their own, the gap between what the child could initially do alone and subsequently do unaided would be reduced. This development is referred to as the Zone of Proximal Development (ZPD) (Vygotsky, 1978).

Vygotsky placed a far higher priority on cooperative and collaborative learning experiences with peers than did Piaget; he viewed the ZPD as the most opportune moment for cognitive development, as it enables the child to learn and use new skills and mental processes with assistance. These can then be used independently in the future. These ideas were further developed by Bruner and his notions of 'scaffolding' and the 'spiral curriculum' (Bruner, 1996) which encourage carefully constructed steps in teaching allowing for ideas to be revisited at more advanced and challenging levels.

Neuroscientific approaches

Neuroscientific evidence appears to show that, while there is some 'hard wiring' before birth, there are spontaneous neural firings occurring in young babies; these contribute to the production of new synapses and thus create the 'fine wiring' required for the human capability to adapt in response to their environment and to cognitive challenges. The rapid growth of neurons at birth is followed by significant 'pruning' in the first few years of life, with a further growth spurt in adolescence. Studies have identified that certain parts of the brain respond to specific stimuli. For example, a significant growth of neurons in the left hemisphere when babies and young children are in a language-rich environment has been observed, yet if they are subjected to radically impoverished experiences there is significant impairment to brain development, which can on occasions be irreversible (David, 1990). There is growing evidence to support the view that certain periods of maturation are more sensitive to adaptation than are others, such as during the Early Years and in adolescence. This factor is of particular interest to those planning the learning of young children, since this appears to be a crucial opportunity to maximise potential through stimulation and lays the foundations for the development of logical reasoning.

Neuroscientists and cognitive scientists suggest the existence of sensitive periods when playful interaction with parents and significant people benefits neural activity; this involves talking to babies in a conversational style and making facial expressions. Early Years practice is undergoing pedagogical changes as a result of practitioners gaining a deeper insight into aspects of cognitive development and social construction, including the deliberate planning of opportunities for child-to-child interactions and adult-to-child interactions to extend learning.

Education as a holistic practice

Although the Early Years Foundation Stage sets six learning goals to help the Early Years workforce plan their pedagogy, there is a need to emphasise the requirement for a holistic approach to early learning and development, rather than a rigid adherence to one policy or view. While an ecological approach recognises the interrelationships between different environments – and the behaviourist approach is beneficial in adapting behaviours – a

Table 3.1 Comparison of the development theories of Piaget, Vygotsky and Bronfenbrenner

age	Piaget's stages of cognitive development	age	Bronfenbrenner's ecological models	age	Vygotsky's three stages of language development
0–2 yrs	**Sensory Motor stage.** Simple reflexes develop into sensory and motor skills used to explore the world. Knowledge is based on their limited physical experiences. Infants are thinking, but language not used for thought. Thought and language developing separately.	0–2 yrs	**Microsystems.** Interaction between the growing person and their direct environment is dynamic. Only really aware of immediate surroundings, immediate needs, immediate family. Focus of attention is limited to direct happenings. Emotional stability draws heavily on positive relationships with 'mother'. Biological factors including good physical health influence general well-being and development.	0–3 yrs	**Social Speech.** Language is used to control behaviour of others. Curious and active in exploring their world, where actions evolve into meaning and become part of the communication process. Around the age of 2 years language and thought become related, start to impact on elementary mental functions; can express simple thoughts and emotions. Memory is limited by biological factors. Language develops through active interaction with more knowledgeable others, e.g., adults engaging babies in conversation aids progress.
2–5 yrs	**Pre-operational thinking.** Symbols used to represent objects and events. There is a capability to label things such as 'dog' and recognise basic characteristics of 'dog' in other dogs. They can manipulate concrete objects to assist their thought and sort objects into simple observed features, such as colour. They view the world only from their own perspective; egocentric until about 4–5 years of age and they do not question their own thoughts. Language can describe their thoughts yet does not aid their thinking. They attribute feelings and intentions to inanimate objects such as 'stars twinkle because they are happy'. They are able to initiate simple symbolic games and use simple rules. They are unable to conserve. Thinking is not logical or reversible.	2–4 yrs	**Mesosystems.** Wider circle of influence. Family stability important. The evolving nature of the infant means they are more aware of their own interaction with and influence on other people and objects within their physical and social environments. More aware of relationships between people and events that do not directly involve them from the outset, such as school, parents' work, family influences. Growing awareness of the significance of spoken and written language. Creativity developing; able to understand settings they have not encountered for themselves, such as fantasies through stories and symbolic play. Can become very frustrated when physical capabilities do not match intentions.	3–7 yrs	**Egocentric speech.** Children talk to themselves regardless of other individuals who are listening. Their talk is used to guide their own behaviour. Children are able to move through their ZPD through well-structured, stimulating activities with other children and an adult to mediate. Culture plays an important part in language development and memory is enhanced using cultural tools such as chanting, singing, and remembering by counting thoughts on fingers.
5–11 yrs	**Concrete operational stage.** An ability to think logically and systematically is starting to evolve	5–11 yrs	**Exosystems.** Evolving concept of themselves in relation to systems beyond their own direct	7+ yrs – adult	**Inner speech.** This is silent and is used to direct behaviour and thought. Only at this

(Continued)

Table 3.1 (Continued)

age	Piaget's stages of cognitive development	age	Bronfenbrenner's ecological models	age	Vygotsky's 3 stages of language development
	and egocentric thought diminishes. Classification systems are developing and conservation of number is possible. They can put things into a series of more than three items. They can understand reversibility and compensation.		interaction affecting them and *vice versa*, such as society, social values, legislation, welfare, community and cultural beliefs. A construct of reality within their immediate and remote environments which effect them indirectly such as the school their elder sibling attends, or their parents' network of friends, which includes the impact of wealth or poverty on daily life.		stage can they engage in all types of higher mental functions. Thought is enhanced through language. Socio-cultural tools continue to be developed to enhance memory such as 'mind mapping', note-taking, and mnemonics.
12 + yrs	**Formal operational stage.** This stage is only possible if maturation, genetics and suitable experiences have occurred. They are now capable of multivariable thinking and abstract thought, i.e., they can move beyond the concrete situation and think about the future. They can reason and hypothesise beyond their actual experiences. They can hold a number of variables in their head at one time. They can do complex conservation tasks such as volume density and area.	11 yrs – adult	**Macrosystems.** Adolescence brings with it a wider sphere of influences outside of their direct environments and includes global, economic and ecological factors that influence family and individual ideologies and lifestyle choices that define the individual.		**Key principles:** Full cognitive development requires **social construction** as thought and language are integral to each other. The interaction with a more knowledgeable other (**MKO**) creates the Zone of Proximal Development (**ZPD**).

constructivist approach, however, focuses on the construction of knowledge through interaction and challenge, and could arguably be the most significant approach to developing an individual's potential.

Viewing education as a holistic approach concerns the cultivation of moral, emotional, physical, psychological and spiritual dimensions of development, with the view that holism is all about human possibility and the nurturing of a passion to learn. This approach would be recognised by those influenced by the work of Steiner or Montessori, where the overriding perception consists in learning being a journey taking many different paths rather than an academic curriculum consisting of the delivery of specific instructional packages.

Specialists such as Steiner and Montessori would also actively veer away from the labelling of children in a manner that restricts possibilities, such as 'special educational needs', 'hyperactive' or 'lower ability'. While most settings do not subscribe fully to a holistic approach to education, many try to foster a collaborative approach and use real life experiences with children.

There is also a growing trend towards planning in opportunities for reflection and fostering curiosity by encouraging child-led investigations; this is in contrast to the promotion of children as passive recipients of knowledge. The work of Reggio Emilia has been influential in the design of learning environments and builds on the premise that learners are actively engaged in their own learning through sustained exploration.

In Early Years education the exploration is underpinned by the essential role of play in children's learning and development. Despite the debate about the role, the purposes and the values of play as an exploration tool for young children, curricular approaches in Early Years education have demonstrated evidence of endorsement for a 'pedagogy of play'.

Early Years educators use structured and unstructured play sessions to develop social and physical skills, and with carefully mediated adult intervention children's natural curiosity can be enhanced and their understanding of their world challenged (DCSF, 2008; Harrison and Howard, 2009; Siraj-Blatchford et al., 2004). In this manner 'play' has long held a major role in early childhood development, as was proposed in the models of development of Piaget, Vygotsky and Bronfenbrenner. Symbolic actions and representation are believed to be the ways in which the child learns to make sense of their surroundings and their thoughts. Vygotsky states that: 'children solve practical tasks with the help of their speech as well as their eyes and hands' (1978: 26). While authors such as Claxton recognise that direct teaching forms part of the curriculum in the Foundation stages, the dangers of over-teaching in a formal manner too early are well articulated (Claxton, 2008); they claim that too formal a learning experience for young children may prevent them from achieving their full potential in later years. Claxton goes on to say that play-based learning instils a desire to learn and leads to greater achievement throughout life. He supports this with evidence from European experiences allowing for play-based learning up to age 7, beyond the age that most UK schools encourage it (Claxton, 2008).

Learning through play and child-initiated activities are central to any Early Years setting, and can be enhanced with appropriate resources, for example, the use of ICT (such as digital cameras, tape recorders and video cameras). Laptops are ergonomically suited to very young children as their portability means they can easily be used to increase interaction and support a range of child-initiated activities both in and out of doors. Where adult mediation occurs in guiding and enhancing interaction with the ICT, children's higher order thinking capabilities can be significantly enhanced, and an opportunity for further dialogic interaction can occur as part of an intrinsically engaging and motivating environment. ICT, such as computer use, not only increases self-confidence and raises self-esteem, but has also been found to promote a positive desire to learn, along with the development of the fine motor skills required to operate the technology.

Neuroscientific evidence demonstrates that the brain learns best when it is challenged in an atmosphere of relaxed alertness, thus creating the optimum emotional and physical environment in which to take risks and to explore new experiences. Freely chosen play activities often provide the ideal opportunities for adults to extend children's thinking, as these capitalise on the learners' interests and self-motivation in engaging them in 'sustained periods of thinking' (Siraj-Blatchford et al., 2004). Bruner termed these 'joint involvement episodes', whereby an activity is created in such a way as to make demands on working memory capacity and challenge the child's internal processing systems.

Structured programmes of sustained periods of thinking have been created for the Early Years based on the work of Adey, Shayer and Yates (1995); in turn, this builds on the Piagetian and Vygotskian principles of cognitive development, including utilising the ZPD through social construction (Howard, 2006; Robertson, 2005). Within the Early Years setting these reasoning patterns would primarily be based on patterns associated with the schema of classification and its subset of sorting, ordering and grouping by observerable features. Each cognitive acceleration activity in the intervention programme has an element set deliberately to challenge the children's thinking beyond their initial response. In order to work through a problem the trained practitioner ensures that the children are part of a socially constructed group of peers. Together, they agree the appropriate language to name items, and ensure the challenge is set in a context found to be intrinsically motivating. Through careful adult mediation and scaffolding, in the form of questioning, the young children have the opportunity to engage in discussion with their peers and test out ideas, talk about the processes, relate their talk to prior experiences, and ultimately refine their initial thoughts (Shayer and Adey, 2002).

Meeting the requirements of EYFS in a flexible manner

When considering what effective practice involves, the findings from the longitudinal study of effective pre-school provision are worth noting (Siraj-Blatchford et al., 2004). This extensive UK study examined the long-term impact of pre-school provision upon children's learning. Having focused on the role of language the study found a correlation between the type and quantity of adult–child verbal interaction; furthermore, settings that viewed cognitive and social development as complementary made better learning gains than others. From observing these settings the research was able to identify effective pedagogy, noting, for example, that settings implementing intelligent discipline policies (which focused on the youngsters' taking responsibility for their actions and talking through conflict) were found to be far more effective than those using distraction techniques or simply ignoring antisocial behaviour. The study concludes with an important factor in relation to good Early Years provision: it was not just what children receive, but the duration of their attendance, with those having had an early start making comparatively much better intellectual development than others, and those children classed as 'disadvantaged' making significant gains, especially in settings containing a mix of social backgrounds (Siraj-Blatchford et al., 2004).

Helping children to gain in confidence and take greater responsibility for their learning requires the shift of control from the teacher to a shared partnership with the child. With only minor alterations to existing practice, most practitioners can develop a 'have-a-go culture' and encourage the collaboration of ideas, such as 'turn to your partner and talk about different ways we can try to solve Teddy's problem in the story'. Using supplementary questioning strategies, such as 'Say a bit more' or 'Then what?', children are subsequently encouraged to think more deeply about a question or task. Altering familiar activities to include greater challenge (such as using prompt cards, e.g., 'What …' 'How …' and 'Where …') can develop child-led questions in activities such as 'show and tell' sessions. These may then become 'show and ask', during which pairs of children use a question prompt card and, with assistance, think up a question starting with the prompt word (Harrison and Howard, 2008). All practitioners play a crucial role in the mediation process, and learning is further enhanced when practitioners use specific focused praise such as 'Well done for trying both cubes in each hole', as opposed to bland generalised comments like 'Good' or 'Well done', or the overuse of reward stickers which emphasise competition among individuals rather than promote learning (Harrison and Howard, 2008).

Although 'thinking' cannot be taught, it can indeed be developed and improved by trained practitioners' creating the right habits and opportunities for engaging in thoughtful dialogue as part of the normal practice within the setting.

Where practitioners use age-relevant strategies with the aim of helping the children to self-regulate their behaviour, they have found it reduces the 'telling tales' aspect of group work (e.g., too many children at the water table could be controlled by the allocation of coloured bands: no more bands, no more people). When a child comes to 'tell a tale', the teacher can mediate self-regulated learning through questioning, which will encourage the child to think about its own reasoning. This could be: 'How do you know there are too many people?' followed by a supplementary question such as 'So what could you do as a good member of our team to help that group sort it out?' Such methodology is more effective in the long term than is redirecting their attention or taking control and resolving the situation, unless of course the children's safety is at risk.

The whole notion of the nature of intelligence involves a complex dynamic relationship between biological and environmental factors, including the role of structured and unstructured play opportunities. This recognises that each child is unique and has differing rates of development (DCSF, 2008); however, there are basic principles that can be applied, although the actual practice will need to be adapted to meet the diverse needs of babies and young children, the variations found in socio-economic and cultural backgrounds, and considerations of personality and preferences.

Early Years education today needs to be far more creative than it has been in the past, as it needs to equip children with the skills and processes required for an unknown tomorrow. It entails a shift from a content-driven curriculum to one that uses content as a vehicle to tantalise and provoke an overt awareness of 'effective thinking' and problem solving strategies. To achieve this effectively, practitioners need to have an understanding of a range of learning theories, a sound grasp of the curriculum pedagogy, especially in the core goals such as communication, language, literacy, problem solving and reasoning, knowledge and understanding of the world, and creative development, as well as a sound knowledge of normal child development. Together, this will help practitioners to observe children effectively, in order to plan and instigate an appropriate degree of cognitive and physical challenges building on the unique nature of each child, to move learning forward.

 ### Key points to remember

- Practitioners need to be mindful that children are the product of their family and home, which will have a profound influence on their development and behaviour.
- An effective learning environment needs to be emotionally ordered and secure, yet encourage risk-taking and creativity.
- Opportunities to develop dialogue and collaboration need to be planned as part of the normal learning environment.
- Cognitive development requires regular carefully mediated opportunities that utilise the ZPD.

 ### Points for discussion

- With the help of Table 3.1, identify the similarities and differences among the views of Piaget, Vygotsky and Bronfenbrenner regarding child development, and consider how their theories are reflected in your own practice.
- Reflect on the quality of your questioning by observing an activity you undertake with a small group of young children. Keep count of how many times you ask a question that is more dialogic and beneficial to learning.
- Consider the principles and the themes of the curriculum within which you are working. Discuss the role of play and how you can promote play experiences with young children.

Further reading

Alexander, R. (2008) *Towards Dialogic Teaching: Rethinking Classroom Talk*, 4th edn. Thirsk: Dialogos.

Useful websites

A number of pieces of research are taking place looking at the implementation of EYFS and appropriate pedagogies:

Teachers TV – Using Puppets:
http://www.teachers.tv/video/215

EPPE, REPEY and EYTSEN Projects:
http://www.ltscotland.org.uk/earlyyears/resources/publications/resourcesresearch/eppe.asp

The Effective Provision of Pre-School Education (EPPE) Project: Final Report: A Longitudinal Study Funded by the DfES 1997–2004:
http://www.surestart.gov.uk/publications/?Document=1160

Bronfenbrenner, U. (1990) 'Five critical processes for positive development', from 'Discovering what families do', in *Rebuilding the Nest: A New Commitment to the American Family*, published by Family Service America
www.montana.edu/www4h/process.html

CHAPTER 4

ASSESSMENT IN THE EARLY YEARS FOUNDATION STAGE

Ioanna Palaiologou and Maura Bangs

Chapter Aims

As mentioned in Chapter 1, one of the important procedures within EYFS is observation and assessment as an integral element of children's learning and development. There is a wealth of literature that stresses the importance of assessment in the Early Years (Carr, 2001; Clark and Moss, 2001; Drummond, 2003; Smidt, 2005). This chapter discusses assessment in the Early Years Foundation Stage; it narrates the personal experiences and views of the realities of EYFS Profile assessments for an Early Years teacher. It claims neither that what is suggested is the only way assessment can be implemented, nor that this is exemplary practice, but instead aims to help you to understand:

- the statutory requirements for assessment in EYFS

- the eProfile

- what strategies can be implemented for organising and planning assessments

- the complications involved in assessing children in early years.

The statutory requirements for assessment in EYFS

The *Statutory Framework for the Early Years Foundation Stage* (DCSF, 2008: 16) states: 'Ongoing assessment is an integral part of the learning and development process. Providers must ensure that practitioners are observing children and responding appropriately to help them progress from birth towards the early learning goals.'

Individual EYFS settings catering for children below Reception age track progress against the Early Learning Goals, yet do so in a variety of ways, appropriate to the age and needs of the child. However, every school or setting must submit to its local authority data from the EYFS Profile (hereinafter 'the Profile') for children who are in the final year of the Foundation Stage, i.e., those who attain their fifth birthday during the current academic year. The Early Years Foundation Stage Profile Handbook (QCA, 2008) provides a detailed explanation of the Profile and the related statutory obligations.

The Profile was devised as a way of summing up the attainment of a child at the end of the Foundation Stage, providing clear baseline data for entry to Key Stage 1. The Profile is intended to inform Year 1 teachers so that effective planning can take place. Results from the Profile are now also part of the calculation of a school's 'value added' score, showing pupil improvement across the age range of the setting. Increasingly, it is also used to predict children's scores in the SATs tests.

Since its initial introduction, the Profile has evolved into the main focus for assessment in Early Years settings. Before the introduction of the Profile, local authorities had been required to submit baseline data for children on entry to school, although they had the freedom to choose which published baseline system to use; data could thus not be matched like for like. As there will now be homogeneity across England, it seems likely that the Profile will increasingly be used as an instrument of educational (and social) monitoring and planning in order to meet the five outcomes of Every Child Matters.

The EYFS Profile is divided into 13 scales across the six curriculum areas, and derives its statements from the Early Learning Goals. Although the government insists that the six curriculum areas have equal importance in a child's development, the assessment scales are not evenly spread:

- Personal, Social and Emotional Development – three scales: Dispositions and Attitudes, Social Development, and Emotional Development
- Communication, Language and Literacy – four scales: Language for Communication and Thinking, Linking Sounds and Letters, Reading, and Writing
- Problem Solving, Reasoning and Numeracy – three scales: Numbers as Labels and for Counting, Calculating and Shape, Space and Measures
- Knowledge and Understanding of the World – includes ICT in its one scale
- Physical Development – includes gross and fine motor development in one scale
- Creative Development – one scale to cover all aspects of creativity, including art and design, music, dance, imaginative games, role-play and stories.

Within each of the 13 Profile scales, there are nine scale points:

- Points 1 to 3 describe the approximate attainment of an average child on entry to Reception. These three scale points describe developmental stages on the way towards the Early Learning Goals, and children are required to have achieved 1, 2 and 3 before being assessed as having attained 4, 5, 6, 7 or 8.
- Points 4 to 8 are the Early Learning Goals. The scale points are not hierarchical, although the Communication Language and Literacy, Problem Solving, Reasoning, and Numeracy scales are laid out in roughly the order they are normally attained. A child may be assessed as having attained any of scale points 4–8 in any order.
- Point 9 indicates a child who has attained all the Early Learning Goals (scale points 4–8), and who is functioning independently at a consistently higher level than would normally be expected for a child of Reception age.

Almost all of the Profile scales may be assessed in a language other than English. The exception is Communication Language and Literacy, where assessment of points 4–8 across the four CLL scales must take place in English.

What is the eProfile?

Early Years settings now use the eProfile programme to record children's progress within the Profile scales. There is scope within the programme to highlight when assessments are made: there would be a significant difference between planning for the needs, on the one hand, of a child who is attaining some of the Early Learning Goals on entry to the setting and, on the other, for one who is working at the level of the first three scale points for most of the year. Early Years settings must be prepared to show how planning is differentiated as a result of Profile assessments.

The eProfile can be used to track the progress of a group of children in their first year of school, and can generate graphs and charts that act as a snapshot of attainment, e.g., for the whole class on entry to the setting, as a baseline to future attainment, or for Communication Language and Literacy Writing at the end of the Spring Term, to see whether boys and girls are making equal progress. An individual child's attainment may be recorded across the six areas of the EYFS, or group assessments may be entered – perhaps after a series of focused assessments in a curriculum area.

In practical terms, information can most usefully be gathered and entered onto the eProfile at four points in the year:

- Within a few weeks of entry to the setting: to find out as much as possible about each child so that his or her needs are understood and, equally importantly, to have all the relevant information required by Ofsted
- End of the Autumn term

- End of the Spring term
- Also, at the 'end' of the Reception year (actually around the half term of the summer term, as results are required by school administrators in time for these to be forwarded to the local authority, who themselves have deadlines for DfES collation of national statistics).

The information gathered by the Early Years practitioners and professionals is transferred into a computer program in the following stages:

Stage 1 – load eProfile data from computer A onto memory stick
Stage 2 – load data from memory stick onto computer B
Stage 3 – enter most recent assessment results
Stage 4 – load data back onto memory stick from computer B
Stage 5 – transfer old and new data back to computer A
Stage 6 – check everything is still in place.

There is the facility within the program for a report to be generated. However, in practice the language of the report is very formal and, in fact, it merely lists the Early Learning Goal statements within each of the six areas. It might be felt that a more personal summary of a child's achievements and next steps, written by the practitioner, would be more informative to parents. Alongside this, the eProfile is capable of producing a one-page summary of Profile results (with or without a numerical score), and this is helpful towards meeting the statutory requirement to inform parents of their child's attainment.

Organising and planning for assessment

Assessment is arguably the most useful tool in organising and planning Early Years practice (Carr, 2001; Draper and Duffy, 2001; Driscoll and Rudge, 2005; Drummond, 2003; Elfer, 2005; McClennan and Katz, 1992). In Early Years settings a number of different techniques of assessing and recording children's progress are used, before this information is translated into the formal statutory requirement of EYFS. The most common ways of gathering information on children to assess their progress are the Learning Stories Pedagogical Documentation and the Ferre Laevers Scales of Involvement and Well-being.

Learning stories

Carr (1998, 1999, 2001) has introduced learning stories as a means of ongoing observation and assessment in Early Years. This process reflects the principles of the Te Whāriki Curriculum in New Zealand. As will be discussed in detail in Chapter 5, learning stories, or learning journeys, focus on documenting learning episodes in children's everyday worlds with a view to extending these episodes and furthering children's development. Early Years teachers gather information (stories) over time for either each child or for a group of children; a learning story becomes a window into understanding children's learning and development. These learning stories inform planning, help Early Years practitioners to share information with the parents and, most importantly, become a useful tool through which to discuss this planning with the children. Similarly to the Profile in EYFS, learning stories are a way of communicating with children and parents, while being less formal and with no descriptive assessment scales.

Learning stories are used widely in Early Years settings to collect information on individual children and then to inform the individual Profiles. The next chapter offers a number of examples of how learning stories or journeys are used in Early Years settings.

Laevers Scales of Involvement and Well-being

Ferre Laevers at the University of Leuven introduced the Scales of Involvement and Well-being in 1976. The instrument was developed at the Research Centre for Experiential Education (Leuven University, Belgium). The aim is that these scales will measure and monitor children's involvement and engagement in activities as well as their well-being. Such an approach relies on the constant monitoring of children and helps practitioners to identify children who need extra care. As EYFS aims to help children to achieve the Every Child Matters five outcomes, the scales are becoming popular as they focus on children's well-being and involvement, and of course help to identify any additional needs for an early intervention.

The scales aim:

1   to serve as a tool for self-assessment by care settings
2   to focus on quality, taking into consideration the child and its experience of the care environment
3   to achieve appropriateness for the wide range of care provision.
    (Research Centre for Education, Leuven University, 2005)

After the scales have collected information about children through observations, the Early Years team can identify strengths and weaknesses. The results from the scales will enable the Early Years team to create the best possible conditions for children to develop.

There are three steps in the process:

Step 1 – assessment of the actual levels of well-being and involvement
Step 2 – analysis of observations
Step 3 – selection and implementation of actions to improve quality of practice in the Early Years setting.

Laevers (2005: 5) claims that this approach to the assessment of children can lead to significant changes in the setting as well as in the professional development of Early Years practitioners: 'Through the process [the practitioners] learn to take the perspective of the child in their approach and because of this to create optimal conditions for the social, emotional and cognitive development of the children.'

As EYFS suggests, assessment scales are provided for each area of development, thus the reasons for the popularity of the Laevers scales can be understood.

Pedagogical documentation

Reggio Emilia is an alternative and flexible pedagogical approach to a pre-defined and pre-described curriculum, in which children, parents and teachers are working together through a variety of activities. Children express their ideas and lead the activities according to their interests. One of the main questions about the Reggio approach concerns the way in which children's making meaning can be assessed. Instead of traditional assessment methods, such as scales, Reggio suggests, similarly to the Te Whāriki approach of learning stories, pedagogical documentation as an effective way of recording children's learning and development.

The concept of pedagogical documentation in Reggio is a way of collecting children's experiences during activities through materials, photographs, videos, notes and audio recordings. This information becomes visible to others (children and parents) through exhibits, DVDs, books, posters and pamphlets. The teachers act as recorders/documenters for the children, helping them to revisit their actions and self-assess their own learning. In the Reggio classroom documentation is an integral part of the procedure and it aims for a pedagogy in which children are listened to.

Rinaldi (2005: 23) stresses two important aspects of documenting children's activities:

1. [Documentation] … makes visible the nature of the learning process and strategies used by each child, and makes the subjective and intersubjective process a common parsimony;
2. it enables reading, revisiting and assessment in time and in space and the actions become an integral part of the knowledge-building process.

Similarly to learning Stories, the narrative of the documentation can be translated into assessment scales in order to create the Profile of each child, as is statutory in EYFS. This is a creative and advocacy approach to children's assessment that can enable not only teachers but also children and parents to participate in the process.

The role of observation

As has been shown, there are different approaches to children's assessment. No matter which approach (or mixture of approaches) Early Years settings adopt, observations are central to all of them. There are a number of observation techniques available to the Early Years workforce (participant observation, narratives, checklists, diagrammatic, sampling, and media techniques) that can be used to record children's learning and development.

The systematic collection of information about children's learning and development in either a formative or a summative way is important, as it helps professionals to:

- collect and gather evidence that can offer an accurate picture of children, their learning and development
- understand the reasons behind children's behaviour in certain situations
- recognise stages in child development
- inform planning and assessment
- provide opportunities for collaboration with parents and other services
- find out about children as individuals
- monitor progress
- inform curriculum planning
- enable staff to evaluate their practice
- provide a focus for discussion and improvement.

(Palaiologou, 2008)

Case Study

Assessment in my Reception class: the voice of an Early Years teacher

As soon as children start school in September, I begin to make notes against children's attainment, mainly with the first three points of each assessment scale in mind, as this is the expected level on entry to school. I focus on two children each day, and try to observe them unobtrusively so as to gain a picture of their interests and their developmental level. I also chat to them informally while they are playing, both to assess each child's language attainment, and also to get to know them and to win their trust. Obviously some children will have significantly higher attainment than others, and some will have self-evident gaps. I have a meeting with my Headteacher and SENCO [Special Educational Needs Co-ordinator] before half term, as soon as all the children have started school, and we look through my early assessments in order to identify any specific needs, e.g., children with English as an Additional Language, or those with major gaps in their Personal Social Emotional Development scores, who might be having difficulty adjusting to school life or to our behavioural expectations. We agree plans and coping strategies, and the SENCO might decide to enlist advice from outside agencies.

In order to assess each scale point during the year, e.g. Problem Solving, Reasoning and Numeracy: Numbers as Labels and for Counting 7 (Orders numbers up to 10), the

(Continued)

(Continued)

ideal would be to observe each child spontaneously ordering numbered objects in the context of self-directed, self-initiated play. However, within a class of up to 30 individuals, it is just possible that the teacher may not see each child do this independently. It might be necessary, therefore, to devise an enticing game or challenge, and invite children, alone or in small groups, to come and work with the teacher or other trained Early Years practitioner.

For this area of Problem Solving, Reasoning and Numeracy – numeral and number recognition and ordering – I have a set of large, laminated card 'lilypads' numbered 1 to 20, a soft toy frog, and a small plastic fly. The challenge to the group of children is: to share out the cards fairly and take turns putting them down (good also for Personal Social and Emotional Development opportunity); to work out what the numbers on the cards are, and put them on the floor in order (potentially going beyond the Early Learning Goals by ordering to 20, so as to assess children of higher attainment); the intrinsic reward for successful completion is to make the toy frog jump from one end to the other and 'eat' the fly (there is a role-play opportunity here that may also feed into Communication Language and Literacy or Creative Development scales, depending on the interest and enthusiasm displayed by the children – some will project a whole personality onto the frog, complete with 'froggy' sounds and dialogue).

The task may be differentiated by giving only the 1 to 10 cards to a group who are known, anecdotally, not to be working with larger numbers yet; or an adult might prompt the task step-by-step for children who find working in a group challenging (this could be the teacher or another practitioner who is making the assessments – participant observation); a more able group might take turns to lead the activity themselves, giving additional Personal Social and Emotional Development opportunities, and a Communication Language and Literacy: Language for Communication and Thinking focus, as the leader explains to the others what they are to do.

If an activity like this is set up, it is essential to share the assessment goals with the group, so that the children understand what the teacher is looking for. This is in contrast to more open-ended observation where children are being observed while deeply involved in self-initiated play. In that case I would try extremely hard to be unobtrusive, and not show the children that they are being watched, in order to have as frank and candid a picture of their development as possible.

While I am working with a group, I have to be aware of the other children in class (or outside, if I am working there), and may notice that a boy is reading *Dinosaur Roar* [Paul and Henrietta Stickland, Dutton Juvenile, 1997] from memory to a friend in the small world area, and that they are finding plastic dinosaurs to match the ones in the book, making them move in ways that match the descriptions of dinosaurs in the book, and playing with the alliterative and rhythmic phrases from the text as they do so, repeating 'Dinosaur grumpy, dinosaur lumpy' and laughing together. As this kind of golden moment ticks so many EYFS Profile boxes, I find the simplest way to record it is to take a photo, and I keep a small digital camera beside me all the time (used without flash). Early in the school year, the children learn not to put on 'holiday grins' every time they see me pick the camera up, and I tell them I am taking photos so I can show their grown-ups how well they are working in school. This is perfectly true – I run a slideshow of photos on the interactive whiteboard during open-evenings and on other occasions.

Later on, at the end of the school day, I load the photos onto my computer and look through them, noting any significant milestones, or evidence of consolidation of learning – children doing something in self-initiated play truly demonstrate the security and permanence of their learning. Often, too – like the background scene in a film – I notice other events; perhaps a child making repeating patterns with Knex, when my earlier visual scan of the room failed to pick this up.

I find this is a more manageable method than attempting to write it all down at the time – children deserve a larger share of my attention than I can give if I am frantically writing labels or Post-It notes (I think this is distracting to the children, too – unless I have explained beforehand what I will be doing); it is also faster, and picks up more of what is going on in the classroom.

As far as working through the EYFS Profile scales goes – the sheer volume of potential assessments is daunting, but diminishes as the year progresses, i.e., once a child is assessed as being secure on a point of the scales, it does not need to be repeated.

As discussed above, during the few weeks until the end of September whilst the children attend school during the mornings only, I focus on two children each day, and try to get a picture of their overall attainment against the first three points on each of the scales – just as a starting point. I then use these early assessments to group the children for focused teaching – mixed ability for some areas, but banded by attainment for, e.g., phonics or writing. Once I know the range of the new children's interests, I can plan effectively to extend their learning by introducing activities they hopefully will find irresistible and challenging.

Attainment and confidence on entry to school varies enormously, depending on the child's home life, and their experience of pre-school, if any. It also depends on whether they have secure attachments or not (for more information on attachment, see Chapter 9). It is very difficult to make a complete and accurate assessment of children on their entry to school, as you do not know the child, you have not yet established a trusting relationship with the parents for good communication. Once again, planning and preparation are crucial for these children so the parents and the child are involved and the child finds my class life interesting, and the parents feel confident leaving their child in my class.

Planning for assessment is cyclical, and I try to concentrate on assessing points from one set of scales each week, building my teaching around setting up situations where this might be possible, and using activities that I know will appeal to the interests of the

(Continued)

(Continued)

children I am assessing. By the end of the first term, I have sufficient information to add to the initial assessments made on entry – these have to be quick and decisive, as time is so limited, and I do not know the children well at this early stage – and create a more rounded picture of each child. Usually children are beginning to attain some of the Early Learning Goals (scale points 4 to 8) across the six areas by this time.

In the Spring Term, the cycle is repeated, and once more in the Summer Term, when final assessments are made. Time is also spent assessing whether individual children are working independently at a sufficiently mature and confident level to attain point 9 on any of the scales. Point 9 in each of the 13 scales indicates a child with significantly higher attainment than the average, and should be considered very carefully. In Problem Solving, Reasoning and Numeracy, for example, it would indicate a child with real flair for, potential and interest in Maths, not just a child who has learned how to complete some mathematical operations accurately.

Some assessment continues year-round, e.g., informal notes made after each child reads from the reading scheme or in a Guided Reading group (Communication Language and Literacy 3), or a brief note made on the independence or otherwise of the 'sounding-out' process when a child attempts to caption his or her drawing. I keep an assessment grid in the front of each child's writing book, where I note their level of understanding against the Profile scales for Linking Sounds and Letters and Writing (Communication Language and Literacy 2 and 4) – every week I work with the children to write 'News' and a writing activity suggested by a book read to and discussed by the class.

Additionally, I also continue to have two children each day uppermost in my mind, and known to the other practitioners in class, so that a bank of informal, anecdotal information might be amassed. This is achieved by having two children each day be 'helpers' and undertake small administrative tasks like taking the register to the school office, or collecting the milk cartons from the kitchen. The helpers' names are displayed in class each day, and the other adult practitioners report back to me on what those children have been doing and anything they consider noteworthy. We do not, in this case, share our agenda with the children, as it is the child's natural, unforced behaviour I hope to capture. Using this system, in a class of 30, each child is the focus once every three weeks, twice each half term, four times each term. This is a way of keeping track of children's changing interests, and of making sure that the most quiet, reserved and self-contained individuals are not overlooked in such a large group.

I work in a two-form intake school, and moderate my assessments with my partner teacher informally on a regular basis during the year, and scale for scale at the end of the year, to ensure we are assessing at a roughly similar level, given any differences in our respective groups of children (e.g., Special Needs).

Our assessments are moderated within my local education authority by three meetings each year attended by all Reception teachers (or at least one teacher from each school). The focus of these meetings is one or two curriculum areas at a time, on a continuous cycle. We are asked to bring evidence of top, middle and lower attainment to the meeting, and compare these with those brought by other teachers. Evidence can be: photos; paintings, drawings and writing by the children; video clips; or written notes. In alternate years, we get a moderation visit from a member of the Early Years advisory staff, who looks at the range of evidence we are keeping in school.

Recent training has stressed that an 'average' score on the Profile scales would be about 6 out of a possible 8. Children are not expected or driven to attain every scale point, nor to reach the description for scale point 9. The Early Learning 'Goals' are just that: they are where we are all aiming. Every child is different: each has individual talents and skills, and also areas where they lack understanding. It may be that their development has yet to blossom, or it may be that they are very young (children with August birthdays, for example, are assessed alongside those almost a year older, born in September). However, the absence of a wide range of Early Learning Goals, and a very low Profile score at the end of a year in Reception may indicate cause for concern.

The challenges to effective assessment

Where does assessment take place?

Assessment can take place both inside and outside the classroom. One adult may be inside the classroom and another outside, so each practitioner must fulfil multiple roles, supporting and stimulating development through play, actively teaching or consolidating skills, and assessing the ephemeral aspects of children's attainment by observing their self-initiated play.

Assessment may also take place anywhere around the Early Years setting: while the class is moving from place to place; during ICT in the computer suite; or in the playground at break time. Chapter 5 offers examples of the assessment of children during the daily routine of the setting.

Who makes the assessments?

All involved in the learning and development process of children should be able to make an assessment in collaboration with the parents. However, the challenging issue is the ratio of staffing and the training of the staff to be able to perform observations effectively, in order to inform the assessment process.

Parents, of course, are the child's first and best teachers and assessors, and there is a great deal to be contributed by them, especially in building up a picture of children's interests and needs when they start school. A family-friendly booklet to fill in – 'Who is in my family?'; 'What is my favourite toy?'; 'What do I like to do at home?'; 'Where do I like to go when we go out?', etc. – can provide many talking points while it is being filled in, e.g., at the Home Visit (if it is your local authority's policy to make one).

The purpose of the eProfile

The profile aims to become a way of sharing information about children in an Early Years setting and school. The eProfile aims to reach:

- The School Leadership Team, as discussed above. The eProfile can generate an assortment of graphs and radar diagrams that can be helpful to practitioners as they illustrate the progress of a child or a group of children. It can also generate compatible reports and summaries that can be forwarded directly to the LEA for inclusion in their statistics.
- Early Years team: attainment of children on the scales, e.g., for Writing within Communication Language and Literacy (writing is a whole-school focus area for 2009/10), is used to set one of the Performance Management targets. The eProfile can become a tool of communication information among the Early Years team, sharing achievements and concerns.
- Children: assessment findings and plans for the next steps in their learning journey can, and should, be shared with children using language appropriate to their understanding. In the *Practice Guidance* for EYFS the concept of listening to children is strongly promoted. Children's involvement in any decision-making that affects them creates 'learning communities … where children [can] take an interest in an activity, become involved in it over a sustained period of time, persist when they meet difficulty, challenges or uncertainty, express their ideas or feelings in a range of ways and finally take responsibility to change the way things are, to teach others, and to listen to another point of view' (Carr, 1998: 15).
- Parents: will recognise the character sketch it is possible to draw after a year of careful study for the Profile. Report writing is made easier by the detail of the Profile assessments. As discussed above, the eProfile will produce a report, but it can be in technical language – all that is delivered is a list of the descriptions of the Early Learning Goals achieved. It is important to communicate this report to the parents and help them to understand what is meant in each of the points of the report. The eProfile will also generate a one-page summary that, in conjunction with a written summary of each of the six curriculum areas and a brief narrative about the child's strengths and next steps, makes a more rounded report.
- Local authorities.
- Ofsted.

Key points to remember

- In the *Practice Guidance for the Early Years Foundation Stage* (DCSF, 2008) a detailed and descriptive assessment section is included. All settings providing care and education for children from birth to 5 have to implement the assessment requirements. There are 13 assessment scales derived from the Early Learning goals.
- Assessment in a classroom setting is a very helpful tool in organising and planning practice, as well as in communicating with parents and staff. However, the effective implementation of assessment requires the participation of all staff and the improvement of staffing ratios.

Points for discussion

- What are the advantages and disadvantages of narrated assessment in comparison to the use of scales?
- Visit the National Assessment Agency website, find the EYFS Profile Handbook and familiarise yourself with its layout. Navigate the site to explore the other EYFS resources available for download. Consider why the Profile scales are so heavily weighted towards Personal Social and Emotional Development, Communication, Language and Literacy, and Problem Solving, Reasoning and Numeracy. Look at the scale point descriptions in these areas and think what the implications might be for a setting's future planning with regard to an individual child's Personal, Social and Emotional Development; his or her grasp of spoken and written language in Communication, Language and Literacy; and attainment in Problem Solving, Reasoning and Numeracy.
- After studying different ways of organising and planning for assessment, during your placement try to devise a single page assessment form to be used. Focus on one of the six learning areas and try to investigate how you will gather information, what observation techniques you will be using, how you will record your information. Discuss your assessment with an experienced Early Years practitioner.

Further reading

Abbot, L. and Nutbrown, C. (2001) *Experiencing Reggio Emilia: Implications for Pre-School Provision*. Maidenhead: Open University Press.

Carr, M. (2001) *Assessment in Early Childhood Settings*. London: Paul Chapman Publishing.

Drummond, M.J. (2003) *Assessing Children's Learning*, 2nd edn. London: David Fulton.

Useful websites

The Early Years Foundation Stage Profile Handbook: www.naa.org.uk
Click on 'Assessments', then 'EYFS Profile Handbook' to download.

E profile
www.teachernet.gov.uk/management/tools/schoolsdataportal/eprofile/
Teachernet has a portal that opens onto the website of Suffolk County Council (who devised the eProfile). The programme and its manuals may be downloaded.

Practice Guidance for the Early Years Foundation Stage:
www. standards.dcsf.gov.uk/eyfs/resources/downloads/practice-guidance.pdf

CHAPTER 5

USING LEARNING STORIES IN THE EARLY YEARS FOUNDATION STAGE

David Coates and Wendy Thompson

Chapter Aims

The previous chapter explained the assessment requirements in EYFS. Learning stories were mentioned as having become a useful tool in gathering information to inform planning and assessment in the Early Years environment. This chapter aims to discuss the use of learning stories as a tool for observing and assessing children in EYFS.

This chapter aims to help you to:

- indicate how provision based on children's interests and motivations can be analysed and used to enhance children's learning

- illustrate how learning stories may be used to record progress within the Early Years Foundation Stage

- encourage analysis and reflection of children's learning

- consider the significant role of the Early Years practitioner in facilitating children's learning.

What are learning stories?

Learning stories can be described as approaches to observational assessments that explain the 'narrative' of children's learning. The 'narrative' in this context, taken from a social constructivist perspective, describes and analyses children's active involvement in activities (Carr, 2001). Learning stories allow practitioners to use multimedia tools to make learning visible, for example through the use of digital cameras.

In recording development and progress, relationships and actions become significant and illustrative of the progression in children's learning. The 'actions' described by Carr (2001) demonstrate children's readiness for learning through dispositions that include: children taking an interest; being involved; persisting with difficulty or uncertainty; communicating with others, and taking responsibility (Carr, 2001). Practitioners subsequently analyse the strategies applied by children, consider their levels of motivation, and observe their abilities to recognise, select, edit, respond to, or resist learning opportunities. Assessment, in this context, becomes more than just a record of the individual child's isolated skills and structured observation is a key to success (Anning et al., 2004: 73).

How can learning stories be used?

Practitioners working within play contexts search for and construct learning opportunities that will lead to more meaningful understanding and development (Anning and Edwards, 2006: 52). Carr (2001) describes this process as encompassing four elements of effective practice:

- describing
- documenting
- discussing
- deciding upon the next steps.

This process also avoids concentration on deficit models of children's development and learning, as the learning story seeks to understand what a child *can do* and is therefore a more positive affirmation of his/her capabilities than are some forms of assessment (for example, standardised testing).

Stories are complex as they are collected in natural contexts and include reference to the environment in which the learning takes place, including the respective roles of peers and adults working within the same environment or activity (Anning et al., 2004: 73). They are particularly focused on what makes sense to the child. Broadhead (2001) noted that as children get older they show enhanced levels of mutual understanding; they begin to see other children as intentional agents and begin to accommodate their ideas. This supports the concept of a developed sense of 'memory in action' (Bruner, 1983), which highlights the complex nature of children's learning to adapt and respond within unfolding play scenarios.

DATE:	AREA OF PLAY ENVIRONMENT:	CHILDREN INVOLVED:
KEY DISPOSITIONS Carr, M. (2001)	**LEARNING STORY OBSERVATION**	**AREAS OF** **LEARNING** (DCSF, 2008)
Taking an interest Finding an interesting topic, activity or role. Recognising the familiar, enjoying the unfamiliar. Coping with change.		*Select from:* Personal, Social and Emotional Development; Communication, Language and Literacy; Problem Solving, Reasoning and Numeracy; Knowledge and Understanding of the World; Creative Development; Physical Development.
Being involved Paying attention for a sustained period. Feeling safe, trusting others. Being playful with others or materials.		
Persisting with difficulty Setting and choosing difficult tasks. Using a range of strategies to solve problems when stuck.		
Expressing an idea or a feeling – in a range of specific ways. For example; oral language, gesture, music, art, etc.		
Taking responsibility – responding to others, to stories and imagined events, ensuring that things are fair, self-evaluating and helping others.		
HOW DID PRACTITIONER/S FACILITATE LEARNING?	**CHILDREN'S COMMENTS ABOUT THE ASSESSMENT**	
WHAT LEARNING DID WE THINK TAKE PLACE? (Discussions with other practitioners if necessary)	**HOW TO BUILD ON THE INTEREST/NEXT STEPS?** (Discussions with other practitioners if necessary)	

Figure 5.1   Examples of how learning stories are recorded (adapted from Carr, 2001)

This process of formative assessment is embedded within the statutory framework setting out the legal requirements for Learning, Development and Welfare of the 0–5 age phase in England, i.e. the Early Years Foundation Stage (EYFS) (DCSF, 2008). As explained in Chapter 4, the EYFS documents include guidance for assessment and monitoring standards to ensure the starting point is the 'unique child'.

Within EYFS (DCSF, 2008: Card 3.1) 'Observation, Assessment and Planning' provides examples of describing and documenting in such ways as noting children's responses in different situations, as part of the daily routine, and finding out about their needs, what they are interested in and what they can do. This approach complements the methods used in documenting learning stories. The EYFS (DCSF, 2008) guidance continues with recommending analysis of the observations to help plan what next for individuals and groups of children. Practitioners are advised to create records 'that are clear and accessible to everybody who needs them [to ensure] the views of parents and practitioners are reflected in children's records' (DCSF, 2008: Card 3.1).

The discussions between children and their peers and between children and practitioners form an integral part of learning stories. When documented, they may be used as a tool for engagement in talk with both the children and their parents/carers. Examples of the strategies employed by practitioners, whilst engaging with children, involve using recall, and drawing out patterns and connections in order to enhance children's learning. Thus, as Moss (2004) highlights, the practitioner is a 'co-constructor of knowledge' and values together with children; she/he is a cultured and curious person, which means an inveterate border crosser; and she/he is a researcher, with an enquiring and critical mind (Moss, 2004).

The learning story provides positive affirmation of children's capabilities as subtle actions and interactions are recorded and noted. The decision making (Carr, 2001) stems from this analytical approach, which helps move forward children's thinking. This involves processes aimed at different levels. There is the immediate feedback given to children whilst they are engaged in activities; there is the process of thinking about the next stage in their learning that will include sharing the results of observation with other practitioners and parents. Finally, there is the modification to the learning environment to ensure children remain motivated and engaged. As Seifert (2006) emphasises, it is not sufficient simply to know or observe the behaviour of the children: it is what the practitioner does to ensure interest is sustained that is important. 'To call myself a teacher of the young, I must connect with them somehow, which means interacting, relating, and touching their lives in valuable ways' (Seifert, 2006: 9).

Personalised active learning

EYFS suggests that 'active learning' occurs when children engage with people, materials, objects, ideas or events, and test things out and solve problems (DCSF, 2008: Card 4.2). Personalised learning and the consideration of children's involvement in their learning, as well as the nature and quality of adult and peer interaction in children's learning, is emphasised. A number of studies that examined play and learning (Wood and Bennett, 2000) indicated that children are capable of developing structured and purposeful play upon which educators can base future planning. Moyles (2005: 9) describes the process of learning through play as providing opportunity 'for learning to live with not knowing' and allowing for 'independence in thought and action' where children are operating in an open frame of mind and are engaging in 'what if' situations. In this sense play is a process and not an activity in its own right (Smidt, 2006). This process allows children to create alternatives to reality, producing new combinations described by Bruner as memory in action (Bruner, 1983).

The developmental potential of play can be maximised where children perceive the activity as play and subsequently approach it in a playful manner. Studies showed that children chose to distinguish play from other activities and to refer to certain indicative characteristics such as play being fun, noisy and spontaneous, occurring on the floor rather than at a table and also being free from rules (Howard, 2002; Howard et al., 2006; Westcott and Howard, 2007). The value of play as a learning medium in relation to enthusiasm, motivation, creativity and willingness to participate (Moyles, 1989) is inextricably linked to the way in which the player perceives the activity. Playfulness is an internal state comprised of the personal qualities that children bring to an activity. It is therefore important to understand what children believe to be play, how such perceptions may have developed, and how feelings of playfulness can be evoked. Wiltz and Klein (2001) found that regardless of classroom quality, self-selection and choice are important determinants of a child's perception of an activity as play. Children in a more teacher-directed and structured setting separated play from learning, describing teacher-directed activities as learning and self-initiated activity as play, and consequently not as learning (Howard et al., 2006). It could be argued that children are more intrinsically motivated and thus sustain interest and involvement when they perceive an activity as play and 'not work'. Children who are used to teacher involvement in play activity will be more likely to accept adult involvement and retain a sense of playfulness. This is important if practitioners are to be accepted as 'committed co-players' to facilitate learning (Rich, 2002). It is the role of the practitioner to recognise, intervene and facilitate where and when it is appropriate and 'encourage play that is emotionally, intellectually, physically and socially challenging' (QCA/DfEE, 2000: 5).

According to EYFS, children need sensitive, knowledgeable adults who know when and how to engage their interests and how to offer support at appropriate times. The role of the practitioner is considered crucial in:

- planning and resourcing a challenging environment
- supporting children's learning through planned play activities
- extending and supporting children's spontaneous play
- extending and developing children's language and communication in their play.
  (DCSF, 2008: Card 4.1)

Appropriateness is key in this respect, as imposing these roles in an insensitive manner could destroy the play scenario. Practitioners need to focus on helping children to become resilient learners, who enjoy learning and feel that they are able to succeed (Anning and Edwards, 2006: 54). They should create the conditions for learning through play (Members of the British Educational Research Association Early Years Special Interest Group, 2003).

 Case Study

Block play in the construction area
(based on discussions with other practitioners)

Five children aged 4 years were involved – Alex, Harry, Chloe, Darshan and James.

The block play area was very popular and after practitioners' observations and discussions it was decided that the five children above often led the play. Other children entered the area and joined in at regular intervals, but the group of five showed sustained high levels of involvement, displayed sophisticated personal and social skills, negotiating for equipment, listening to others' points of view, and were engaged in problem solving. They also seemed very willing to take risks and failure in their stride and accepted it as a new challenge when things did not happen as they expected.

The children began their play by using large pieces of canvas placed on the floor that they decided would make a road. Initially it curled up at the corners as it had been rolled up for storage. Alex immediately turned it over to make it lie flat.

Alex: 'Let's make a ramp. What do we need for a ramp?'

They all looked around.

Harry: 'I know. This.' [Pointing to a basket]

The children lifted the end of the canvas and placed a basket underneath the end, which made it slope for the cars to travel down. They then proceeded to play with the cars.

The next day the group made a replica of the model placing it at a higher level on top of a cupboard. Harry placed a long brick onto the cupboard and added a cylinder into the construction and rolled a car along to see what happened. The children looked carefully at the construction and then began to make minor adjustments to the height. Each time they made an adjustment they tried out the car and then adjusted it again until they felt happy with it.

Darshan: 'It's a big ramp.'

They then decided to add a basket to the end of the construction to catch the car that fell out. The whole group felt happy with this new addition and began to take turns to roll the car down the ramp. They talked about fast, slow and how well it worked. Throughout the sessions all of the children showed a sustained high involvement and excellent problem solving skills.

Harry asked if they could look for something else to make a ramp. When a basket top was suggested Harry tried it and said, 'It's no good. It's too rough. The cars don't move down it.'

One of the practitioners took him to the resource room with Alex and James to find a suitable resource.

Harry found some pieces of thick carpet and brought them back to the classroom. He then tested them out.

'It's no good. It's not strong,' he said.

The practitioners felt at this point that the challenge of finding the right material was a vital part of the learning process and knew the children were confident enough to try and to discuss outcomes. Harry and James tested it independently and the material bent under weight.

The rectangular structure had a small opening housing the trucks and cars. The children began to discuss how to make a door for the cars to get in and out. Harry and Chloe spent long periods adjusting the bricks to allow the 'door' to open without the rest of the building falling apart. They eventually achieved this through a sustained period of trial and error and testing out their ideas.

Decisions made by practitioners

Practitioners (teachers and nursery nurses) working with children in the Nursery School attempted to identify children's interests and motivations through careful observation and documentation. Practitioners felt that observation of the area and the dynamics of the group would be crucial to knowing how to proceed and support learning. The practitioners decided that daily discussions throughout the story would be the most significant factor in extending learning and that it was vital that the play be analysed before rushing to intervene. They accepted that the play could not be conceptually controlled.

> If children's perceptions of play are influenced by experience, the communication of the opportunities for learning in both child-initiated and teacher-directed activities, and teacher participation in a wide range of classroom activities could lead to adult acceptance during play. (Howard, 2002: 500)

For the children, adult involvement did not mean 'work' as they were used to practitioners being present and involved in their activities. By considering the children's perspectives the practitioners were able to motivate the children's learning by providing enjoyable and challenging experiences that the children believed were play.

Analysis of the learning story

The play experience allowed the children to explore and experiment, to discover the dynamics of cause and effect, to build imaginary worlds, to rehearse new roles, and to practise new skills (Leyden, 1998). As Vygotsky (1978) noted, the play provided the children with an important mental system allowing them to think and act in more complex ways. The pretend play was social and it was essential that children agreed on the reference of pretence. The sharing of focus came about through inter-subjectivity (Smidt, 2006: 53). The 'road' made of canvas involved all children being engaged in an extremely complex cognitive act of shared meaning-making.

Preparing a relevant environment implies that choices are being made by practitioners. The play-based provision may cause children to react to environmental stimuli in different and perhaps unexpected ways. Through play children can develop their higher level thinking skills and problem solving abilities, while monotonous repetitious play, which is simply 'hands-on' and not 'brain-on' (Wood and Attfield, 1996) can offer little cognitive challenge for children. The practitioners in the Nursery School picked up on and developed this child-initiated activity with the purpose of deepening children's thinking about what they were doing (Siraj-Blatchford and Sylva, 2004). It is the role of the practitioner to recognise, intervene and facilitate where and when it is appropriate, in order to promote challenging play experiences. Children, therefore, learn through play when they are in 'a secure but challenging environment with effective adult support' (DCSF, 2008: *Practice Guidance*, p. 8). In the Nursery School the practitioners were seen and accepted by the children as 'committed co-workers' (Rich, 2002). A sense of playfulness was therefore maintained when the practitioners offered advice and discussed ideas with the children.

Case Study

Outdoor play (based on discussions with other practitioners)

During this period the children had also been transferring their skills to outside play. They used large crates to make enclosures. Chloe displayed good spatial awareness of the amount of space needed and good problem solving skills working out how to connect the crates.

In mark making, Alex, Harry and Chloe were also fitting shapes together to make objects and people, making cars, tractors and houses, and drawing people to put in them.

Decisions made by practitioners

An environment where open-ended play is valued and where there is a rich range of resources available to challenge children's thinking is important in this context. The

Practice Guidance for the Early Years Foundation Stage (DCSF, 2008: 8) suggests the environment should allow children to 'explore, develop and represent learning experiences' in order to help them make sense of the world. It suggests children should also 'be able to practise and build up ideas, concepts and skills' and learn how to understand the need for rules. Risk-taking, the tolerance of mistakes made and encouraging creativity and imagination are characteristics that the environment should encourage.

The environment should include a balance and variety of experiences, which are multi-sensory and can be delivered with differentiated learning intentions for children, dependent on their needs. The provision of necessary time for sustained play and exploration is also considered an essential environmental attribute in the support of nursery children. The new EYFS indicates how the environment should be developed to meet the needs of all children when it states:

> Every child's learning journey takes a personal path based on their own individual interests, experiences and the curriculum on offer. (DCSF, 2008: Card 3.2)

The skill lies in providing an environment resourced with challenge in mind and incorporating the facility to encourage sustained play and involvement.

The practitioners allowed the children's ideas to emerge as the children were given the freedom to explore boundaries in an unrestricted manner (DfES, 2006b) and cultivate their interests extensively and in depth. They utilised every opportunity to promote children's self-esteem, confidence, independence and imagination (CCEA, NES and BELB, 2002: 1–2) and provided the scaffolding (Bruner, 1960) essential for children's learning. Through play children can develop their higher level thinking skill and problem solving ability. It is the role of the practitioner to recognise, intervene and facilitate where and when appropriate in order to promote challenging play experiences.

Sustained shared thinking

Practitioners have a crucial role as they should not simply be providing play activities, but should be supportive and interact with the children as they tackle the activities (Coates et al., 2008). The activities should be challenging and achievable, and based on individual interests and experiences. One of the challenges for practitioners is to give children time to think about what they want and to express these wishes, rather than stepping in to 'help' by making decisions for them (DCSF, 2008).

Good outcomes for children are linked to adult–child interactions that involve 'sustained shared thinking', open-ended questions to extend children's thinking, and formative feedback to children during activities. Practitioners should support and challenge the children's thinking by becoming involved with them in the thinking process. Sustained, shared thinking is a process that involves awareness of the child's interests and understanding, and collaboration in developing an idea or a skill (DCSF, 2008). Providing appropriate contexts for thinking, interacting with children and sharing children's small group interactions are just some of the ways in which this can be achieved. Children should be working within their zones of proximal development or ZPD (Vygotsky, 1978), characterised as the gap between learners' current or actual developmental level determined by independent problem-solving, and the learners' emerging or potential levels of development; these should be 'determined through problem solving under adult guidance, or in collaboration with more capable peers' (Vygotsky, 1978: 86). As will be shown in Chapter 3, Vygotsky believed whatever children can do with help today, they will be able to do by themselves tomorrow. The supporting practitioners give help to extend children's thinking and help children to make connections in learning (DCSF, 2008).

A rich learning environment offers cognitively challenging activities. It allows children to investigate in depth rather than moving from one task to another. This open-ended, flexible provision gives children the opportunities to follow their own interests, sustain their active involvement, and pursue their own goals. It is generally understood that children from disadvantaged backgrounds fail to achieve as highly as their wealthier peers (Eyre, 2007).

Learning stories can help practitioners to provide a highly stimulating environment in an attempt to compensate for various deficits in the children's home circumstances (Clark, 2007). Eyre (1997) has highlighted the need for a stimulating environment to maximise a child's natural ability in the following model:

> **Ability + Opportunity/Support + Motivation = Achievement**

The emphasis should be placed on play and oral language for the development of 'literacy, attention, concentration and memory skills, physical confidence and competence, and the children's ability to build social relationships and co-operate with one another' (Walsh et al., 2006: 203). Practitioners should try to maximise learning opportunities that allow all learners to blossom. The classroom should be a place where all children can easily engage in activities and projects at their own respective level and pace (Smutny, 2001).

The environment should allow children to express elements of critical and creative thought. Such an environment would acknowledge both independence and collaboration with like-minded peers and supportive practitioners as necessary components. Opportunity to engage in open-ended exploration and knowledge-generation activities gives children the potential for autonomy and self-selection (Baczala, 2003) and is an essential feature of a nursery environment.

Case Study

Group problem solving
(extract from a group learning story)

The group comprising Harry, Chloe, Darshan and James had been experimenting with masking tape and making enclosures within the home area and nearby book corner. They were very experimental, testing to see how far the tape would stretch before breaking, what it would stick to and how to cut it off at the right moment.

They needed to use scissors to achieve this and previously we had always asked the children to sit down or be still whilst cutting or using sharp tools. The practitioners had a discussion concerning safety versus learning opportunities. They decided to supervise the activity closely, so discussed and emphasised safe use of tools with the children concerned.

The children continued to enclose different sections of the home area each day and their methods became more sophisticated as they became more familiar with handling of materials. They used shorter pieces and stuck them together to make them stronger. There was a considerable amount of discussion and negotiation involved over equipment and the use of space and tools.

Developing the environment

The practitioners were providing an environment that supported children's learning and development. The children were confident in this environment which meant they were 'willing to try things out, knowing that their efforts were valued' (DCSF, 2008: Card 3.3). The learning story shows how the practitioners were flexible enough to recognise and cater for the needs of every child while supporting groups in their learning.

Review of previous experience and building
on interest through a learning story

The practitioners had already been discussing shapes during the week and one practitioner noticed the children were beginning to make shapes within the carpet area. With encouragement from the staff the children could discuss the properties of the shapes — sides,

(Continued)

(Continued)

corners and curves. They knew how many corners and sides were needed for each shape. They also knew that circles had no corners and mastered the art of making one on the carpet. They used positional language to describe where they were putting the next shape. They began by making small shapes within the home area working individually. James became much bolder and began to make large strips across a wide expanse of carpet. Darshan looked on at this point. He joined these up to make gridlines on the floor. He sustained a high level of involvement in this task, seeming totally unaware of the others at this point. Staff continued to observe and noticed Darshan beginning to use long strips of the tape but at a higher level above the floor, attaching it to the bookcase and cupboard. This effectively blocked off the home corner so the children had great fun finding ways of getting through. Lots of positional vocabulary was used in this activity – for example 'over' and 'under'.

The next day Darshan and James moved to the home area and again began to experiment with the tape. Harry joined in, making waist-height gridlines across the home area. Darshan then noticed a musical instrument – a triangle, on the windowsill – and said, 'Should we stick this on?' James agreed. The tape was at waist level so they had a problem as the weight of the triangle made the tape sag on to the floor. They seemed to want the triangle suspended at waist height. At this point two practitioners had a discussion as to whether they should intervene and help the children solve the problem themselves. Given that the children were not getting frustrated and appeared just to be negotiating and discussing the problem, they decided to observe only and intervene when it was thought necessary. The children persisted all afternoon using a process of trial and error in testing their theories. Eventually they discovered that sticking on extra lengths and putting the tape further over the windowsills enabled the triangle to be suspended at the height they wished. The sense of achievement was enormous.

Analysis of the learning story

This learning story is a good example of learners' advanced thinking skills and how the curriculum offered open-ended activities that 'encouraged higher level thinking skills such as analysis, synthesis, evaluation and problem solving, and promoted intellectual risk-taking' (Porter, 1999: 173). These children had the ability to create wonder from unpromising material (the masking tape). They felt safe to make mistakes and use trial and error to solve problems (Porter, 1999). The practitioners played a key role in developing the learning experience for the children, as they were happy not to be in complete control when they allowed the children to use resources in a unique manner (DfES, 2006a). They provided a high quality environment, which provided an open use of resources, and encouraged the children to feel secure and confident to learn for themselves (DfES, 2002) and to pursue their own interests (Clark, 1997).

The practitioners allowed the children's ability to emerge as the children were given the freedom to explore boundaries in an unrestricted manner (DfES, 2006a) and to cultivate their interests extensively and in depth (Porter, 1999). They utilised every opportunity to promote children's self-esteem, confidence, independence and imagination (CCEA, NES and BELB, 2002: 1–2) while providing the scaffolding essential to children's learning (Bruner, 1960).

Key points to remember

- Learning stories can help Early Years practitioners, professionals and teachers to:

  - o develop and monitor the application of effective pedagogy
  - o chart children's development and learning to ensure that the needs of all children are met
  - o work on flexible activities with children of similar aptitudes
  - o become active participants in children's play (this active involvement is crucial if the Early Years team is to be able to analyse children's learning and development purposefully and accurately)
  - o identify the 'next steps' in children's learning and development, and to support them to further their development.

- Learning stories allow practitioners to focus on interventions that are process-oriented and not curriculum-focused (Bennett et al., 1997). The key is the formation of relationships that mutually influence both practitioners and children. The children were involved in activities that they perceived as play. Through these activities children could extend their interests, motivation and abilities (Seifert, 2006). Perceived playfulness in children can therefore be effectively supported by the skilful documentation and analysis of learning stories.

Points for discussion

- How do learning stories correlate with other forms of assessment and record keeping?
- Try to design and implement a learning story with a group of children. Reflect on this activity and try to investigate the advantages and disadvantages of using this technique for assessment of the children.
- Compare the learning stories with the pedagogical documentation described in Chapter 4. Can you see how these narrative documentations might help you to complete the assessment scales of EYFS?

Further reading

Carr, M. (2001) *Assessment in Early Childhood Settings*. London: Paul Chapman Publishing.

Clark, A., Moss, P. and Kjorholt, A.T. (eds) (2005) *Beyond Listening to Children: Children's Perspectives on Early Childhood Services*. Bristol: The Policy Press.

Moyles, J. (ed) (2007) *Early Years Foundations: Meeting the Challenge*. Maidenhead: Open University Press.

Useful websites

Learning stories:
www.aare.edu.au/99pap/pod99298.htm

Te Whāriki: He Whāriki Matauranga mo nga Mokopuna O Aotearoa. Early Childhood Education. Learning Media.
www.minedu.govt.nz/web/downloadable/dl3567_v1/ whariki.pdf

CHAPTER 6

WORKING IN PARTNERSHIP

Ally Dunhill

Chapter Aims

Central to the principles and aims of the Early Years Foundation Stage (EYFS) is to 'create partnerships between parents and professionals and between all the settings that a child attends' (DCSF, 2008: *Statutory Framework*, p. 7). Historically, the Early Years workforce previously worked alongside other services and communicated with parents and carers, yet this was often fragmented and sporadic. Working in partnership with parents and carers is now a legal requirement. The Childcare Act of 2006 provided the context for the delivery of EYFS and clearly states the importance of working – and necessity to work – in partnership. This raises new challenges for the Early Years workforce as new ways of working together and new skills have to be developed. The new Early Years workforce has accountability to deliver policies, and as well as working in partnership, to observe regulatory standards laid down in legislation.

This chapter aims to help you to:

- understand the need and the value of working in partnership with parents, carers and other professionals

(Continued)

(Continued)

- be able to identify and reflect on your own practice when working in partnership
- understand the role of the Early Years practitioner when working in partnership.

Partnership in context

As mentioned in Chapter 1, the overarching aim of the Early Years Foundation Stage (EYFS) is to support children in achieving the five outcomes of Every Child Matters (ECM): staying safe, being healthy, enjoying and achieving, making a positive contribution and achieving economic well-being (DfES, 2003). The principles for EYFS are directly linked to the ECM outcomes and are concerned with the unique learning and development of each child. The guiding themes for EYFS – a Unique Child, Positive Relationships, Enabling Environments and Learning and Development (DCSF, 2008) – endorse a holistic approach to learning and care, where children's needs are addressed through a range of integrated services, supporting all areas of child development while working in partnership with children, parents, carers and other professionals.

Working in partnership requires a range of different skills, and the Early Years workforce has a duty to ensure that the required skills are approached and developed positively and effectively. Key elements when working in partnership are:

- communicating information effectively
- establishing an on-going dialogue with children
- establishing an on-going dialogue with parents
- establishing an on-going dialogue with other professionals
- sharing planning and curriculum implementation, as well as sharing children's progress.

Within EYFS, this can be carried out informally with a discussion with the parents and carers or formally through the EYFS Portfolio. Only effective communication will lead to truly effective partnerships. The Early Years practitioner's daily routine is a very busy one; new curricular approaches are being implemented and these changes are having a positive impact on practice. Children's experiences in the family context are interlinked with the children's experiences in Early Years settings. These links between home and setting need to be addressed by the Early Years workforce and enhanced as a key element for working in partnership. Additionally, children's prior experiences or out-of-setting experiences are now equally important and valid within the educational programme, and thus are essential elements in working in partnership. These experiences need to be communicated between the Early Years workforce and parents. Effective partnership requires the use of appropriate language, respecting individual values and cultures, sharing experiences and practices, and sustaining an on-going dialogue with all members involved.

All participants in children's learning need to interact in harmony, and share concerns, problems and issues in a way that will permit them to achieve mutual understanding and agreement about how to proceed. In many ways Freire's (1972: 53) vision of student–teacher interaction, where 'the teacher is no longer merely the one who teaches, for the teacher is also taught in a dialogue with students. And students, while being taught, also teach. In this way, teacher and students become jointly responsible for a process in which all of them grow', can be transcended as pedagogical routines under EYFS.

Partnerships in teams

It is important for partnerships in teams that all team members have built relationships that respect each other, trust each other and are fair to each other. The starting point for working in partnership begins with effective communication within the Early Years team at setting level. Partnership working starts with all members of staff establishing good working relationships among them.

Failures in effective communication among practitioners and professionals can result in a lack of involvement and professional contribution; consequently, working in partnership is put at risk. Staff should be able to examine their personal practices, routines and activities and be constructively critical with each other. Professionals should take the time to have direct informal conversations about their daily routines, roles and responsibilities within the settings. Teams should establish working relationships where:

- roles are clear
- there is clear understanding of responsibilities
- systematic sharing of information among all team members takes place
- everyone respects each other
- everyone in the team has the opportunity to be heard.

Partnerships with children

The focus of the Early Years workforce is to work with children, yet it is equally important to form partnerships with children. Chapters 4 and 5 demonstrated how practitioners listen to children and how children can be observed, for us to assess their progress. The following section aims to focus on how practitioners involve and invite children as partners in Early Years settings, with an emphasis on observations as a communication tool. For a successful partnership with children it is essential to communicate with them at all levels.

Starting with children's interests

Involving children in the planning and decision making and changing the planning of activities on a daily basis allows the practitioner to be flexible and spontaneous when responding to children's needs, while being equally important for working in partnership with children. For example, the weather could change suddenly and the children might be curious or frightened. They will learn more from talking about these changes, interesting to them at the time. The practitioner can also reassure and comfort the child if this event has been a frightening experience. Unplanned learning opportunities should be seen as valuable experiences and many are memorable to the children.

Thus, observations are central to establishing successful communication and partnerships with children. Observations hold a central and important role throughout the on-going dialogue with the parents (as mentioned in Chapter 4) and with other professionals. Observations are key to identifying where children's developmental and learning needs, as well as their strengths, lie. However, observations cannot offer the Early Years workforce the complete 'picture' of a child; additional information must be gained from the parents or other carers. This information is usually gained over time and is more effective when a constructive relationship is formed with the parents and/or other carers.

There are several types of observation; a practitioner should choose the method that suits the activity and accurately record what the child is doing while observing. This can be in the form of notes, photographs, or tape and video recordings (as explained in Chapter 5). Observations can be carried out while working directly with the child. These are called 'participant observations'. They are usually planned observations where the practitioner writes down brief notes while being involved in an activity or session, writing a fuller description afterwards. Other methods are more impromptu and the practitioner should be ready to note down these significant (or 'wow') moments when they occur (DCSF, 2008).

Only after observing a child can a practitioner analyse, review and plan to meet a child's needs. The child's interests should be at the centre of short-term plans; links should not be made to the six areas of learning and development before the child's interests have been established. Plans should be thought of as guidelines rather than as a set timetable for the day or week. This will allow the practitioner to be flexible and spontaneous and to respond to the child's changing needs and interests.

Observation to inform future planning for children's interests is a concept that can have many interpretations, as each child is as unique as each practitioner. To attempt to anticipate the pathway along which a child's thinking processes will turn next requires the practitioner to be open-minded and to 'listen' for cues from the child engrossed in play or attempting to master new learning. The emotional cues can be shown in a variety of ways, including as excitement when a child does something that exhilarates them, or as frustration when a child demonstrates a negative emotion or response.

Taking children outdoors provides endless opportunities for future planning. A walk in the park stimulates all five senses as the weather is felt on their skin; warm sunshine, cooling wind or cold rain as it causes a sharp intake of breath as it falls on a child's face.

The colours of the sky, the trees, the buildings, the different people and animals are seen. The sounds of the traffic, the birds singing, the falling rain or grass being cut are heard. The smell of damp tree bark, freshly cut grass, different blossom perfumes, damp rotting leaves, the smell of the pond as you near the ducks and swans: all stimulate another sense. There is also taste: that of bread, a sneaky piece meant for the ducks is eaten, a picnic or, if lucky, an ice cream.

While walking, children will see objects for which they do not yet know the names. These objects can be identified by an older child or by the practitioner. Hearing those words that begin to give meaning to the 'things', together with listening to birds singing, the wind rustling the leaves, or the splashes made by the ducks when they are scrabbling for the bread: the opportunities for children to connect to their emotional inner selves are endless.

Children will learn more from their social environments and relationships with adults and each other than from anything that is taught directly to them. Children are constantly receiving messages and signals from the world around them. How these messages are interpreted depends upon the way in which the messages and signals are given.

Case Study

Children's learning

Whilst talking outside with a group of 2–4-year-old children at a local pre-school, the practitioner and the children stood looking over a fence and locked gate. The other side of the fence was very overgrown with nettles, with a path leading to a large tree and shrubbery. The area was due for further development; word was being awaited whether the bid for funding had been successful, therefore the area was kept out of bounds to the children for safety reasons. On closer inspection, the only reason children should have been discouraged from entering the area was found in the large nettles. If a short amount of time had been invested in clearing the nettles, a whole new world was waiting to be explored by the children. The practitioner asked the children playing outside if they would like to go into the garden area. The response was an excited 'Yes', and then she asked what they thought they would find, as it was very overgrown. The children excitedly told her that there would be squirrels that would bite them and, when further prompted, ladybirds, spiders and worms. She asked them if they could hear the birds and they immediately quietened to listen; they could. One boy showed a vivid imagination as he described the monsters that could be in the area, and he would catch them and bring them out and kill them.

When the nettles were finally cleared, the children were taken to the grand opening of the gate! Children were allowed to enter the still overgrown area and explore the

(Continued)

(Continued)

grassy pathway. They were not given a predetermined task to do, e.g., look for worms, insects, snails, etc., but they were allowed to venture in and discover the area for themselves. Adults accompanied the children; they did not lead any of the play, only providing support, encouragement and a means to answer queries.

After almost two hours had lapsed the children were asked what they thought of the garden area. This provoked much discussion and many excited exchanges relaying their discoveries; they were asked what they would like to have in it. Eventually, the children decided upon two items, a table for the birds to feed from and somewhere nice to sit and have a picnic.

The children were asked to draw their ideas of how either the bird table would look or the place where they could sit. Adults supported the children by bringing in magazine and catalogue pictures for the children to look through to inspire them, and the children's drawings were placed carefully on the wall. Clay was then provided for the children to model their bird tables using their hands, with wet sponges and wooden lollipop sticks as tools to shape the more intricate details. The children persevered until they were satisfied that each tabletop would balance on its stand.

The collection of clay bird tables was kept safely, along with the first drawing designs, in full view of the children. The next step in the process was to make the table. Through dialogue with the children it was decided that parents' help would be needed. The children were asked what they thought should be said; they dictated a letter to a staff member to be sent out to the parents asking for their help. Parents volunteered to build the birdhouse with the children and it was erected in the grassy area.

Listening to children: the role of observation

When working with children in any setting or environment an Early Years practitioner will be observing children continually, and will probably not realise they are doing this. The Early Years practitioner will work closely with children at certain times and have the advantage of knowing each child's background, developing this knowledge on a daily basis and liaising with those closest to each child. To record the constant stream of information effectively the Early Years practitioner will need to learn how to observe objectively and record the findings accurately. This can also allow children with a limited language repertoire to communicate their interests and inform planning.

Although EYFS provides clear and useful advice on observations and assessments, along with detailed information with examples to meet the needs of children's learning, development and welfare, the Early Years practitioner needs to use these in a way that informs their own practice and further develops their knowledge, understanding and skills.

Effective practice in EYFS provides each child with the support they need to develop and learn. The EYFS documents (DCSF, 2008) provide the Early Years practitioner with information and guidance to reflect on the experiences children receive at home, on the provision received in the setting and on the individual needs of the child. Through effective on-going observations and assessments using the EYFS guidance, children can be supported individually to make progress at their own pace, and the Early Years practitioner can use this evidence to plan continual progress. This can meet the needs of each child only if the Early Years practitioner understands the basic needs of each child in their care. In turn, this understanding can be gained only through a two-way communication process with the child's parents, carers and other professionals. There is no point in observing children if the information is filed away and is not shared with children, parents, carers, other practitioners or external professionals in such a way that it will improve practice.

The holistic child and EYFS

To support all areas of development an Early Years practitioner will focus holistically on the whole child and not just on one aspect. A child does not learn or develop a skill in isolation. This is not a new concept. Theorists such as Vygotsky (1978) emphasised the social nature of cognitive development and suggested a non-compartmentalised approach to childcare. When a child is being observed they do not segregate their learning and development. They automatically manoeuvre from one skill to another: from communication skill to physical skill to mark making. For example, a child may talk to their peers about getting the chalks and going outside with them, then skip outdoors and start to draw large circles on the ground. Children do not identify these skills in isolation or give themselves scores after carrying them out.

The four guiding themes and related principles of EYFS (DCSF, 2008: *Statutory Framework*, pp. 8–9) are:

- A Unique Child
  Principle – Every child is a competent learner from birth who can be resilient, capable, confident and self-assured
- Positive Relationships
  Principle – Children learn to be strong and independent from a base of loving and secure relationships with parents and/or a key worker
- Enabling Environments
  Principle – The environment plays a key role in supporting and extending children's development and learning
- Learning and Development
  Principle – Children develop and learn in different ways and at different rates and all areas of learning and development are equally important and inter-connected.

Each guiding theme is unique and interlinked. For example, when observing a child, the practitioner would take into account the skills being developed by the child, the area of the setting in which the child has chosen to be, the equipment the child has chosen and the children and adults with whom the child is interacting. The information from each observation can then be analysed and reflected upon. Further information may be sought from other practitioners, the child and the parents or carers. Only then can a practitioner make an informed decision regarding the child's development needs and plan to meet them.

> Observing what children are doing and are interested in, to match provision to individual learning needs, interests and styles of learning. Close, informed observations using various assessment techniques will inform, plan and improve practice and provision. (CWDC, 2007: 27 S10)

The EYFS themes support the Early Years practitioner holistically to sustain the developmental needs of each child. The documentation can provide the practitioner with the confidence and guidance to provide a child-centred environment. Play is central to EYFS; it can provide evidence for the six areas of learning and development of life skills for today's society. The Unique Child Principle guides the Early Years practitioner towards nurturing the unique nature of every child.

Positive relationships (children learn to be strong and independent from a base of loving and secure relationships with parents and/or a key worker) are one of the most important aspects of EYFS. The four commitments of this theme are:

- Respecting each other: understanding feelings, friendships, professional relationships, effective practice, challenges and dilemmas and reflecting on practice
- Parents as partners: communication, learning together, effective practice and facing challenges and dilemmas
- Supporting learning: positive interactions, listening to children, effective practice and facing challenges and dilemmas
- Key person: secure attachment, shared care, independence, effective practice and facing challenges and dilemmas.
(DCSF, 2008: *Statutory Framework*, p. 9)

The new professional standards for teachers (TDA, 2008) lay down the requirements for qualified teacher status (QTS) through a range of study routes. The statements of the professional attributes, professional knowledge and understanding, and the professional skills that teachers are required to demonstrate, underpin the five key outcomes for children identified within Every Child Matters (DfES, 2003) and the six areas of the Common Core of Skills and Knowledge for the children's workforce (DfES, 2005).

Teachers are required to demonstrate at each stage of their career that they have achieved these standards in order to progress to posts with greater responsibility. Each standard and its requirements have some reference to Early Years, yet the terminology presented in these standards refers only infrequently to very young children from birth to 3 years; rather, the terminology used mirrors the language of the primary and secondary school sectors and the National Curriculum. These standards suggest that a teacher 'teaches' a lesson. The emphasis in an Early Years setting is on continuous provision for children that enables the child, with or without the support of practitioners and other children, to explore their world and ideas, through a diverse range of expertise and using a range of materials.

> On-going assessment is an integral part of the learning and development process. Providers must ensure that practitioners are observing children and responding appropriately to help them make progress. (DCSF, 2008: *Statutory Framework*, p. 16)

This emphasis from the teaching standards lies on the teacher's teaching, not on starting with the child and their needs; it may create a conflict for settings and trainees between, on the one hand, the teacher's achieving the standards and, on the other, meeting the individual needs of each child (Miller and Cable, 2008).

How observation informs planning

Practitioners observe children to identify the nature of the support needed by each child for their play and development. Practitioners need to be aware of the children's individual needs and current preferences in order to provide the appropriate environment and, furthermore, to ensure that children are engaged in play opportunities that each child finds interesting and rewarding. Stages are more important than ages. Every area of development is equally important.

> Assessment should be based on practitioners' observations of what children are doing in their day-to-day activities. As judgements are based on observational evidence gathered from a wide range of learning and teaching contexts, it is expected that all adults who interact with the child should contribute to the process, and that account will be taken from information provided by parents. (DCSF, 2008: *Statutory Framework*, p. 16)

Listening to and recording children's views through observations or conversations can enhance the planning process. The information gained from observations could determine whether an activity has been successful; the practitioners would then decide to repeat, adapt or extend that activity. Children's comments should also be taken into account through taking the time to share children's views at that time, writing down the language they use and the exact phrases they present. This will give the practitioner the opportunity to identify the stage at which the children are in their development and what interests them. Only then can the practitioners build on children's previous understanding (Afrey, 2003).

Case Study
Children's planning

To ensure the activities provided by a setting meet the individual needs and interests of all children, input from the children is essential. One way in which this is happening in a private nursery in Hull is through mind mapping (2–3 years age range).

The practitioner started with a large blank piece of paper and many coloured crayons, pencils and pens on the floor. She then explained to the children that she would like them to help in deciding what activities to prepare for their group. The children interested in joining her were asked to go and get their photos from their drawers then place them onto the middle of the paper. This set the scene, as the photos were the central image on the mind map. The practitioner then asked the children if they wanted to draw something they enjoyed doing or playing with and gave examples of her own. The children drew and chatted while the practitioner listened and, if required, answered questions. The next stage was to see how each of the children's drawings could be linked. In what ways were they similar and in what ways were they different? The children started to discuss similarities and differences and the practitioner noted likes and dislikes from the discussion. The children were then asked to draw examples of activities that they wanted to do from as many of the drawings as they could. From this the practitioner identified resources, themes and activity ideas that could be implemented in the setting.

The mind map was kept as a record for the practitioner to plan the activities, to share with the parents and for the children to continue to add to and develop.

Partnerships with parents and carers

Parents are children's first and most enduring educators. When parents and practitioners work together in Early Years settings, the results have a positive impact on the child's development and learning. Therefore, each setting should seek to develop an effective partnership with parents. (QCA/DfEE, 2000: 9)

 Every child has individual needs; in Early Years settings the child's 'key person' should oversee those needs. The key person system allows the child to make a strong emotional attachment with one adult in a setting. This helps the child to feel safe and cared for and gives the practitioner the opportunities to build relationships with the child and their parents or carers. A key person plays a vital role in a child's life through being consistent and sensitive, as well as bearing the responsibility for meeting the needs of each child in their care. To do this they must actively engage, interact, connect and build trust with each child and their family.

Parents and families are central to a child's well-being and practitioners should support this important relationship by sharing information and offering support for extending learning at home. (DCSF, 2008: *Statutory Framework*, p. 10)

There are numerous benefits to be derived from this relationship. Parents and carers can feel supported and reassured that someone who is committed to their child is caring for their child in an environment of which they feel a part. This can be very important for parents, as they may need to go to work and thus feel reluctant and upset when leaving their child in a setting, or can feel uneasy when sharing intimate information or asking for advice. Information is shared between the home and the setting by adults who have a mutual respect for one other. This creates professionalism within an Early Years setting; additionally, it has resulted in a reduction in staff sickness and absence because of increased job satisfaction and fulfilment.

A manageable, trusting relationship between a key person and parents and carers supports and develops the relationships between the parent and child, and can establish and sustain the relationships between the practitioner and child. A child who observes their parents or carers interacting with their key person can find it easier to form links between home and the setting. This is especially valuable when encouraging the learning experience to be continued at home, or when drawing on the child's experiences from outside the setting. The impact of a positive relationship with parents and carers upon a child's development has been widely acknowledged since the 1958 National Child Development Study (NCDS, 1958), Bronfenbrenner's evaluation of the US Head Start Program in the 1970s (Ryan and Bronfenbrenner, 1974), and the DfES (2003) Effective Provision of Pre-School Education (EPPE) project (Sylva et al., 2003).

The start of the day can be tense and difficult for both the child and the parent. A key person can make this transition time as easy as possible: parents, carers and children may need to inform them what happened the night before or during the previous day. This information is vital for the key person to understand what the child has experienced and to ensure that the child's needs are met. This approach takes time and effort. An Early Years practitioner takes on the role to ensure the safety of the child – not only because the law requires it but also because young children are vulnerable and practitioners are accountable for them while they are in their care.

Partnerships with other services

Early Years practitioners work with a range of services beyond the setting to ensure that the needs of the children are met. A child can move between settings over a month, a week or even daily. A child may be with a childminder first thing in the morning and attend a private nursery in the afternoon. Communication among these settings is vital if the child is to feel secure. Coherent, joined-up provision improves the outcomes for children as well as enabling and encouraging professionals to work together to meet the needs of the children in their care.

 An Early Years practitioner should build up a strong partnership with a range of professionals and services, including the coordinated and joined-up working between education, social work, health and relevant voluntary organisations, to ensure that the specific needs of the children and their families who attend the setting are met and that the service is more cohesive. Working with other services can support high quality provision for children and improve their life chances. Being receptive to other professionals' different approaches can also improve parental and carer confidence and self-esteem, leading to parents and carers feeling less anxious about interacting with other professionals. The Early Years environment cannot always meet all the needs of the child or family, yet it can 'signpost', i.e., direct, parents and carers to other services they might require.

Key points to remember

- Planning starts from the child's experiences and interests at that time.
- Holistic learning and development take place when children learn physically, intellectually and emotionally, and can experiment and express their ideas in a non-threatening environment.
- Working in partnership with parents, carers, children and other professionals is crucial to ensure the practitioner meets the needs of the child and the family.
- Working in partnership is a two-way process and allows the practitioner and parent/carer to have a shared vision and shared goals.

Points for discussion

- Supporting children to represent their inner thoughts and express their imagination is dependent on the resourcefulness of sensitive adults. Consider a recent opportunity you created or supported to allow children to represent their inner thoughts and express their imagination. Reflect on how you did this.
- Think about what messages your setting gives to parents, carers and children at dropping-off and collection time. Is your environment parent/carer-friendly? Do all the parents/carers know their child's key person? Are all the key persons present at these times? Do the key persons have the time and somewhere to go if a parent wants to have a chat? Are all key persons aware of their roles and responsibilities? How effective are your key persons in meeting the needs of the parents, carers and children?

- Fitzgerald and Kay (2008: 14) list some characteristics of effective communication which are essential when creating an effective partnership:

    - Being an open and honest communicator
    - Keeping information confidential when necessary
    - Providing accurate and balanced information
    - Sharing all news even when it is difficult and/or unpleasant
    - Avoiding making assumptions
    - Ensuring that agreed actions are followed up and completed.

To this list we could add more, such as being objective. Can you think of any other characteristics and actions for effective communication with parents, carers and other professionals?

Further reading

Clark, A. and Moss, P. (2001) *Listening to Young Children: The Mosaic Approach*. London: National Children's Bureau.

Fitzgerald, D. and Kay, J. (2008) *Working Together in Children's Services*. London: Routledge.

Smidt, S. (2005) *Observing, Assessing and Planning for Children in the Early Years*. London: Routledge.

Useful websites

Implementation of EYFS:
www.teachernet.gov.uk/teachingandlearning/EYFS/
www.foundation-stage.info/forums/index.php?showforum=125

CHAPTER 7

Effective Transitions into and out of the Early Years Foundation Stage

Ioanna Palaiologou and Alex Hallowes

Chapter Aims

It is clearly stated within the EYFS that it is 'crucial to their future success that children's earliest experiences help to build a secure foundation for learning throughout their school years and beyond' (DCSF, 2008: *Statutory Framework*, p.10). However, in order to build effective and strong foundations in children's lives it is important for the Early Years workforce to understand the importance of transitions in children's lives and try to accommodate these transitions. Early Years settings and schools maintain a critical role in delivering a coherent approach both to the continuation of EYFS and when children are moving from EYFS to Key Stage 1. The smooth transitions into and out of EYFS are important for children's well-being and, therefore, for their development. This chapter deals with the key issues around transitions and discusses actions for effective transition such as: sharing information, assessment and record keeping, leading in partnership, and Early Years team meetings. Briefings will also be addressed.

This chapter aims to help you to:

- examine what transitions are

- understand the impact of transitions upon children's well-being and development

- examine how effective transitions can be implemented in EYFS.

What transitions are

EYFS states that:

> Children may move between several different settings in the course of a day, a week, a month or a year.
>
> Children's social, emotional and educational needs are central to any transition between one setting and another, or within a single setting.
>
> - Some children and their parents will find transition times stressful whilst others will enjoy the experience.
> - Effective communication between settings is the key to ensuring that children's needs are met and there is continuity in their learning.
>
> (DCSF, 2008: Card 3.4)

Children's experiences when they are growing up are full of changes, such as changes in their own bodies, and changes in family circumstances: moving house, the breaking up of the family, the loss of a family member, going from home to a playgroup or from home to a nursery, then from nursery to school. All of these changes in a child's life can be regarded as transitions. The EPPE project revealed that children do actually experience a number of these transitions during the first years of their lives. The EPPE project has described two types of transitions: the 'horizontal' and the 'vertical'. Traditionally, moving from home to school (a horizontal displacement) was considered as the most important transition in children's lives. However, it is now recognised that children move vertically in their lives, for example, from home to playgroup with a member of the family; also, as it is increasingly common that both parents have to work, from home to that of grand-parents, or half-day nursery and half-day playgroup, or during childminder care.

As has been shown in Chapter 3, Bronfenbrenner (1979) identified 'systems': layers that we move into and out of throughout our lives. He claims, for example, that the microsystem (of home, playgroup, or childminder) of a child's life is rich in transitions, and these have an effect on a child's well-being. Bronfenbrenner emphasised, for the child's well-being, the need for links in between the systems:

> The developmental potential of a setting is increased as a function of the number of supportive links existing between the setting and other settings (such as the home and the family). Thus, the least favourable condition for development is one in which supplementary links are either non-supportive or completely absent, when the mesosystem is weakly linked. (1979: 215)

Also, as will be seen in Chapter 9, attachment theory as introduced by Bowlby (1969) has an impact on Early Years education and care. Attachment is the process where babies and parents or carers form a relationship and this leads to emotional bonds. Bowlby (1969) suggested that babies show stranger anxiety, a fear of unfamiliar persons or unfamiliar contexts, and these often cause stress to babies and young children. They also show separation anxiety at about the age of 6 months. This is a fear of being separated from care-givers (Vondra and Barnett, 1999). Babies appear to be upset when their parents or carers are leaving them and this can again cause distress. Early years practitioners who work with babies and toddlers are familiar with the signs of a child being distressed when the child initially arrives in the unfamiliar Early Years setting. Early Years practitioners find the first few weeks in the Early Years settings the most difficult and challenging for children, who are anxious, distressed and disturbed until they settle down.

Working within the EYFS framework, it is important for children's well-being to support transitions. The following sections attempt to discuss some steps towards effective transitions.

Steps towards effective transitions

Develop a transition action plan

The Early Years workforce have realised the significance of transitions in children's well-being and development. Thus, many Early Years settings and schools have developed 'transition programmes' consisting of a range of activities occurring throughout the year and constituting a process for preparing the children to accommodate 'horizontal' transitions. However, it is important that the Early Years settings developing action plans or transition programmes also prepare the children for 'vertical' transitions.

An action plan is essential to make sure that the process of transition is indeed implemented; it must not be forgotten or left too late in the hurry of the daily routine of the setting. All members of the staff should participate in this action plan as each has an important role to play. Within this action plan practicalities need to be considered, such as completing the Profile of the child for it to arrive at the new setting in time, determining who is going to work with the child (i.e., the key worker), how many hours during the first couple of weeks a child will stay in the setting, etc.

This action plan needs to involve the staff, children and parents. Brooker (2008) stresses the importance of this relationship and she describes it as 'a caring triangle'. She identifies three key processes for effective planning:

- Understanding routines in the nursery and at home, such as sleeping habits, feeding habits (for younger children) or children's interests (for example, whether they like to play outdoors or with construction materials)
- Enjoying relationships and having pleasurable interaction with other children. Friendships in the nursery should be encouraged amongst children
- Making links with the outside world. 'Enabling environments' is a principle within EYFS; the outside-of-the-class life of children is important, for example, little items such as a photograph of parents or a little toy help children to 'transfer' their own environment into the class setting, as will be explained later in this chapter.

Involve the children

During transitions it is important for children to be actively involved in the process. Throughout the EYFS one of the key issues is to listen to the children, to ascertain how they feel about the setting, which activities they like to participate in, and in which area in the setting they prefer to be. Observations are important in listening to children and involving them in the transitions. As was explained in Chapter 4, observations are a useful tool for assessment, while they also enable Early Years teams to listen to the children by understanding their needs. Observations help the Early Years team to recognise what the children like or dislike, especially where younger children (0–2) are concerned, with their limited spoken language repertoire, and thus they cannot always effectively express what they want.

Case Study

From home to nursery

Harry is 18 months old. He is starting private nursery care for three days a week for not more than three hours per session. The parents have decided to send him to the nursery as he is the only child in the family and they have noticed that he is not interacting with other children of his own age. His mother is not working so she can be reached any time. Prior to the official starting date, there were a few visits to the setting so that Harry could familiarise himself with the place.

During the first 'official' day at nursery Harry and his mother enter through the main door and Harry immediately runs to the outdoor area. He takes out his little red car and starts playing with it. The Early Years practitioner invites him into the class but he declines to enter. His mother says goodbye and she leaves. Harry seems fine when his

(Continued)

(Continued)

mother has left but he still does not want to go inside. He enjoys playing in the outdoors area on his own.

The Early Years practitioner leaves the door open in case he wants to come inside and join the other children. Harry is observing what happens in the classroom area yet he does not want to come indoors.

Harry spent the first month in the outdoors area observing what was happening indoors, sometimes joining in with a nursery rhyme and making moves to accompany them, although still on his own outside. It took him a month to come inside the class, and the first activity he joined in with was singing.

In this case, the Early Years team did not force Harry to come indoors; they were 'listening' to Harry's needs. He was ready to be in the nursery although he was not ready to be indoors with others. When he was indeed ready, he moved of his own volition. During this transition from home to nursery Harry was listened to and involved in the transition – he was not forced to be indoors, but was given appropriate time in which to feel comfortable to join in with indoor activities at the moment of his choosing.

Another key issue for effective transitions is to understand and respect the objects brought by children into the class from home. These objects – the little toys that children carry with them – offer emotional comfort to young children, who carry and regard them as symbols: the items symbolise the continuation from home to nursery. Examining the theory of attachment, and focusing on the work of Bowlby and Ainsworth, the importance of these objects carried by children during transitions is that they are essential for the children's well-being. In the above case study of Harry, he had a little red car with him for two months. For the first month it never left his hands. During the second month, when he was coming into the nursery, he wanted the toy for a while, and then, at the Early Years practitioner's suggestion, he left the car with the practitioner to 'sleep'. However, he always remembered to take it away with him when he left the nursery. Harry was observed again after seven months. He was still bringing in his little red car, but as soon as he arrived in the nursery he immediately gave it into the safekeeping of the Early Years practitioner.

It is very important that practitioners make every effort to ensure that children feel both confident and supported when they are still new to the environment. Make sure vocabulary is appropriate and that the children understand what it means. Each setting uses different terms to describe certain items or activities; for example, in a nursery the staff may call the construction area something different from the term used in the Foundation Stage, so it is important to find out and clarify that everyone knows what items and locations are going to be called and therefore prevent confusion.

It is essential to explain what words mean – 'assembly', for instance, and 'corridor': words and concepts that adults use unconsciously yet that may not be familiar to children. Another example is the instruction, 'Sit in a circle': 'But what is a circle?', 'How can I sit in a circle if there isn't one?'

As soon as children establish a relationship in the Early Years setting or school then they are ready to leave behind the objects they carry. Still, many children might feel the need to have them in their bags, such is the emotional attachment to these objects. Working in the Early Years it is important to respect the children's need to bring little objects from home, and what these objects mean for the children. It is also essential to allow them to choose the materials they want to play with, to respect a child's daily routines, and not to discourage constant links with home.

Involve the parents

Throughout EYFS the role of parents is highly emphasised. It is suggested that parents should be part of children's education and care, and be encouraged to remain actively involved in all educational processes. The 'curriculum' of family life is vitally important because this is where young children spend much of their time. It is essential that we engage the parents in school life so that there is a 'joined-up' aspect to the child's experiences.

What it is important to understand when practitioners involve parents is that they themselves are also going through transitions. For example, they move between home and work and back again, changing 'hats' from parent to teacher, from daughter to mother, from son to father, and so on. As with Early Years staff, parents are as strongly influenced by the 'transition effect' as are their children. It also needs to be acknowledged that parents feel anxiety about their children's transitions. Of course, they see the effect of the stress in the children at home in ways that may not be reported to the Early Years setting or the school, especially if the relationship with staff has not been established. Perhaps a child has started bed-wetting, or using 'baby talk'; perhaps a child is misbehaving, unusually, or perhaps they spend a lot of time hiding under their bed. All these may be signs that a child is stressed and the cause of this could be their transition. It is imperative that the parents are involved in the process of preparing the child to 'go up'. As mentioned above, Bronfenbrenner (1979) has shown that the more practitioners can combine the interactions of settings that the child has in his life (i.e., not just 'him-and-school' or 'him-and-parents', but 'him-*and*-school-*and*-parents') the more effective the child's development will be. Since the child's family home is the most important setting (because this is where he/she spends most of his/her time and is most strongly emotionally influenced) it is important that the nursery or school communicates with the parents in a practical and positive way.

Building positive relationships with the parents helps effective transitions. It is important to involve parents directly by making them feel really welcome in the setting or school by inviting them into the class, inviting them to sit with their children in the class, and getting to know them (i.e., involving them not only in times of a crisis or trouble).

Documenting children's activities and sharing them with the parents (as has been shown in Chapters 4 and 5) helps to involve them indirectly.

Case Study

The Danish example: enabling the family life

At an Early Years setting in Denmark the children each had a very personal way of identifying their locker and their clothes peg – sometimes a photograph, sometimes a small toy – and in every case it was something from and about the home (e.g., a picture of the child with their parents). The child could see this picture or artefact whenever they wanted, thus helping to allay the fears of being left behind or forgotten.

Here are some activities that parents can be involved in during the transition period:

(1) A 'family display' with photographs of children's lives from home. Early years practitioners can organise a space for a display of photographs from or of parents, grandparents, or activities the child did at home. This way parents will feel part of the life of the Early Years setting. The display can be extended with the use of modern technology. Practitioners can take some photographs of what happens in the setting on the day then download these into the computer as a screen saver. When the parents come to the setting the staff can show the images to the parents.

In this way parents know what their children did in the setting and can also ask the child questions about the pictures when at home; thus, the setting's life is moved into the home. Responsibility for putting the photos into a dated folder during the mid-morning break the following day must be taken by a member of staff, so that 'today's folder' is ready for new photos – simple, inclusive, reflective and effective.

(2) A 'Play and Stay' activity type for one group every morning. This involves the parent's doing an activity with the child for about 20 minutes while the other groups have 'carpet time' with staff. The parents feel they really are making a contribution. Furthermore, they also have the chance to see how the dynamic of the class works with the other children. In this way staff in the setting tend to be able to learn to know the parents better.

(3) Give the children 'something to take or do at home' which involves the parents – taking the gerbil home for the weekend is a type of 'homework', as is taking Barnaby Bear or equivalent, while these involve only individual children. Devise a short, enjoyable, interesting task for the children to complete at the weekend that will also involve the parents or carers. One week it could be quite

serious (or formal), such as making a number wheel, or counting the number of dandelions in the park, and other weeks the task can be as frivolous or silly as you can imagine. The point is simply to get the parents involved with their children's school life, which means that when you need the help of the parents in achieving an important milestone, such as to address a transition, they are used to being involved in co-operating, as are the children.

Case Study

The Danish example: 'the summer box' homework

In Denmark they have a 'summer box' project: the children are given a box at the end of the school year and are asked to collect over the holidays items to put into that box. At the beginning of the new school year they bring their boxes in; the first piece of work is all about the summer and what is in the boxes. This is a really effective way of involving the parents, while it also ensures that the children, who have a limited concept of time, remember about school, so when it is time to go back it is not a shock – indeed, they may even look forward to the chance of showing off the items in their box!

The environment is the third teacher

The environment as a 'third teacher' is part of the ethos of the Reggio Emilia approach, and it can be used for effective and successful transitions for children.

EYFS states that:

- Every setting is part of its community even though not all the children may live in the surrounding neighbourhood.
- The local community may contain many different racial, cultural or religious groups. Even if it doesn't, there will be children and adults of various ages with different views, beliefs and backgrounds using the setting.
- When the setting values the local community, it can encourage the different community groups to work together for the benefit of all. (DCSF, 2008: Card 3.4)

Children have a life before entering the Early Years setting; this life may either be transferred into the class in the form of an activity such as a festival or playing at being firemen, or else the class can be transferred outwards into the community, for example, a visit to the local church or a visit to the local post office. In this way there is going to be a continuation of familiarity between the setting/school and the community in which the children are growing up.

Familiar staff – the key person

As will be shown in Chapter 9, for young children attachment is important to their emotional and social development. EYFS has addressed this by identifying a key person for each child:

- A key person helps the baby or child to become familiar with the setting and to feel confident and safe within it.
- A key person develops a genuine bond with children and offers a settled, close relationship.
- When children feel happy and secure in this way they are confident to explore and to try out new things.
- Even when children are older and can hold special people in mind for longer there is still a need for them to have a key person to depend on in the setting, such as their teacher or a teaching assistant. (DCSF, 2008: Card 2.4)

The children may be able to discuss with their key person fears and concerns they are experiencing, as they will know this person well and they will have started establishing a relationship with them. However, children are sometimes happier talking to a toy or a puppet than to an adult – and if the Foundation Stage and Year 1 teachers use this knowledge to bring questions and concerns out into the open, this will lead to conversations and discussions through which fears can be expressed.

Visits and cross-phase activities

One of the strategies that can be developed in order to smooth transitions is to set up a series of visits in either direction for specific age groups; for example, younger children might go to visit their future class, and the Year 1 children might visit the Foundation Stage settings. These visits can lead to a project such as a 'post office' area, where there are exchanges of letters between the Nursery and Foundation Stage, or between Foundation Stage and Key Stage 1. Visits and cross-phase activities are a helpful technique, not only to ease the transition process but also provide enabling to environments effectively.

Case Study

'Our post office': an opportunity to visit a KS1 class

After a visit to a local post office, the children created a post office area in a Foundation Stage class. In this area there were stamps, pens, envelopes, a set of scales, and other material that one can find in a post office.

> The children started writing letters and cards they wanted to post. The Foundation Stage teacher suggested posting letters to KS1 children. In this way they began a long and complex project where the two groups of children communicated with each other and provided a real opportunity for cross-phase working, which could be built upon during transition discussions.

Shared playtimes

There should be shared playtimes, when the younger children visit the older ones in the playground. In many settings the Foundation Stage children are separated from the rest of the school, so anything that can prepare them for, and assimilate them with, the older children is beneficial. One option is that, after visits, the children could be paired up so that the younger ones had a more experienced child to take care of them and 'show them the ropes'.

Use the outdoors

Many Foundation Stage classrooms and Early Years settings have their own outside space so that there can be freedom to move between the indoor and outdoor areas. The outside is vital for children, so every effort should be made by KS1 regularly to go outside for work to take place there.

Staff liaison and transfer of records

Transfer of records is an important period for KS1 staff to familiarise themselves with the children's needs and the ethos of EYFS, and to see how it can be transferred over to the National Curriculum. As the implementation of EYFS is relatively new, the KS1 staff might be unfamiliar with the concept of 'a unique child', and therefore will not plan for an individual child's needs and pace. KS1 may provide a more 'whole-class' experience, rather than small group opportunities for individual exploration and self-discovery.

Certain skills and abilities are to be expected after transition, however if there is a lack of understanding about a child's previous experience of learning – and therefore a lack of transition of methods – then the skills and abilities acquired by the child during EYFS might not be taken into consideration, with the result that learning opportunities are subsequently lost. Foundation Stage staff need to ensure that KS1 staff have attained the required understanding, in order to ensure that the delivery is appropriate until the children are settled. Otherwise, there is a clear danger that the children may become de-motivated because everything is so different. It is also important that the Foundation Stage staff have an understanding of the National Curriculum requirements in KS1 and can play their part in preparing children for the transition.

Key points to remember

- This chapter discussed the important role of transitions in children's lives. Transitions can become stressful for children and they subsequently have an impact on children's well-being. Transitions cannot be avoided, but they can be effectively planned and organised so that the social and emotional effects of transition will not have a negative impact on children's well-being.
- This chapter offered some steps that can help children to experience effective transitions into and out of EYFS. There is great emphasis on involving the children themselves in the process, as well as involving the parents. Early Years teams should become facilitators in the transition processes of children, involving all staff in the environment of the children, and creating creative and stimulating activities for children.

Points for discussion

- Imagine that a child in your Early Years setting is going away for a month. Can you create an action plan to smooth the transition for when he or she returns? How can you prepare the parents and the child before their departure and how can you welcome the child back?
- Study the EYFS and the KS1 curriculum and try to identify the differences (and similarities) between these two curricula. How can you prepare children for KS1?
- What are the main challenges faced by Early Years teachers when they try to implement enabling the environment, organising visits and shared play, and liaising with other staff?

Further reading

Brooker, L. (2002) *Starting School: Young Children Learning Cultures*. Buckingham: Open University Press.

Brooker, L. (2008) *Supporting Transitions in the Early Years*. Maidenhead: Open University Press.

Dunlop, A.W. and Fabian, H. (eds) (2007) *Informing Transitions in the Early Years: Research, Policy and Practice*. Maidenhead: Open University Press.

Useful websites

The Early Years Transitions and Special Educational Needs (EYTSEN) Project:
www.dcsf.gov.uk/research/data/uploadfiles/RR431.pdf

Transitions in EYFS:
www.standards.dfes.gov.uk/eyfs/site/3/4.htm
www.teachingexpertise.com/articles/transitions-in-the-early-years-foundation-stage-
   eyfs-2863

CHAPTER 8

MEETING EYFS OUTCOMES OUTSIDE OF THE EARLY YEARS SETTING

Wendy Thompson

Chapter Aims

One of the key principles of the Early Years Foundation Stage is that of 'Enabling Environments', instrumental in 'supporting and extending children's development and learning' (DCSF, 2008; *Statutory Framework*, p.10). Outside classrooms, other environments can become helpful contexts for the learning goals of EYFS. Museums, archives, libraries and galleries all become not only an interesting educational context for children; they are also places that can promote a holistic approach to children's development.

This chapter aims to help you to:

- develop an understanding of how the Early Years Foundation Stage principles and areas of learning can be implemented outside of the Early Years classroom or setting, specifically with children of 30–60 months old

- reflect on opportunities for using the local environment as a starting point for initiating and extending learning opportunities for young children

- think about whether 'out-of-setting activity' and experiences can contribute towards children's motivation, interests and creative development

- consider the implications for developing partnerships with parents and widening participation to involve the community learning context.

What does 'out-of-setting' learning mean?

High quality learning experiences can be found outside the classroom or setting and can prove to be a rich resource bank for children and their Early Years practitioners. If the latter are to provide experiences that motivate and encourage young children to achieve their full potential, and also empower and encourage parents and carers to do the same (DfES 2005), then educational experiences need to be viewed holistically. The Qualifications and Curriculum Authority (QCA) provides (via its website) an overview of the 0–16 age phase curriculum, starting from the Early Years Foundation Stage (EYFS) to the end of Key Stage 4. This is titled the 'Big Picture of the Curriculum' and involves the entire planned learning experience, including learning outside the classroom or Early Years setting. In QCA terms this involves community participation, creativity and critical thinking.

The Common Core of Skills and Knowledge (DfES, 2005) suggests practitioners should know how to motivate and encourage children to achieve their full potential, and should know how to empower and encourage parents and carers to help their children to achieve their full potential. Practitioners are encouraged to recognise that play and recreation, directed by young children, performs a major role in helping the children understand themselves and the world around them, as well as helping them to realise their potential.

The Children's Plan, *Building Brighter Futures* (DCSF, 2007), emphasises the need for young children to be involved in positive activities in order to develop personal and social skills, promote well-being, and reduce behaviour that puts them at risk. Article 31 of the Convention on the Rights of the Child (UNCRC, 1992) emphasises that children should be able to participate fully in cultural and artistic life in order to develop talents and to promote respect for cultural identities.

Learning outside the classroom or setting can be interpreted in diagrammatic form (see Figure 8.1); in this context it suggests opportunities for engaging in a wide range of experiences, in order to promote creativity and to stimulate interest and involvement. It is possible for aspects to overlap and interconnect in numerous ways.

Defining the boundaries between recreational and learning activities when working with young children is a difficult task. Proponents of an experiential learning model argue that young children are capable of demonstrating sophisticated levels of complex thinking when provided with an appropriate learning environment. Such an environment will encourage children to engage in reflective processes, problem solving and logical reasoning, and thus develop higher-order thinking skills and levels of creativity (Walsh and Gardner, 2005).

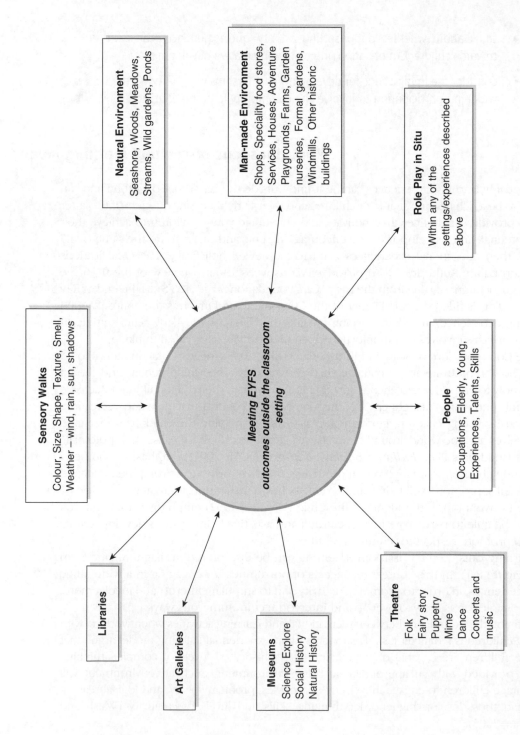

Figure 8.1 Meeting EYFS outcomes outside the classroom/setting

---

The following text is contained within the figure:

Natural Environment
Seashore, Woods, Meadows, Streams, Wild gardens, Ponds

Man-made Environment
Shops, Speciality food stores, Services, Houses, Adventure Playgrounds, Farms, Garden nurseries, Formal gardens, Windmills, Other historic buildings

Role Play in Situ
Within any of the settings/experiences described above

Sensory Walks
Colour, Size, Shape, Texture, Smell, Weather – wind, rain, sun, shadows

Meeting EYFS outcomes outside the classroom setting

People
Occupations, Elderly, Young, Experiences, Talents, Skills

Libraries

Art Galleries

Museums
Science Explore
Social History
Natural History

Theatre
Folk
Fairy story
Puppetry
Mime
Dance
Concerts and music

Young Children and creativity

Creativity will be discussed in detail in Chapter 13, although the focus will be on constructing the pedagogy for creativity in the class. Here, creativity is approached in an attempt to investigate how it can be extended to out-of-class environments. Loveless (2005: 29) describes creativity as involving the interaction between people and their communities, in social processes and subjects, and in wider social and cultural contexts. Adult creativity can often lead to a product, such as a work of art or a solution to a problem, whereas very young children's creativity, by contrast, may produce no tangible product or result. Because of this, young children's creativity has been described as being 'fundamentally different [from] the creativity of adults' (Runco, 2006: 121). It may take the form of imaginative play and self-expression, or a new understanding of the world. The opportunity for widening children's experiences is thus essential.

If children do not fully utilize their imagination, explore possibilities, try new things, consider new actions, invent understandings, and experiment, they will not be able to discover who they are, what they are capable of, and what is acceptable in their family, school, peer-group and culture (Runco, 2006: 121).

Similarly, EYFS also emphasises widening children's experiences (DCSF, 2008). It states that children in the 30–60-month age phase are becoming more aware of their place within a community and are beginning to build a stronger sense of their own identity; also, of their place in a wider world. A competent learner needs an enabling environment that offers both outdoors and out-of-setting experiences. These will provide freedom for young children to explore, use their senses, and be physically active and exuberant (DCSF, 2008: Card 3.3). In terms of wider contexts, EYFS suggests the need to develop multi-agency working, including working with librarians and local artists: 'When the setting values the local community it can encourage the different community groups to work together for the benefit of all' (EYFS, 2008: Card 3.4).

It is 'sustained engagement with experience' that leads to a different relationship with the world from that based on 'a succession of brief encounters' (Riley, 2007: 205). Sustained engagement can lead to new discoveries and different ways of viewing people, social situations and objects. Highly skilled and motivated professionals working within community learning environments (such as museums, libraries and galleries) may help to give depth to experiences and promote the type of learning that enables children's creativity to flourish. It is also possible for children to become active co-constructors of knowledge, if the adult positively enhances the learning experience (Riley, 2007). It is suggested that children are supported by adults who:

- highlight the critical features of the activity
- buffer the child's attention through distractions
- channel the child's activities to ensure success

- use errors to encourage learning
- enable procedures to be commented upon and explained.
  (Riley, 2007: 20)

In order to provide a focus for illustrating how EYFS outcomes can be met outside the classroom or setting, it is necessary to consider a beginning point or initial stimulus. The Museums, Libraries and Archives Council (MLA) will be selected, as it provides significant opportunities for developing higher-order thinking skills and creativity in young children.

Museums, Libraries and Archives Council and training opportunities

The MLA argues that it is best placed to serve communities and deliver local agendas to maximise local impact in neighbourhoods. Its aim is to provide new learning opportunities and to create partnerships across a number of sectors. The MLA offers a whole variety of initiatives and programmes in order to help individuals and settings develop accessible, inclusive and educational resources and services. As can be seen in Table 8.1, the MLA has created Generic Learning Outcomes applicable to working with a range of partners in EYFS such as Early Years Professionals and Early Years teachers. As is shown in Table 8.1, the MLA Generic Learning Outcomes can be linked with EYFS learning areas.

According to Salaman and Tutchell (2005: 1), museums and art galleries can offer unique opportunities to motivate children. Engagement with 'authentic' objects allows them to understand principles previously only available through books or verbal descriptions. They suggest that problem-solving activities can develop through a simple questioning approach: 'What does it look like? (Form) What is it for? (Function) What is it made of? (Material) Where does it come from? (Provenance)' (Salaman and Tutchell, 2005: 5).

The Early Years Foundation Stage reminds us that children's engagement with people, materials, objects, ideas or events allows them the opportunity to test things out and to solve problems, stressing that children need the co-operation of adults to challenge and extend their thinking (DCSF, 2008: Card 4.2). The wider partnership, developed through Early Years practitioners working with experienced museum, gallery or library staff, should enable a dialogue to take place that will extend the knowledge base and enrich the interactions and experiences provided for children.

In order to build on experiences, the observation of children by professionals is essential. EYFS (DCSF, 2008: *Practice Guidance*, p. 11) urges practitioners to *look, listen and note* the progress children are making. In the context of museums, libraries, galleries and archives, the general advice given by Smidt (2005: 11) to practitioners regarding aspects to observe, seems particularly apt:

What is this child paying attention to or interested in?
What experience does the child have of this?

Table 8.1   Museums, Library and Archives Generic Learning Outcomes

MLA GENERIC LEARNING OUTCOMES	Example of which EYFS Learning areas are linked with MLA Generic Outcomes:
Knowledge and Understanding Knowing about *something* (for example a fact information). Learning facts or information, which can be subject-specific, interdisciplinary or thematic. Making links and relationships between *things (or facts)* and using prior knowledge in new ways. Learning how museums, archives and libraries operate.	Knowledge and understanding of the world
Skills Development Knowing how to perform an action. Intellectual, information management, social, emotional, communication and physical skills.	Personal Social and Emotional Development Communication Language and Literacy Physical Development
Attitudes and Values Feelings and perceptions. Opinions about selves and others. Positive and negative attitudes in relation to experience. Reasons for actions or personal viewpoints, empathy and capacity for tolerance.	Personal Social and Emotional Development Problem solving, reasoning and numeracy
Activity, Behaviour and Progression What people have done, do, or intend to do. Actions (observed or reported) and changes in behaviour. Progression towards further learning.	Personal Social and Emotional Development Problem solving, reasoning and numeracy
Enjoyment, Inspiration and Creativity Having fun, being surprised and inspired. Innovative thoughts and actions including creativity. Exploration and experimentation.	Creative development

What does the child already know about this?
What does the child feel about this?

Further analysis can connect observations to EYFS areas of learning and development, and thus provide a focus for future planning and resourcing, linked with what is already considered to be effective practice (DCSF, 2008).

Early Years Foundation Stage and Areas of Learning and Development

The Early Years Foundation Stage (DCSF, 2008) advocates key principles when planning experiences for children. These relate to the distinctive needs of individual children. EYFS stresses the importance of children developing secure relationships in positive and enabling environments, and being involved in active learning through play, exploration and critical thinking. It is suggested that it is possible to cover all six areas of learning when using out-of-setting learning contexts (DCSF, 2008):

- Personal, Social and Emotional Development (PSED)
- Communication, Language and Literacy (CLL)
- Problem Solving, Reasoning and Numeracy (PSRN)
- Knowledge and Understanding of the World (KUW)
- Physical Development (PD)
- Creative Development (CD).

In fact, EYFS (DCSF, 2008) stresses that none of the six Areas of Learning and Development can be delivered in isolation from the others, as all are equally important and interdependent. The actual focus during the out-of-setting event will, to some extent, depend upon children's needs and interests, and the type of stimulus offered.

For illustrative purposes only, Personal, Social and Emotional Development, Communication, Language and Literacy, Knowledge and Understanding of the World, and Creative Development will provide the main focus for this chapter, as those areas specifically link with Museums, Library and Archives experiences. Questions will be raised and group activities suggested to highlight the other two aspects of learning and development: Problem Solving, Reasoning and Numeracy, and Physical Development.

Within Personal, Social and Emotional Development the aspects of 'Disposition and Attitudes' and 'Sense of Community' are particularly significant, as the first is concerned with how children become interested, excited and motivated to learn. A sense of community relates to how children understand and respect their own needs, views, cultures and beliefs, and also those of other people (DCSF, 2008).

Communication, Language and Literacy aspects, 'Language for Communication' and 'Language for Thinking', are significant in the context of 'out-of-setting' learning. 'Language for Communication' is concerned with how children become communicators and the skills that develop as children interact with others and listen to and use language (DCSF, 2008). 'Language for Thinking' is concerned with how children learn to use language to imagine and recreate roles and experiences. It is also concerned with how talk is used to clarify thinking and ideas or to refer to events children have observed and are curious about (DCSF, 2008).

All of the Knowledge and Understanding of the World aspects are relevant. 'Exploration and Investigation' focuses on how children investigate objects and materials and learn about properties, change, patterns, similarities and differences; they question how and why things work. 'Designing and Making' is about the ways in which children learn about the construction process and the tools and techniques that can be used to assemble materials creatively and safely. 'ICT' is concerned with how children find out about and learn how to use appropriate information technology to support their learning. 'Time' concerns finding out about past and present events relevant to their own lives or those of their families. 'Place' focuses on how children become aware of and interested in the natural world and their local environment. 'Communities' is concerned with how children begin to know about their own and other people's cultures in order to understand and celebrate the similarities and differences between these in a diverse society (DCSF, 2008).

All of the Creative Development aspects are relevant. 'Being Creative – Responding to Experiences' and 'Expressing and Communicating Ideas' are concerned with how children respond in a variety of ways to what they see, hear, smell, touch or feel, and how they express and communicate their own ideas, thoughts and feelings. 'Exploring Media and Materials' is about children's exploration of and engagement (both independent and guided) with a widening range of media and materials. 'Creating Music and Dance' encourages children's independent and guided explorations of sound, movement and music. 'Developing Imagination and Imaginative Play' focuses on how children are supported to develop and build their imaginations through stories, role-playing, dance, music, design and art (DCSF, 2008).

Preparing children for the learning experience

Preparing children for an out-of-setting visit through describing the narrative in terms of the where, the why, and what processes are involved in the event, is especially important. This does not suggest taking away the elements of surprise and serendipity that may be an outcome of the experience; rather, it ensures that children know the fundamental features of what is likely to happen. Some children find unpredictable sequences and events particularly disturbing, and thus emotional security is essential for learning during out-of-setting contexts. To help alleviate distress a picture diagram of the events likely to happen throughout the day may help children to feel secure and in control of the situation.

Storytelling is also a useful technique for introducing the subject or theme attached to the event. This can be in the form either of published literature or of spoken stories, made up by the practitioner. Children particularly love made-up stories linked with actual places within their community. According to Riley (2007), emotional development hinges on the ability to make meaning of experience in an often-bewildering world, and storytelling is one way of highlighting (within controlled boundaries) significant experiences.

> Stories provide a landscape in which children can confront and reflect on emotions and experiences too frightening to confront in daily life, feelings of anger, jealousy and confusion. And good stories are not over in an instant but continue to speak to the child and 'interact' with her developing experience. (Riley, 2007: 59)

Made-up stories, developed alongside the child's ideas, can also promote the process of sustained shared thinking (Siraj-Blatchford et al., 2002), to a similar extent that sustained engagement with objects can promote deep-level thinking. Sustained shared thinking is embedded within the EYFS (2008) *Practice Guidance* and the Early Years Professional National Standards (CWDC, 2006: S16), where it is advocated as a way of helping to develop children's thinking skills and for providing a context for effective language development. Practitioners are encouraged to share a genuine interest in what seizes children's imaginations and ensure that mutual meaning-making takes place. The imaginative story context is an ideal starting point for this process.

Case Study

A seaside community

This case study is based on a seaside town in the north of England. There is a community library, natural history museum, art gallery, seashore, harbour, and lighthouse within short walking distances of one another. A short journey by bus along the sea front passes a lifeboat station, a harbour, a castle, and cliffs full of seabirds, a marina of yachts, and a sea life centre. Any of the first three MLA sites (library, museum or art gallery) could be the starting point for learning outside the classroom, as could the stimulus provided by both the natural and man-made environment. This exemplar has been chosen as its MLA provision is not as extensive as that found in inner city areas, yet is nevertheless a rich resource for meeting the needs of the local community. The community library offers story sessions, puppet performances and an extensive range of electronic resources, as well as providing children's literature. The art gallery offers both weekend and after-school workshops for children, and a dressing up and interactive area for young children. It also houses a number of large historical paintings of the town's sea front and its fishing industry. There is a museum within the locality that features earlier lifestyles and the changing role of the fishing industry within that community.

The art gallery has a variable programme of visiting exhibitions and the current display is focused on illustrations from 'children's fairy tales and fantasy'. A room has been set aside with games, fairy tale books, dressing up clothes, swathes of flimsy, colourful fabrics, and drawing and modelling materials specifically related to the theme. One of the larger Fantasy illustrations, rich in detail, is an illustration of a children's fairy tale based under the sea, with both wonderfully imaginary and realistic sea creatures.

A group of 3- and 4-year-olds are visiting the art gallery; a musician has been invited to create musical sounds representing the feelings associated with the under-sea picture and the creatures depicted within it. The children are keen to contribute their ideas to the musician, suggesting sounds that depict the characters and how the characters are behaving, for example, happy, sad, fierce or frightened, etc. The children imagine whether the creatures will make high, low, loud or soft noises. Discussions surrounding the size and shape of the musical instruments and the type of noise they are able to make are all part of this dialogue.

After this discussion, an Early Years practitioner supports the musician by creating a musical story. The remaining Early Years practitioners encourage children to express their feelings by improvising physical movements and by selecting sea-coloured materials to swathe around themselves as they move to the music. A group of children eagerly takes part in the imaginative dance. One or two children choose to express themselves through pictures, rather than participate in movement and dance. Smidt's (2005: 11) observational questions are a useful tool to analyse and note individual responses: *What is this child paying attention to or interested in? What does the child feel about this?*

Added to this, there would be questions about the child's use of vocabulary and her/his awareness of differences between objects and their creative responses to music and sound.

It is useful to refer back to the MLA Generic Learning Outcomes in Table 8.1 and reflect on the child's experience by questioning: What knowledge and understanding has been developed? What are the skills, attitudes and values that the child has demonstrated? How has she/he shown her/his enjoyment, inspiration and creativity?

There are links with the learning outcomes for the EYFS (DCSF, 2008: *Statutory Framework*, Appendix 1) from this out-of-setting experience:

- **Personal, Social and Emotional Development**: seek and delight in new experiences; understand that people have different needs, views, cultures and beliefs that need to be treated with respect;
- **Communication, Language and Literacy**: build up vocabulary that reflects the breadth of their experiences; use language to imagine and re-create roles and experiences;
- **Knowledge and Understanding of the World**: show curiosity and interest in the features of objects (musical instruments); look closely at similarities, differences, patterns, and change;
- **Creative Development**: develop preferences for forms of expression; express and communicate their ideas, thoughts and feelings by using a widening range of materials, suitable tools, imaginative role play, movement, designing and making, and a variety of songs and musical instruments.

Continuing to build on the experiences encountered in this case study would depend upon both the children's responses and their interests. Reflection in thinking about the activities, behaviour and progression encountered in out-of-setting contexts is important to children and practitioners for developing effective, interesting and stimulating Early Years practice. It could be that the visit has been planned for a whole day, where during the afternoon the children are taken on a visit to the harbour and the nearby beach area. Children could look at the fishing boats, various types of fish, ice trays, lobster pots, buoys, nets, and lighthouse. This offers extensive scope for developing the area of learning through Knowledge and Understanding of the World (DCFS, 2008: *Practice Guidance*, pp. 77ff). It provides an opportunity to encounter creatures, plants and objects in their natural environment, and people in 'real-life' situations. It enables children to show curiosity about why things happen and how things work, and it provides opportunity for problem solving, for example, looking at the lobster pot one could ask, 'What do you think it is used for?' or 'How does it work?'

Developing creative and imaginative reasoning through questioning helps children to seek meaning from their experiences (DCSF, 2008: *Practice Guidance*, pp. 77ff). According to Runco, the most important feature a practitioner can allow a child to develop is 'ego strength' (Runco, 2006: 128). This allows the child to believe in his or her own thinking and ideas, which is essential in developing creative thinking because the child has been able to withstand pressures to conform. It is important that Early Years practitioners should listen to children and value their ideas, while they should also encourage critical reflection by interpreting, analysing and helping to clarify children's ideas.

Being outdoors also gives children first-hand contact with the weather and the seasons; it helps them to understand how to behave by talking about personal safety, risks and the safety of others. It could be that the beach area offers opportunities for beachcombing for stones, shells, seaweed, driftwood, or for creating sand structures, thus continuing the morning's theme of homes and palaces for sea creatures.

Parents (or carers) as partners

Working with parents presents challenges, as Smidt (2006: 51) acknowledges, although it is important for the practitioner to rise to these challenges. Research has demonstrated how the home learning environment can have a significant impact on children's learning and development (Sylva et al., 2003). The Effective Provision of Pre-School Education Project found that home environments where children were involved in a range of activities – such as visiting the library or going on visits – were associated with higher intellectual, social and behavioural scores (Sylva et al., 2003). Providing a partnership with parents is thus crucial for continuity in the educational experience for children.

The EYFS *Practice Guidance* (2008: 6) suggests that Early Years practitioners have a key role to play in working with parents to support children through the shared identification of learning needs. The 'Parents as Partners' guidance acknowledges that parents are children's first and most enduring educators and that 'parents and practitioners have a lot to learn from each other' (DCSF, 2008: Card 2.2.).

In a wider context, Smidt (2006: 51) questions whether parents can be taught to be 'good parents' as viewed from the practitioner's standpoint, as this implies the adoption of a model of parenting that is universal. What is considered essential for children's learning is to some extent culture-specific, and practitioners need to be careful not to impose their views without careful consultation and an opportunity to listen to the views of the parents. Within EYFS the need for effective communication with parents, as well as the need to respect the contribution made by parents and carers to the development and well-being of children, is emphasised. It is important to learn about and consider children within their respective family relationships and communities, including their cultural and religious contexts, and their place within the family (Zwozdiak-Myers, 2007).

Informing parents about the nature and value of out-of-setting learning is crucial to its success. Notice-boards within settings containing MLA website information and events relevant to young children are important for ensuring the development of an awareness for learning of community contexts. EYFS suggests that regular information should be provided about activities undertaken by children through visual displays, documentation and photographs. Newsletters informing parents about particular visits and linking these with the EYFS can help develop understanding and a transfer of knowledge. Seeking feedback from parents and asking for suggestions on ways to build on the children's experiences helps to promote a two-way flow of information, and it also shows that practitioners respect parental views. EYFS suggests that in a true partnership parents understand and contribute to the policies in the setting, thus influencing future planning and development (DCFS, 2008: Card 2.2).

To summarise, EYFS has four guiding principles that are grouped thematically and are crucially important in developing curricular opportunities for young children (DCSF, 2008: *Practice Guidance*, p. 5). Each aspect needs to be considered in order for out-of-setting learning to be successful and for the holistic needs of children to be met. Links have been made with MLA Generic Learning Outcomes:

- **A Unique Child** stresses the positive nature of the child, being a competent learner from birth who can be resilient, capable, confident and self-assured. It is the practitioner's role to build confidence or 'ego strength' (Runco, 2006: 128) and to ensure that a child is ready to face new challenges in out-of-setting contexts. MLA Generic Learning Outcomes: 'Attitudes and Values' and 'Skills Development'.
- **Positive Relationships** emphasises that children learn to be strong and independent from a basis of loving and secure relationships. It is the practitioner's role to provide out-of-setting learning, which develops from a secure and consistent base. Developing opportunities for sustained shared thinking (Siraj-Blatchford et al., 2002) ensures that practitioners are alert to the learning needs of young children, and are sensitive to children's interests and motivational aspects. A two-way dialogue with parents/carers is essential in order to provide for the 'unique child'. MLA Generic Learning Outcomes: 'Activity, Behaviour and Progression' and 'Attitudes and Values'.
- **Enabling Environments** acknowledges that the environment plays a key role in supporting and extending children's development and learning. It is the practitioner's role to make the environment, within and outside the setting, both stimulating and motivating. MLA Generic Learning Outcomes: 'Enjoyment, Inspiration and Creativity' and 'Activity, Behaviour and Progression'.
- **Learning and Development** acknowledges that children develop and learn in different ways and at different rates, and that all areas of learning and development are equally important and inter-connected to one another. It is the practitioner's role to map children's learning and development in order to ensure a broad and balanced curriculum, which builds upon children's experiences and provides for the unique child. Part of this process is through actively seeking partnerships with those professionals who are experts in their given field. MLA Generic Learning Outcomes: 'Knowledge and Understanding of the World' and 'Skills Development'.

The definition of meeting EYFS, as explored in this chapter, considers that children gain much from out-of-classroom or out-of-setting experiences. This chapter has highlighted the importance of observing children and noting their interests and motivations in order to support their learning. It also stresses the importance of listening to children and encouraging them to express their views. According to Smidt (2006: 117), allowing children to express their thoughts and ideas can be contentious, as the 'language of education must express some stance' and invite those joining in either to agree or adopt a different stance. When children are allowed to reflect on what they think they are involved in 'metacognition'. This means that they are involved in understanding what it is they already know.

Katz (1998) implies that young children need opportunities to express, improve, transform, validate, develop, refine and deepen their own constructions of their worlds – the worlds of here and now, but also times past and times to come, and of people like and unlike themselves (Smidt, 2006: 117).

Practitioners are urged to promote a wider partnership with the community and with those professionals who have expertise in specific areas, in order to enrich children's experiences and to promote a deeper understanding of the world. The EYFS (DCSF, 2008: *Practice Guidance*, p. 10) adds force to the notion that high quality Early Years experience provides a firm foundation on which to build future academic, social and emotional success. High quality experiences can be found outside the classroom and add richness to the curriculum, as they provide a source of stimulation and motivation for young learners.

     Key points to remember

- This chapter explores how the six learning areas can be met outside of Early Years settings. A number of independent organisations such as museums, libraries and archives can be used to promote children's learning and development alongside the EYFS requirements for learning.
- It is important for Early Years practice to include parents in activities outside of the classroom. Parents' participation can be of great help to the Early Years practitioners.
- Partnerships with local communities can enrich children's experiences and promote the six learning areas of EYFS.

     Points for discussion

- When planning any out-of-setting activity a careful risk assessment needs to be carried out. Obviously, the intended location will have an impact on aspects that need to be considered. Your local authority will have specific guidelines regarding which compulsory checks need to be made. The key aspects include: pre-visit analysis and completion of risk assessment documentation; parental consent forms; level of supervision (including ratios of adults to children); behaviour (including safety rules); health and hygiene rules (including food, toilet and hand-washing facilities); and first aid provision and documenting incidents (including emergency procedures). The Teaching Resource Site (TRS) has information produced by the government and the Central Council of Physical Recreation (CCPR) on planning for out-of-setting contexts. Think about a location for a visit and consider the risk assessment that needs to be carried out in advance.

- Try to identify opportunities for meeting the Communication Language and Literacy and Personal, Social Emotional Development areas of learning and development of EYFS outside of the setting. Use the MLA Generic Learning Outcomes to extend and to build on ideas for learning and development in the following areas:

Communication, Language and Literacy: Language for communication; language for thinking; linking sounds and letters; reading, writing and handwriting
Personal, Social and Emotional Development: Dispositions and attitudes; self-confidence and self-esteem; making relationships; behaviour and self-control; self-care, sense of community.

- Think of an out-of-classroom experience that is possible within your own community. For example, this could include: a farm museum, a traditional working windmill, or a natural history museum. Focus on Problem Solving, Reasoning and Numeracy (DCSF, 2008) and look at the following aspects: *Numbers as Labels and for Counting, Calculating, Shape, Space and Measures*, and think about favourable conditions or opportunities for developing children's learning and development. This could be during the visit or back in the setting through the provision of role-playing or by other play experiences. How could this planning incorporate the required outcomes of the Common Core of Skills and Knowledge (DfES, 2005)?

Further reading

Griffin, J. (2000) 'Learning outside the classroom', *Investigating: Australian Primary and Junior Science Journal*, 16 (4).
Riley, J. (2007) *Learning in the Early Years*, 2nd edn. London: Sage.
Salaman, A. and Tutchell, S. (2005) *Planning for Educational Visits for the Early Years*. London: Paul Chapman Publishing.
Smidt, S. (2006) *The Developing Child in the 21st Century*. London: Routledge.

Useful websites

Inspiring Learning for All:
www.inspiringlearningforall.gov.uk

Describes what an accessible and inclusive museum, archive or library, which both stimulates and supports learning, looks like. It invites you to: find out what is learned by those using your services; assess how well you are achieving best practice in supporting learning; improve upon what you do. Learning is now high on local, regional and national agendas. Inspiring Learning for All will transform the way in which museums, archives and libraries deliver and engage users in learning;

Creative Partnerships:
www.creative-partnerships.com/
The government's flagship creative learning programme, designed to develop the skills of young people across England, raising their aspirations and achievements, and opening up more opportunities for their futures. This world-leading programme is transforming teaching and learning across the curriculum.

24-Hour Museum:
www.show.me.uk
This is the 24-Hour Museum's zone for children where places, counties and cities are listed, allowing for immediate contact with a huge range of museums and galleries. Designed for children aged 4 to 11 (or KS1 and 2 in the English National Curriculum), this site is packed with online interactive resources produced by museums and galleries.

Part 2

THE AREAS OF LEARNING AND DEVELOPMENT IN EYFS

CHAPTER 9

PERSONAL, SOCIAL AND EMOTIONAL DEVELOPMENT

Ioanna Palaiologou

Chapter Aims

It is emphasised in EYFS that the early years in a child's life are important for the formation of personal, social and emotional development. An environment that is safe, affectionate and encouraging for children promotes positive feelings and social skills. From the moment that children are born they are engaged in interaction with adults, in the attempt to become both independent and social beings. The early stages of their lives are important for children's acquisition of social and emotional skills that will enhance their personal development.

The tendency is for social and emotional development to be studied together, as they are linked and reinforce one another. This chapter aims to explore children's personal, social and emotional development; it aims to help you understand:

- personal, social and emotional development in the Early Years

- the importance of attachment and its implications for the key worker

- the role of the environment and its implications for children's personal, social and emotional development.

Personal, social and emotional development in EYFS

The Early Years Foundation Stage stresses the importance of personal, social and emotional development for young children's well-being. This view was supported by the EPPE study (Sylva et al., 2003), which found that when educational settings view social development as being complementary and equal in importance, children make better progress in their processes of learning and development. The EPPE study also suggested the existence of strong links between the quality of Early Years provision and the children's personal, social and emotional development.

As has been shown in Chapter 1, more than ever, at policy level, the personal, social and emotional development of young children is becoming a key issue and a priority in the government's agenda. The National Childcare Strategy, Every Child Matters and the Safeguarding Children policy aim to protect children from harm and to promote children's well-being. EYFS aims to deliver the Every Child Matters outcomes (of personal, social and emotional development) as a learning goal. As these areas of development are broad, EYFS (DCSF, 2008: Card 4.4) clarifies what is meant by describing these following aspects:

- **Dispositions and Attitudes** – is about how children become interested [in], excited and motivated about their learning.
- **Self-confidence and Self-esteem** – is about children having a sense of their own value, and also understanding the need for sensitivity to significant events in their own and other people's lives.
- **Making Relationships** – is about the importance of children's forming good relationships with others and working alongside others companionably.
- **Behaviour and Self-control** – is about how children develop a growing understanding of what is right and wrong (and why), together with learning about the impact of their words and actions upon themselves and others.
- **Self-care** – is about how children gain a sense of self-respect and concern for their own personal hygiene and care, and how they subsequently develop independence.
- **Sense of Community** – is about how children understand and respect their own needs, views, cultures and beliefs, and those of other people.

The importance of personal, social and emotional development as key aspects of pedagogy in Early Years has been emphasised. The EPPE project showed that adults involved in an Early Years setting have a significant impact on children's well-being. The Reggio Emilia pedagogy, for example, focuses on children's well-being and personal development, and that activities are organised around promoting children's well being. A number of theorists researching effective pedagogy within the Early Years have linked pedagogy with children's social relationships (Dunn, 1993; Elfer et al., 2002; Howes, 1990, 1992; Hymel, 1983; Hymel et al., 1990; Rubin, 1982; Rubin et al., 1983). It is a positive factor that EYFS addresses the key issues of personal, social and emotional development as being of equal importance to education as children's learning. However, it can be argued that in pre-set goals and descriptive curriculum approaches such as EYFS, personal, social and emotional development can be seen as measured achievements, rather than as children's journeys towards self-awareness, well-being and building relationships.

The journey made by children on entering the world can be seen as a two-sided process, in which children simultaneously become integrated into their larger community and are also differentiated as distinctive individuals. One side of social development is socialisation and the process by which children acquire the standards, values and knowledge of their respective community (behaviour and self control, making relationships and a sense of community). The other side of social development is personality formation: the process through which children come to have their own unique patterns of feeling, thinking and behaving in wide circumstances (dispositions and attitudes, self-confidence, self-esteem, and personal care and hygiene).

Personal development: self concept

When babies are born they have a very long way to go before becoming independent. If they are safely to survive, consistent care must be provided over an extended period of time. It is here that the social skills of infants come into play. Part of their development can be characterised as a process to differentiate themselves and to construct the concept of 'self' (or personal identity) in order to be able to be 'interested, excited and motivated about their learning', to acquire a sense 'of their own value and understanding [of] the need for sensitivity to significant events', to have self-respect and to take care of themselves. (DCFS, 2008: Card 4.4)

In the case of developing the self, babies have, as one of the major developmental tasks in this area, the gradual awareness of a sense of themselves as distinct and separate entities, clearly differentiated from all other entities (human and non-human) that populate their everyday world. This process of articulation and definition of self begins in early infancy. At first babies do not recognise themselves. For example, when a baby is placed in front of a mirror there is no reaction; the baby does not recognise the reflection as being of itself. At about the age of 18 months babies begin to have a clearer idea that this reflection is a representation of themselves.

The acquisition of the concept of identity is important for children's well-being. Selleck (2001) claims that the parent or carer in an Early Years setting plays an important role in this formation of infant identity. A baby's crying is a form of expressing how they feel (such as discomfort, stress, hunger, or tiredness) and at the same time is a way of attempting to communicate with the parent/carer. Gradually babies develop their 'social smile'. In the beginning of their lives, a baby's smile is a form of expressing their comfort, as it is related to their biological needs. When their biological needs are

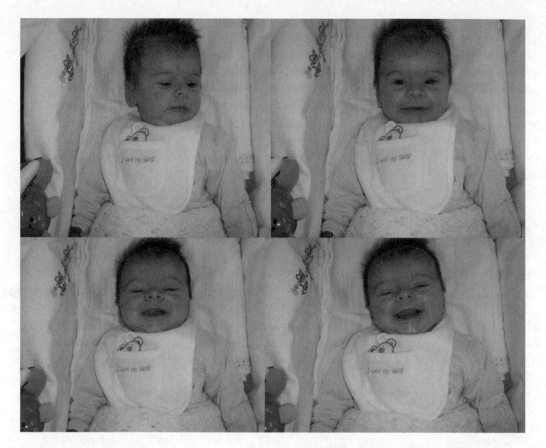

Figure 9.1   A baby's social smile

covered, they feel comfort, and the muscles in their faces relax and they appear to smile. They also appear to smile when the mother strokes and comforts them. However, at between 6 and 10 weeks infants start to show a clear preference for certain human beings, and especially for familiar human faces.

A 'social smile' indicates the progress of babies in differentiating themselves as individual human beings, and they respond to the face of another human being by smiling back to them. It is a major developmental stage in babies' lives towards the process of identity formation, and towards the acquisition of a repertoire of social skills.

In the sequence of photographs in Figure 9.1, the social smile of a baby is captured. The baby is lying in his cot and an adult is approaching him. The baby looks at the adult's face and soon afterwards his lips form a smile (shown in the last photo of the sequence) and the expression becomes one of happiness as the smile becomes more intense.

Gradually, when infants become more mobile and explore the world around them (alongside cognitive development) they begin to acquire self-recognition by becoming self-aware, an element central to children's emotional and social lives.

When working with young babies in an Early Years setting it is important that babies are offered opportunities to develop a concept of themselves. Activities such as nursery rhymes combined with physical movement, mirrors in which babies explore their reflections, and games such as when an adult hides their face with their hands in front of the baby ('peep-bo'), are activities that sound simple yet actually help infants in their process of acquiring their concept of self.

Attachment

The dominant theory in the emotional development of children is that proposed by Bowlby (1960, 1969, 1973, 1980, 1986, 1999, 2005) and Ainsworth (Ainsworth, 1969, 1979, 1985, 1989; Ainsworth and Bell, 1970; Ainsworth and Bowlby, 1991; Ainsworth et al., 1971a, 1971b, 1978) regarding 'attachment'. All these studies proposed that when babies are born they are 'pre-programmed' to form close relationships with the mother/carer. This bond is attachment. The ideas of Bolwby and Ainsworth have influenced the way mother–child and carer–child relationships are perceived. Bowlby and Ainsworth have each described in detail the stages of attachment and how the formation of the relationship between the mother (or carer) and the baby take place. They have also discussed the consequences of the separation of the child from the mother/carer.

Bowlby (1969) proposed four main stages in the development of attachment. First, he claims that when babies are born and at about the age of 2 months they are in an 'orientation' stage, where the infant shows orientation to social stimuli such as grasping, smiling and babbling. The babies will stop crying when they are picked up or when they see a face or hear a familiar voice. These behaviours increase when the baby is in proximity to a companion or another person, mainly the parent or the carer, although the baby cannot distinguish one person from another; for example, they cannot yet distinguish the mother from the father. Evidence of discrimination begins at about 4 weeks, when the baby is listening to sounds such as the mother's voice, and at about the age of 10 weeks the orientation becomes visual: the baby tends to recognise the face of the mother and smile towards her.

Second, when babies grow to about the age of 3–6 months, their orientation to signals is directed towards one or more discriminated figures. It has been observed that slightly older babies direct their orientation to the primary caregiver.

Third, when babies are 6–30 months old, their repertoire of responses to people increases to include: visually following a departing mother, greeting her on return, and using her as a base for explorations. It is at that age when babies treat strangers with caution and may evince alarm or withdrawal expressed through intense crying.

At the final stage, and at about the age of 24 to 48 months, the child begins to acquire insight into the mother's feelings and goals, which leads to cooperative interaction and partnership (Bowlby, 1969).

What is important with attachment theory is that:

> [T]he infant and young children should experience a warm, intimate and continuous relationship with his mother (or permanent mother substitute), in which both find satisfaction and enjoyment. (Bowlby, 1951: 13)

This has considerable implications for Early Years settings. As increasing numbers of women enter the workforce, more children are from a very young age attending Early Years settings. It is necessary that the EYFS emphasises the importance of the role of the key worker in relation to children. Young children need such emotional warmth as that provided by practitioners when they enter Early Years education and care, and need a continuous and stable relationship with the Early Years practitioners also for their personal well-being.

Bowlby claims, 'If a community values its children, it must cherish their parents' (1951: 84). Not only the children form attachment with parents; parents form strong attachments with their children. Consequently, when children join Early Years settings, parents can feel guilty for not being with them, and may experience anxiety as to whether their children will have an enjoyable time in the nursery and make friends. It is essential to support the parents during this process, and the role of the key worker is continually to reconfirm that children are forming stable relationships within the settings.

Transitional objects

Winnicott (1986, 1987, 1995, 2005) started his career as a paediatrician; he tried to understand how children develop the concept of self into the context of the bonds they have with their parents. He investigated how children develop a healthy 'genuine self', as opposed to a 'false self', by looking closely at the relationships parents form with their children.

Winnicott uses the term 'self' to describe both 'ego' and self-as-object. He describes the self in terms of 'genuine' or 'true self', and 'false self'. For Winnicott, the 'genuine' or 'true self' is developed when the babies form their personalities by developing the capacity to recognise their needs and to express these. When babies are able genuinely to express their needs and their emotions, they are in the state of genuine or true self. For example when a baby is hungry s/he usually cries. The mother responds to the crying by feeding the baby. Upon repetition of this behaviour the babies will realise that when they are hungry, they cry; the mother will feed them, thus their need will be met. A stable, consistent response or reaction by the mother to the baby's needs will help the baby to develop the genuine self. True self develops successfully only when the mother responds to the baby's spontaneous expressions and needs.

However, if the babies are growing up in an environment where their needs are not covered they will build a 'false self'. Their real needs will not be expressed, which is a kind of mechanism for defending their 'true self' and is an unconscious process. Through the interactions with the mother or primary carer the babies are learning through experience and they begin to make sense of the world or, as Winnicot called it, acquire 'object reality'. The baby and carer enter what feels like a place of their own. Winnicott named that space a 'holding environment', which includes language and psychological and physical interactions between a mother and an infant. Thus, a holding environment is a space that is emotional and physical, where the babies are protected without knowing they are protected. He claimed that for a child to form a healthy sense of self it is important for the child to know that the mother will be there when she is needed. Such a relationship with the mother makes the infant feel secure and protected, then the child will be well equipped to form a healthy self-concept.

The study of the 'holding environment' led Winnicott to develop his influential idea of the 'transitional experience'. He suggested that when children start becoming independent, for example, when moving from the home to the outside world (such as to a nursery or a school) they need to represent their mothers when they are absent in order to feel secure. Children use objects such as teddy bears, blankets and dolls as transitional objects, through which they facilitate a symbolic representation of the mother. In this way children can start enjoying the new environment into which they are moving (e.g., the nursery or the school) and become creative and independent; at the same time, the comfort provided by the transitional objects makes them feel protected.

As discussed in Chapter 7, the importance of transition objects has implications for children's transitions into and out of EYFS. This also raises the issue of respecting the objects brought with them from home by the children when they come to the nursery.

Making relationships

An important aspect of children's social development is how they form relationships with others, how they behave during these interactions with either other children or adults, and how they make attempts to become part of the community and the wider social environment.

Children attempt from a very young age to make relationships. For example, small children are interested in the activities of others of a similar age, or they smile at other human beings (familiar faces in particular). Making relationships during early childhood is a major developmental task for children. It is essential to understand that children's perceptions and criteria for forming relationships differ in many ways from those of adults. Young children choose friends and to make relationships with other individuals on the basis of their pleasurable interactions with them. This does not mean that they are selfish. When children first begin to form relationships they lack abstract thinking, so are unable to conceptualise the meaning of mutual friendships. However, as they grow older and their cognitive development advances, they evolve into being able to form a more abstract relationship based on mutual consideration and psychological satisfaction.

For example, a child can be a friend with another child during outdoors play time as they have fun riding bikes, running or jumping; when in the class, though, each may be friends with another child as they enjoy playing in the construction area. Phrases such as 'You are not my friend' or 'I do not want to play with you' are common in Early Years settings. As Damon (1988) suggested, there are different levels at which children develop their friendships. Damon describes friendships in early childhood as a 'handy playmate', where children choose a friend on the basis that they do together those things each enjoys.

As children grow older and develop their own concept of self, self-awareness and an awareness of others' thoughts and feelings, they are able to form relationships involving mutual trust.

Sociometric status studies have shown that in Early Years settings children tend to fall into four major categories. Sociometric studies ask children to rate the other children in their respective group. Numerous sociometric studies (e.g., Black and Logan, 1995; DeRosier et al., 1994; Dunn, 1993; Howes and Matherson, 1992; Hymel, 1983; Hymel et al., 1990; Rubin,1982; Rubin et al., 1983) have investigated how children form relationships within Early Years settings. It has been shown that children in a classroom setting display the following tendencies:

- **Popular** children are liked by their peers. These children are very active, direct or lead activities, and make suggestions and structure activities.
- **Rejected** children are those who are actively disliked by and receive many negative comments from their peers. Others do not want to invite them into their play. These 'rejected' children often demonstrate aggressive behaviours, such as hitting, biting, or kicking, none of which helps them.
- **Controversial** children get a large number of positive and negative comments from their peers.
- Finally, **neglected** children are seldom chosen to join in with activities, either positively or negatively. Their peers normally ignore these children, who then find themselves in isolation. Subsequently, neglected children do not participate in activities; they demonstrate isolated behaviour.

The degree of peer acceptance is a powerful predictor of current (as well as later) psychological adjustment. Rejected children, especially, are unhappy, alienated, and poorly achieving children with a low sense of self-esteem. Both teachers and parents view them as having a wide range of emotional and social problems. Research claims that peer rejection during middle childhood is also strongly associated with poor school performance, antisocial behaviour, and delinquency and criminality in adolescence and young adulthood (De Rosier et al., 1994).

With age, children come to develop a number of skills, such as perspective thinking and the ability to understand the viewpoints of others; therefore, they become better at resolving social conflicts and their relationships with others improve. Taking turns in activities helps children to develop social problem solving skills, while serving one another during snack times helps them to develop a perspective of others. It is important to create activities within which children are offered opportunities to develop all of the necessary social skills and encouraged to form relationships.

Play and social development

When children enter their early childhood education, they begin with non-social activity and *solitary play* (i.e., unoccupied, onlooker behaviour). Then, they shift to a form of limited social participation, called *parallel play*, in which a child plays near other children using similar materials, but does not try to interact with or influence their behaviour (Barnes, 1971; Dunn, 1993; Rubin, 1982; Rubin et al., 1983; Smith, 1997).

As children grow older they reach a higher level of social interaction, characterised by two forms of true social interaction: *associative play*, in which children engage in separate activities, although they do interact by exchanging toys and commenting on one another's behaviour, and *co-operative play*, a more advanced type of interaction involving work oriented towards a common goal, such as acting out a make-believe scenario or working on the same product, for example, a sand castle or patchwork quilt (Barnes, 1971). All of these types of play co-exist during early childhood, as is illustrated in Table 9.1. Furthermore, although non-social activity eventually declines with age, it is still the most frequent form of behaviour among 3- and 4-year-olds. Even among young children it continues to take up as much as a third of children's free playtime. The occurrence of both solitary and parallel play remains fairly stable between age 3 and 6 years (Howes and Matheson, 1992).

Make-believe play is developed in parallel with representation. Piaget (1951) believed that through pretending, children practise and strengthen newly acquired symbolic schemes. Make-believe play also allows children to become more familiar with social role possibilities by acting out familiar scenes and highly visible occupations (e.g., police officer, doctor or nurse). In this way play provides young children with important insights into links between themselves and society.

However, Piaget's view of make-believe play as being mere practice of symbolic schemes is now regarded as too limited. More recent research indicates that play

Table 9.1   Examples of all types of play in early childhood

Play type	Examples
Non-social activity	Solitary play A child is sitting alone in the writing corner using the table as a motorway to play with his cars. He plays there for about six minutes. Parallel play Four children are sitting at a table, trying to put together some puzzles. Each child does a different puzzle. Functional play Simple, receptive motor movements with or without objects.
Unoccupied	A three-year-old boy sits for a long time in a chair doing nothing. He was not obviously engaged in anything, but after close observation he is aware of other children and he watches them very carefully.
Associative play	Constructive play Children are sitting on the carpet playing with Lego. They try to make a farm with animals. Each has his or her own pieces, and the children exchange pieces and talk about what animals the farm will include. Make-believe play Two girls are in the doll's house, pretending that they are friends and that they have invited each other for tea; they talk about their dolls as if these are real babies.
Comparative play	Four children are in the yard looking at some lentils that they planted in the morning. Suddenly, they see a tortoise and try to stop it because they think that the tortoise will eat the lentils. Games with rules Two boys and a girl are in the outdoor area and they want to play in the sandbox area. They make a motorway in order to race their cars. They set two rules: not to damage the motorway by shifting the sand with the cars, and, secondly, not themselves to step on the sand .

not only reflects but also contributes to children's cognitive and social skills (Nikolopoulou, 1993).

Vygotsky offers a slightly different view of make-believe play. In accordance with his emphasis on social experience and language as vital forces in cognitive development (as will be shown in Chapter 10), Vygotsky (1986) granted make-believe play a prominent place within his theory. He regarded it as creating a unique, broadly influential zone of proximal development, during which children advance themselves as they try out a wide variety of challenging skills:

> In play, the child always behaves beyond his average age, above his daily behaviour; in play it is as though he were a head taller than himself. As in the focus of a magnifying glass, play contains all developmental tendencies in a condensed form and is itself a major source of development. (1986: 102)

During make-believe play, pre-school children act out and respond to one another's pretend feelings. Their play is rich in references to emotional states. Young children also explore and gain control of fear-arousing experiences when, for example, they play the role of a doctor or a dentist, or pretend to be searching for monsters. As a result, they are better able to understand the feelings of others and also to regulate their own. Finally, collectively to create and manage complex narratives, pre-school children must resolve their disputes through negotiation and compromise – skills they develop when they become older (Howes, 1992; Singer and Singer, 1990).

The role of resources in the environment

The quality and quantity of play materials has a major impact upon young children's personal, social and emotional development. In an interesting study, Smith (1997) showed that fights and disruptions increase in Early Years settings where children were confined to a relatively small space in which to play, and where there were not enough toys to share around.

It is important to make sure that children have a variety of toys and play materials available to them. Construction materials, building blocks and puzzles tend to be associated with solitary play, but these are important materials to have available when children choose to move into solitary activity. As has been demonstrated, all types of play co-exist in children's daily routine within the class. Children choose what type of play they want to join in according to their needs at that time.

In order to encourage participation from all children, open-ended activities and relatively non-constructed objects (such as using fabrics or instigating face-painting) can facilitate both co-operative and imaginative play. Children will need to use their negotiation, problem solving, communication and listening skills.

Using realistic toys such as trucks, dolls, telephones and tea sets helps children to act out everyday roles, and this also promotes role-playing. Role-play requires complex interactions, especially when children try to recreate 'real' events that have happened to them. Additionally, role-play is essential for enabling children to express and articulate their feelings within a safe environment.

Classroom activities need to be adapted in order to increase the participation of all children present. Regular systematic observations of the different areas of the class are required; the members of staff need to be prepared to change the organisation of their classroom, to ensure that children can move around and use all areas to the maximum.

Planning for outdoor activities helps to promote social interactions. Games that need space and where children can move freely helps children to develop respect for their peers by waiting to take turns or, for example, by playing in pairs.

The role of the adult in all of these situations is highly important. The adult can help children with activities, or can suggest activities where peer collaboration is required. The adult can monitor interactions amongst the children, and make sure that all children are encouraged to play with one another.

In a supportive class or outdoor environment where the social behaviours of children are promoted, and in an environment where children feel safe to express their feelings, the children's developmental journey will be supported effectively.

Sense of the community

When children develop their self-concept alongside their self-awareness, and begin forming relationships, they try to develop an understanding of themselves and the wider world. Again, it is a developmental task: to make sense of the world and transfer new experiences gained from their environment into their personal constructs of what the world is about.

It is important for children's social development to acquire a sense of the community, and its values and knowledge. As mentioned in Chapters 7 and 8, children need to be offered opportunities for activities outside of the Early Years setting. However, within the setting they can also be offered opportunities to develop an understanding of values, cultures and beliefs. Awareness of the world around them has a beneficial impact upon children's processes of the concept of self, as well as in their forming relationships with others. By understanding the environment children make attempts to fit into their own part of it, and consequently make better and more successful relationships.

For example, the use of 'persona' dolls helps children to understand equality and diversity, and helps them to develop discriminatory attitudes and behaviours, thus helping them to understand different cultural backgrounds and behaviours. Kay Taus developed persona dolls in the 1950s in the United States. The role of these dolls in a setting is to raise awareness among young children regarding ethnic, racial and other social differences. The use of these dolls is part of the curriculum and are employed by adults in the class to help children to understand issues about anti-discriminatory practice and cultural differences, as children come to empathise with the stories of these dolls.

In a number of Early Years settings festivals are observed as another method for introducing children to different customs, for example, during a celebration of the traditional Chinese New Year.

Case Study

Australia's living heritage

A 3-year-old boy and his parents are planning to emigrate to Australia. This child is very popular amongst the other children in his class. During a sociometric interview of the group he was highly rated.

The Early Years practitioners have observed that the boy and the other children are anxious about his departure, and they have also observed that the boy is becoming withdrawn from a number of activities. They decided to create a project about Australia's lifestyle and its heritage as a way to smooth the transition for the young boy and the rest of his group.

An area was created using photographs from Australia, and there were discussions about how to go to Australia, the different means of transport and where Australia is. There were also opportunities to discuss its aboriginal art and culture. Children became particularly interested in rock carvings and rock paintings, after seeing photographs from a cave near Marrota in New South Wales. This cave overlooks a fern-filled valley and has interesting rock carvings that resemble children's drawings.

The class decided to create their own cave outdoors and the children started painting rocks to put into the cave. They also created shell necklaces and re-created body painting, which is a typical feature of the aboriginal art.

At the end of these activities there was a festive celebration involving the dances of aboriginal Australians, to which the parents were invited, and everybody together celebrated one aspect of the Australian way of living.

Using the arts within an Early Years setting is undoubtedly beneficial to young children's sense of community. Paintings from the school of Cubism, where the conceptual reality is represented in an abstract way, can become a tool in Early Years classrooms for children to express their anxieties about the world. As these paintings themselves are abstract, children have the opportunity to express how they feel about certain paintings or sculptures. In this way they can create pictorial images of their feelings and this in turn helps the children to conceptualise them. Through the arts children can articulate their personal feelings about others, and about certain events in their community, for example, the death of another child in the group. Thus, art-based activities, although sometimes abstract, can help children to articulate their feelings and emotions and to reflect upon their personal social values.

Key points to remember

- This chapter looked at the personal, social and emotional development of young children. Although these three aspects of development are studied separately, they are interlinked, and they form the foundation for the other areas of children's cognitive development.

(Continued)

(Continued)

- When working with very young children it is important to understand their relationships with the family and with other children, and how they form relationships in the Early Years setting.
- The organisation of the Early Years environment and the materials and resources used play a crucial role in children's personal, social and emotional development.

Points for discussion

- Observe the toddlers in an Early Years setting and try to investigate whether young children bring any objects from their home to the nursery. Observe during the day how often these children refer back to these objects. In the light of Winnicott's idea about transitional objects, what can you observe, and thus deduce, about these children?
- Consider the implications of attachment when you are planning for the arrival of a new child into your setting. How are you going to help with the transition? How are you going to allocate the key worker? How are you going to plan for involving this child in the setting's daily activities?
- Using the different definitions of social positions of children in the class (i.e., 'popular', 'rejected', 'controversial' and 'neglected') try to identify in which category the children in your group belong. How can you help a rejected child to form relationships with other children? How can you help a controversial child? How can you involve a neglected child?

Further reading

Dowling, M. (2005) *Young Children's Personal, Social and Emotional Development*, 2nd edn. London: Paul Chapman Publishing.

Papatheodoropoulou, T. and Moyles, J. (eds) (2009) *Learning Together in the Early Years: Exploring Relational Pedagogy*. London: Routledge.

Sheppy, S. (2009) *Personal, Social and Emotional Development in the Early Years Foundation Stage*. London: David Fulton.

Useful websites

How to use 'persona' dolls:
www.persona-doll-training.org/

Information about multicultural books and video materials:
www.multiculturalbooks.info

Information and materials on festivals:
www.festivalshop.co.uk

CHAPTER 10

COMMUNICATION, LANGUAGE AND LITERACY

Ioanna Palaiologou

Chapter Aims

The second learning and development area described in the EYFS is Communication, Language and Literacy. EYFS emphasises that communication is important for children's social relationships, as well as in developing the important skills of listening that form the foundations for literacy development.

The focus of this chapter is on young children's communication, language and literacy development. Research has shown that children's experiences in the Early Years of language and literacy are not and cannot be restricted only to formal schooling, but are also a consequence of children's outside-of-school learning experiences. This chapter aims to help you to understand:

- language development in the Early Years as important background to the discussion that follows, concerning the differences between spoken and written language

- what 'literacy' and 'emergent literacy' are

- the role of the environment in the development of language and literacy.

The development of language

As EYFS states, and a vast body of research agrees, language is a social process, something that children use to communicate with others. Learning a language is also a social process facilitated by interaction with others (Bruner, 1983; Vygotsky, 1986; Wells, 1981, 1985).

Language is only one of many aspects of the world that children come to understand. The principles that account for cognitive mastery in general should therefore be useful when an attempt is made to explain the mastery of language in particular. Within this general framework a number of specific positions have been proposed, the most influential being those of Piaget, Vygotsky and Bruner.

Piaget and language development

The starting point of Piaget (1948) concerns the issue of which needs a child tends to satisfy when talking. Piaget begins with the functions of language, dividing these into two large groups: (1) egocentric and (2) socialised.

He explains what egocentric speech is and how it functions in a situation:

> When a child utters phrases that belong to the first group [egocentric], he is not interested in knowing to whom he is speaking or whether he is being listened to. He talks either to himself or for the pleasure of associating with anyone who happens to be involved in the activity of the moment. This talk is egocentric, partly because the child speaks only about himself, but chiefly because he makes no attempt to consider the point of view of his hearer. Anyone who happens to be available will serve as an audience. (Piaget, 1948: 9)

According to Piaget, there are three categories of egocentric speech:

1   Repetition (or echolalia): the child repeats words or sounds only for the pleasure of talking. When the child repeats words or sounds, she/he is not aware that she/he is in fact talking or whether she/he is making sense.
2   Monologue: the child talks to him/herself as if she/he were thinking aloud.
3   Dual or collective monologue: this is a conversation between or among children; the other person is never taken into account, but serves as a stimulus.

On the other hand, socialised speech falls into four categories:

1   Adapted information: at this stage the child starts to talk with another child or an adult, in order to influence the child's actions.
2   Criticism: children use language to make remarks about the work or behaviour of others, although in the same way as in adapted information.
3   Commands, requests, threats and questions: in all of these there is interaction between one child and another.
4   Answers: these are answers to real questions and to commands.

As Piaget writes (1952), the growth of language can be predicted from an understanding of children's cognitive skills. Piaget believed that children must understand concepts before they can use words describing those concepts. For example, a toddler should begin to talk about objects when she/he has achieved the realisation that the objects continue to exist even when they cannot be seen. This has been named 'object permanence'. In Piaget's view, children can be 'taught language', but they will be unable to understand the words until they have developed object permanence. He also claimed that thought is necessary to language development. Since Piaget, other researchers have attempted to investigate the relation between object permanence and language development. It has confirmed that children were able to talk about absent objects only after they have demonstrated an advanced level in a test for object permanence (Bjorklund, 1995; Flavell, 1999; Gelman and Williams, 1997).

To conclude, the Piagetian approach is extremely useful with regard to questions of how children use words and why they use particular words to convey particular meanings, while it is much less successful in addressing the issue of how children master the rules of a language such as grammar and syntax.

Vygotsky and language development

Vygotsky's theory emphasises the development of language as 'higher mental processes', including all forms of intelligence and memory (Garton and Pratt, 1998). His aim was to 'describe and specify development of those forms of practical intelligence that are specifically human' (Vygotsky, 1978: 23). Among those forms of intelligence that fulfil useful human functions first and foremost are: speech, perception and attention (Vygotsky, 1978). Thus, Piaget claims that thought comes first and language is relegated to a secondary position. He also believes that language is unable to convey what has not already been established in thought, whereas Vygotsky's view is that language and thought differ in terms of how they are developed. Vygotsky claims that language and thought develop separately and independently in the first years of life and, within the framework he establishes, language allows thought to be both individual and social at the same time. He claims that: 'the child's intellectual growth is contingent on his mastering the social means of thought, that is, language' (Vygotsky, 1962: 51).

Central to his theory of language development is the fact that language is learned through social interaction with others. In social interaction, children learn to use language that will enable them to achieve what they require at a specific time. This is another point of disagreement with the Piagetian theory of language development. Vygotsky (1986) disagrees with Piaget about egocentric speech and points out that children's experiences with language are social from the outset. He claims that when a child is alone she/he uses less egocentric language than is used when playing with others (Vygotsky, 1986). This implies that egocentric speech is influenced by the presence of others.

Vygotsky believes that every new psychological function first appears during children's interactions with others who can support and nurture their efforts. These shared efforts are gradually taken over by the child and transformed into individual abilities. Applied to the area of language, this sequence suggests a progression from social and communicative speech to internal dialogues, or inner speech, in which thought and language are intimately interconnected. This is the exact opposite of the way language, cognition and the social world are related within the Piagetian framework, and, as might be expected, Vygotsky's interpretation of collective monologues (or egocentric speech) also differs from that of Piaget.

Bruner and language development

Bruner extended the work of Chomsky (1957, 1959), who considered that babies and children are programmed to pay attention to language in the same way as they actively seek to explore the world through direct interaction; humans are thus born with an innate 'language acquisition device' (LAD). As children grow up and interact verbally with their human environment, they are picking up the complex grammatical rules of the language, acquiring vocabulary and the ability to put words together to make sentences, and to understand the meaning of the sentences they hear. According to Chomsky (1976), children are prepared for language by using the LAD to master the structure of language. Consequently, he claims, there is no need to teach language directly: when children are growing up in an environment where language is used constantly, adults use correct forms of language, therefore the children will pick up the correct forms of language.

Bruner (1983) described what he calls the 'language acquisition support system' (LASS), based on Chomsky's idea of LAD. For Bruner the role of the adult is important in language acquisition. He is more concerned with the functions of language, namely, the purposes for which language is used. Bruner emphasises the role of the adult through the term 'scaffolding', which refers to a changing quality of social support over the course of a teaching session (Bruner, 1983). Bruner agrees with Chomsky that direct language teaching in early childhood is less effective than supporting children with their language acquisition. Thus, he argues for a supportive environment in early years.

This has significant implications for Early Years education and re-defines the role of the Early Years teacher, practitioner and professional. In practice, detailed instruction is offered when a task is new, whereas less help is provided as competence increases. Thus, the practitioner in a setting maintains the role of the facilitator of the learning process by providing a 'scaffolding' or support system through which children are able to construct their understanding of language. Bruner (1983) views infants as 'tuned' to enter the world of human action. Bruner's work suggests that an enormous amount of the activity of a child during the first 18 months of life is extraordinarily social and communicative. Bloom (1993), taking this point further, argues that a child's social and emotional development plays a leading role in both the quality and quantity of language.

Language development and the environment

It is essential to address the impact of the environment on children's language acquisition. It is well documented that speech directed at infants and young children usually differs from that directed at adults. Snow (1972, 1983), for example, points out that a mother's speech to young children tends to be simple and redundant; it contains many questions and imperatives, few past tenses and few co-ordinations, is pitched higher and has an exaggerated intonation pattern. Fernald and Simon (1984) described this type of speech as 'motherese'. Fernald (1993) shows us that babies do, in fact, find 'motherese' not only pleasant but interesting as well. Other work has shown us that babies' preference for 'motherese' exists from the first few days of life (Cooper and Aslin, 1994). Not only do adults use a special type of speech when talking to children; as Shatz and Gelman (1973) demonstrated, even 4-year-old children will adjust their speech when talking to younger children.

Crying, smiling and other facial movements are the first means of communication. However, as babies become more mobile and more likely to wander out of sight and reach of their carers, facial expressions become less readily available as a source of information and as a method of interaction. Other ways of contact that allow babies and carers to communicate with each other from a greater distance therefore become an urgent necessity (Bloom, 1993).

Symbolic play performs a crucial role in children's language development. Symbolic thought is the result of the development of object permanency and involves the representation of absent persons, objects or actions. When children reach the stage of symbolic play (roughly 15–18 months of age) they begin to combine two actions in play and use two-word sentences (Bloom et al., 1985). A rich environment where children have opportunities for symbolic play is important in the Early Years setting. An environment where children can play with a number of different materials and objects such as sand, bricks, Lego, painting or large picture books will help children to play and to use language. The outdoor environment can become a great facilitator in children's language development, as children can be involved in a number of activities in small groups where language is the main tool for communication and engaging in sharing ideas.

Literacy

Within EYFS, it is essential to understand the term 'literacy' in the Early Years context. A number of studies have looked at what literacy is in the Early Years. Literacy in Early Years cannot be limited only to the ability to read and write using the conventional system of written signs of a particular language; furthermore, there is no doubt that individuals can be literate in more than one language. In Early Years education practitioners and professionals need to extend the basic notion of literacy to indicate competence that enables literate individuals to function independently and flexibly in a society – a view that underpins the EYFS.

It is important to recognise that literacy is not only part of the language: 'whether it is written or oral, [literacy] is a social event of some complexity. Language did not develop because of the existence of one language user but of two' (Harste et al., 1984: 28). It must also be considered as a whole process through which children's literacy skills are acknowledged and are taken into account in the daily activities of the classroom. Literacy should be part of a child's development, not isolated from the society and culture in which that child grows up. Hillerich (1976: 53) argues that children are literate when they are able to:

> [D]emonstrate competence in communication skills which enables the individual to function, appropriate to age, independently of society and with a potential for movement in society.

Goodman (1980) proposes a model of literacy development where the child is a competent cognitive and social learner who can develop, on his/her own, knowledge about, and abilities with, literacy. She claims that it is

> [I]mpossible to consider literacy development without understanding the significance of literacy in the culture – in both the larger society in which a particular culture grows and develops, and within the specific culture in which the child is nourished. (1980: 4)

Literacy should also be viewed as a gradual process that takes place over time with constant social interaction within the environment and in a contextualised way. For example, a common practice in the Early Years setting is that words on cards always bear pictures of the object represented by the words. In a context that supports, facilitates and respects children's development, children's cognitive skills can develop; if this context also provides opportunities for engagement in literacy, children can emerge with literacy skills.

Comber and Cormack (1997) state that there are no ways of teaching or learning literacy that are simple or 'natural'. They claim 'literacy teaching is not neutral' (1997: 28). Literacy is 'socially constructed', and Early Years practitioners or teachers make choices about the instruction of literacy in their setting; therefore the ways in which children develop affect the progress they make.

The research and theoretical developments have changed our understanding of young children's movement into literacy. The term 'literacy' relates to both reading and writing, and suggests the simultaneous development and mutually reinforcing effects of these two aspects of communication. Literacy development is seen as emerging from children's oral language development and their initial, often unconventional attempts, at reading (usually based on pictures) and writing (at first, scribbling): hence the term 'emergent literacy' (Holdaway, 1979; Sulzby, 1985, 1989). Within an emergent literacy framework, children's early unconventional attempts at reading and writing are respected as legitimate beginnings of literacy.

Emergent literacy

Many studies conducted over the past 30 years support the idea of emergent literacy acquisition. Supporters of the theory of emergent literacy consider that it is not possible for children to be unable to read one day, are able to do so the next, then suddenly become readers when they enter school (Heath, 1983). Rather, emergent literacy focuses upon environments where others use reading and writing: children in these environments begin to read and write at a relatively young age (Goodman, 1994; Harste, et al., 1984; Teale and Sulzby, 1989).

Whitehurst (1998), in an attempt to define emergent literacy, starts with the assumption that 'reading is a developmental continuum starting early in life' (p. 23). Thus, the definition of emergent literacy is 'a set of skills, knowledge and attitudinal precursors to formal reading and writing and the environment that supports these precursors' (Whitehurst, 1998: 34).

The main competencies of emergent literacy include:

- awareness of language
- conventions of print
- emergent writing
- phonological awareness
- graphemes
- phoneme–grapheme correspondence
- attitudes such as interest in interacting with books
- environments such as shared book reading, alphabet play and treasure baskets.

Emergent literacy is concerned with 'the earliest phases of literacy development, the period between birth and the time when children read and write conventionally' (Sulzby and Teale, 1991: 728). Thus literacy development begins much earlier than previously thought. Teale and Sulzby (1989) suggest that we should no longer speak of reading readiness or pre-reading but, rather, of literacy development. In preference to 'getting a child ready' to learn to read, the emergent literacy perspective emphasises the child's on-going development. It is important to note that reading and writing 'develop currently and [are] interrelated in young children' (Teale and Sulzby, 1989: 3).

As children pretend to read and scribble messages on cards, they are learning about language (Wolf and Heath, 1992). These are the 'foundations for conventional reading and writing and should be celebrated and encouraged at home, in pre-schools, and in the Early Years of formal schooling' (Searfoss and Readence, 1994: 58).

The importance of reading storybooks to young children both at home and in school (Heath, 1983; Neuman and Roskos, 1997), along with opportunities children should have to explore print, words, rhymes, songs, helps children at a very early stage to begin to experiment with a more literate language.

With increased experience, children begin to focus on the information conveyed in print. They begin by using scribbles and progress through increasingly accurate representations of the relationship between letters and the sounds for which they stand. As children think about how to represent the sounds of words through their writing, they are building skills that will be useful for reading as well.

Perhaps the most important concept that children need to develop is that which is frequently referred to as 'functions of print' (Adams, 1990). When children understand this concept, they have begun to understand that printed language is related to oral language, that print is a form of communication, and that print and books are sources of enjoyment and information (Heath, 1983). Young children learn literacy by being actively involved in meaningful literacy experiences in an environment that encourages and facilitates this active learning (Neuman and Roskos, 1990a, 1990b).

Literacy and the environment

There are numerous references to the role of the home environment in children's relationship with literature. For example, Neuman (1992, 1996, 1997, 1999) has investigated younger children's literacy by examining literacy materials in the home and Early Years settings and opportunities for parent–child storybook reading. She concludes that parents' reading proficiency influences conversational interactions with different text types, serving as 'a scaffold' for parent–child interaction. She suggests that parents play a critical role in children's early literacy learning in the context of access to print resources, and opportunities and interaction in storybook reading.

Neuman (1997) examined the Early Years settings, reflecting literacy-related situations in children's real-world environment. She found that literacy in play may become purposeful in an enriched literacy environment. She also found that literacy becomes part of children's play when literacy activities are in context. Additionally, Hall (1999) suggests that play enables children to experience a wide range of different situations within which literacy is appropriately embedded. By providing a relevant and associated literacy within play settings, children are able to experience literacy in meaningful and purposeful ways.

Wolf and Heath (1992) followed the progress of two young children, learning to negotiate between multiple texts, in order to investigate how literature shapes children's cultural performance. This case study of Wolf's two young girls 'demonstrates the innumerable ways in which books and other written texts are beneath much of the everyday life of their family' (Wolf and Heath, 1992: 195). The longitudinal design of the study allowed the authors to capture literacy development in which information was first shared in reading sessions and then later reproduced, often in the voice and words of the original characters in appropriate contexts.

Spoken and written language

Written language differs from spoken language in many respects and therefore it is important to understand these differences when creating activities to help children develop their spoken and written skills.

As mentioned above, Vygotsky (1986), in his attempt to investigate language acquisition, examines whether there are differences between oral and written language. He claims that the development of writing does not repeat the development of the spoken language. He identifies two characteristics of written language that are different from spoken language: context and receiver. He argues that in written language a child has to create a 'situation' in order to make meaning, and then the audience is abstract. The audience is 'absent' and this is a situation that the child is unable to understand when beginning to learn to write. Therefore, writing language differs from spoken language in terms of 'double abstraction: abstraction from the sound of speech and abstraction from the interlocutor' (Vygotsky, 1986: 181).

He concludes his discussion by suggesting an essential difference between spoken and written language based on the motive of using these two forms of language. He points out that spoken language is 'spontaneous, involuntary and non-conscious' whereas written language is 'abstract, voluntary and conscious' (1986: 183).

Garton and Pratt (1998) identify two main differences between spoken and written language: form differences and function differences. Starting with the form differences, they claim that there are two main differences related to the time and the context in which they take place. Spoken language is ephemeral, it occurs in real time and it requires the ear of the listener. In contrast, written language is more 'durable', it is presented in space (rather than time) and requires eyes to read the language. It is thus permanent, spatial and visual (Garton and Pratt, 1998). Spoken language tends to be more fragmentary and sociable; one talks to or with someone and thus tends to involve the speakers. Written language is durable, the process of achieving it is slow and deliberate, allowing editing both during and after the product, and it is frequently a solitary activity: one writes alone, although usually with a readership in mind. Young children struggle to come to terms with this multitude of differences, which is why it is for them a complex process.

A large body of research agrees that for both written and spoken language development children need instruction, assistance and social interaction (Wells, 1985). The child's development of both spoken and written language is facilitated by the child's active interaction with an adult prepared to assist, guide and support the child (Gardon, 1992).

However, oral language is the critical foundation upon which reading and writing is built. Learning the meaning of thousands of words and developing an understanding of the way words are ordered to make sense are extremely complex processes that take place in oral language development and transfer to reading and writing (Minns, 1997). Cognitive activities, such as understanding cause-and-effect relationships or chronological order established through listening and communicated through speaking, are the same processes used in reading.

Becoming a reader

Research has indicated that children become aware of print from an early age as they interact with the environment (Clay, 1975; Heath, 1983; Teale, 1986). These first exposures occur as children encounter print 'embedded' in their environments (Goodman, 1980; Wells, 1986). Harste et al. (1982) concluded that children begin their literacy learning process by observing this embedded print and constructing schemata concerning its meaning in context. Neuman and Roskos (1997) named these schemata 'play schemata' as children try to make sense of the world of print and literature through play. This is a view that has been extended by the work of Athey (1990) and Nutbrown (2008).

However, children need an important skill in order to achieve this construction and organisation of these 'play schemata', which is symbolic representation. This is a view supported by the Piagetians Ferreiro and Teberosky (1983). They investigated the Piagetian theory and suggested that reading depends on and follows a path parallel to symbolic representation. Children need to be able to represent symbols in their mind, thus enabling them to represent illustrations that are the initial, simplified form of written symbols. Only gradually will they be able to start representing letters, which are a more abstract and complex form of written symbols.

Children learn to recognise printed symbols that occur in context, such as a favourite place for them (Sampson et al., 1991). For example, many children today recognise McDonald's food outlets from the two yellow arches that form its logo. Children's print awareness gradually expands and is not limited to learning from the situational context. Their knowledge of print is also enhanced as they are exposed to print in books, magazines, newspapers, letters and other printed materials (Goodman, 1980). These early experiences with all such printed materials directly influence children's awareness of print and can thus be considered as steps towards children's becoming readers.

Children begin to be aware of the fact that to hold a book is to 'read' the pictures. The initial 'literacy event' takes place when a child holds a book and looks at the pictures. Gradually, the child moves from being a 'naïve' reader to being a more 'expert' reader, and learns such things as how to open the book, how to turn the pages, how to pay attention to the text, and so on. Similarly, after these skills have been mastered children start pretending to read or tell stories. This is not simply children's make-believe play, imitating the teacher or the parent who reads a book: it is an actual literacy event.

Becoming a writer

An important element of the literacy learning process is when children make their first attempts to write. Sulzby (1992: 293) notes: 'Children write with many forms prior to developing close to the adult concept that I call conventional writing.'

> At kindergarten, most children are still using emergent forms of writing such as scribble, drawing, non phonetic strings of letters or phonetic ('invented' or 'creative') spelling and few have made the transition to conventional writing as their preferred writing form. (p. 290)

Martinez and Teale (1988) support this idea and argue that it is destructive to assume that children cannot write until they have mastered the mechanisms, or that the only way they should write is through conventional writing. According to Ferreiro and Teberosky (1983), during this developmental process children often rely on concrete representations to facilitate the transfer of meaning to the written page.

Sulzby (1992) suggests that at this age children should be 'encouraged or nudged' and not pushed to start their writing process. When children first spontaneously produce graphic representations, drawing and writing are undifferentiated. When children first experiment with a pencil, what they want to do is to leave their mark everywhere, for instance, on a piece of paper or on a wall (Ferreiro and Teberosky, 1983; Morrow, 1992).

At this stage children (normally from the age of 18 months) experience school-life play with these materials and treat them as toys. Gradually, they realise that they are different 'toys' from the others, and become more creative. Drawing is a form of semiotic function, which should be considered as being halfway between symbolic play and the mental image. It is a free assimilation of reality to the subjects and the schemes according to Piaget (Piaget and Inhelder, 1966), and it is closer to the imitative accommodation. Drawing becomes imitation and image.

According to Luquet's influential study of children's drawings (1959), a child begins to draw by drawing what s/he knows about a person or an object long before s/he can draw what s/he actually sees. Additionally, Piaget states that the first spatial intuitions of the child are, in fact, topological rather than projective or consistent with Euclidean geometry (Piaget and Inhelder, 1966). The child becomes capable of drawing an object not as s/he sees it but as an observer located to the right of, or opposite, the child would see it. This is an interesting point in that three-year-old children, for example, even in their art works, cannot separate themselves from the object, their activities being an expansion of their perception of the world.

Written language is also a symbolic object: it is a representation of an entity. Both drawing and writing are substitutes for another entity; however, the two differ from each other. Drawing maintains a relationship of similarity to the objects or occurrences to which it refers, whilst writing does not. Language, in the form of writing, constitutes a system with its own rules, whereas drawing does not (Ferreiro and Teberosky, 1983; Morrow, 1992). Both the nature and the content of these substitute objects are different. In the drawings of some 3-year-old children shown in Figure 10.1 their attempts to draw and their attempts to make symbolic representations, hence write or imitate writing letters, can be distinguished.

Play as the foundation for communication, language and literacy

Throughout this book the importance of play within EYFS is emphasised. Once again play maintains an important role in children's communication, language and literacy development.

Neuman (1999) and Hall (1999, 2000) suggest that play enables children to cooperate in learning about literacy. In play, children interact closely in order to achieve more

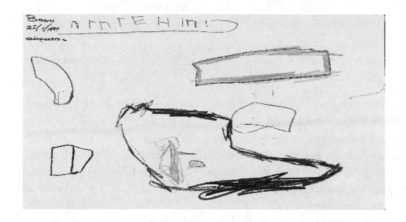

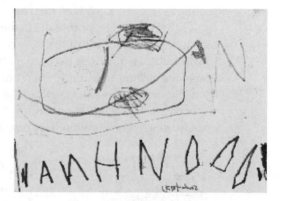

Figure 10.1   Children's attempts to write

satisfying play. Children bring to play different experiences and knowledge and in the course of play these are shared (Neuman, 1997; Hall, 1999, 2000).

The work of Neuman and Roskos (1990a, 1990b, 1998) investigated how play centres, enriched in the functional uses of print, influenced the quality of literacy activities in the spontaneous play of young children. In an earlier study, Neuman and Roskos had examined the common function that reading and writing appeared to serve for children in two pre-schools. These observations indicated that children demonstrated a number of uses of literacy on their own and with others in four functional domains: 'children used literacy to explore the print environment, to interact with others, to express themselves and to transact with text' (Neuman and Roskos, 1998: 214). In their continuing examination of play as a context for literacy, they used the four functional domains as well as the play environment in designing literacy-enriched play areas. The findings of their studies suggest that literacy-enriched play centres can make a difference to children's literacy behaviours through play.

Hall (1999), based on his own research into literacy and play, suggests that:

> [C]hildren bring to play different experiences and knowledge and in the course of play are shared. Play offers a number of valuable opportunities for children to experiment explicitly with, and use, literacy in many different but valid ways. (p. 114)

Based on this conclusion, he describes how a 'literate home corner' should look and how practitioner's intervention encouraged children's play towards their literacy learning. He concludes, based on the evidence of an earlier study (Hall, 1991), that an intervention that aims to increase literacy learning within play should be 'sensitive, appropriate and relative' (Hall, 1999: 124). He claims that such an intervention is the one that does not inhibit the play for the literacy, but that the play becomes richer in order to facilitate children's literacy learning.

This finding in the intervention studies by Hall (1991, 1999) is that when play is central, it enables children to have a holistic experience of literacy. He claims that within a play setting, literacy is not 'fragmented by artificial instructional process' (Hall, 1999: 114). He argues that literacy is appropriate in the play, such as children having a meal in the restaurant area, or visiting a hospital.

Through play children become motivated, try to work together, resolve their differences, are willing to listen to each other (or not), try to make sense of the world, and try to be comforted emotionally; in all of the functions of play, language maintains an important role, so it is essential for Early Years curriculum design to have a wealth of opportunities where children will use language in the form of play.

Case Study

The visit to the open-air market

As part of a visit to the open-air market, a group of 3- and 4-year-old children were asked to draw what they had seen there. While the activity took place, children started to talk spontaneously about their experiences in the open-air market. The practitioner, who was observing the children, seized the opportunity and asked them if they wanted to make their own story about the market:

Early years practitioner: What do you think of having our own story about the visit to the open-air market and then, after lunch, we can invite the other children to listen to our story?

Philip:	I think it is great!!
Vicky:	Yes, and our story in the market will have a dragon.
George:	There are no dragons in the market.
Vicky:	I have been to the open market and one day they had dragons like balloons.
George:	Those were toys, not real dragons.

Vicky:	So what? We can say that they were real dragons. It is a story.
George:	No, you cannot do that.
Vicky:	Oh! Leave me alone, it is our story ... can we have a dragon in the visit to the open-air market?
Early Years practitioner:	Yes, if it is our story it is not real, so we can include whatever we want.
Philip:	Then, if Vicky has a dragon, I will have a knight with a very big and magic sword.
Early Years practitioner:	Okay. What will the knight do with the dragon?
Philip:	The dragon will try to go to the open-air market and eat the people who do their shopping, but the knight will come with his big magic sword and try to rescue the people ...
Vicky:	Yes, but the dragon will hurt the knight first and then will take ...

The open market story illustrates how language is learned in a supportive environment. Children integrate their language and literacy experiences into activities, such as drawing, and into their symbolic play. In the process of using literacy, the child takes ownership of the literacy learning process. Children's play reflects not only their most recent literacy learning, but also their past experiences of literacy (Vicky had been to the open-air market and she recounted everything about her visit in her narration) in the wider print environment where they arise. In this social process, children make their own literacy discoveries. The Early Years practice should be viewed as an 'imaginative mental trip' enriched with opportunities for children to use language and express themselves.

Key points to remember

- This chapter discussed communication, language and literacy development and aimed to illustrate what is meant when these terms are used in the Early Years. Language development is considered important for children's development and learning, as well as critical when literacy is discussed.
- Literacy development in young children begins long before their formal instruction in reading and writing, and play is essential to help children as they bring different experiences, perceptions and knowledge; in the course of play these are shared.
- Literacy-enriched centres can make a difference to children's language and literacy behaviours through play.

Points for discussion

- Observe a group of children during play and try to identify how children use language. How do they use their body language, how do they interact with each other, how do they ask questions, and what range of words do they use?
- Observe children's responses during story time or a nursery rhyme. Is it possible to identify whether children have learned any new words, whether there were any opportunities to interact with each other and share the story, whether there were opportunities to follow up the story and create drawings, or other such activities?
- Consider an activity such as to get pairs of children to discuss their work by giving a creative task, such as asking each child to draw what they might find inside a treasure chest found by a pirate at the bottom of the sea. What opportunities can you create for enriching children's language? What opportunities can you create for literacy development? What opportunities can you create for interaction among children?

Further reading

Bradford H. (2009) *Communication, Language and Literacy in the Early Years Foundation Stage*. London: David Fulton.

Brock, A. and Rankin, C. (2008) *Communication, Language and Literacy from Birth to Five*. London: Sage.

Bruce, T. and Spratt, J. (2008) *Essentials of Literacy from 0–7*, London: Sage.

Useful websites

Communication, language and literacy in the EYFS:
www.standards.dfes.gov.uk/eyfs

Literacy, and family literacy:
www.literacytrust.org.uk/Database/earlyyears.html

National literacy strategy:
www.nls.org.uk/

CHAPTER 11

PROBLEM SOLVING, REASONING AND NUMERACY

David Needham

Chapter Aims

According to the Early Years Foundation Stage:

> [B]abies' and children's mathematical development occurs as they seek patterns, make connections and recognise relationships through finding out about and working with numbers and counting [and] with sorting and matching with shape, space and measures. (DCSF, 2008: *Practice Guidance*, p. 63)

EYFS also emphasises that 'children use their knowledge and skills in these areas to solve problems, generate new questions and make connections across other areas of Learning and Development'. Initially, the purpose of this chapter is to explore why and how children develop their powers of reasoning and numeric abilities, and how such powers help them deal with problems across a range of different contexts. The chapter then focuses upon how individuals can contextualise and develop simple and practical learning opportunities when working alongside young children to help to develop their mathematical understanding.

(Continued)

(Continued)

This chapter aims to help you:

- consider the key role played by the successful development of numeric and reasoning skills in solving problems

- reflect upon how to develop an appropriate pedagogy for EYFS-aged children to achieve their learning goals within the areas of numeracy and mathematics

- develop an understanding of how young children construct and develop numeric and reasoning skills

- appreciate how learning opportunities, though play and social interactions, enable children to develop their mathematical knowledge

- recognise factors that influence learning (such as the indoor and outdoor learning environments)

- consider how the existence of home–school links could support children's learning and development of mathematical skills and concepts.

Problem solving, reasoning and numeracy in context

It is easy to take for granted the multifarious numeric skills that help individuals, whatever their age, successfully to survive each day within any context. The processes of telling the time, spending money, mentally budgeting for the week, measuring, making comparisons, interpreting diagrams, reading timetables, undertaking simple calculations, looking at comparative relationships, applying logic and undertaking simple arithmetic are quite literally inculcated into the myriad of daily decisions that people make. These processes, many of which are social (Munn, 1996a), seem almost instinctive as children learn and develop. Children need to make sense of what they see and what they do. It is a time when children are developing not just their reading skills but also their mathematical skills. They experiment with what they see, particularly symbols, and this is at the centre of their development (Worthington and Carruthers, 2003). They go on to emphasise that 'our central argument is that children come to make their own sense of abstract symbols through using their own marks and constructing their own meaning' (2003: 70). Munn (1996b) further emphasises this link between literacy and numeracy through symbolic activity. She feels that 'their symbolic activity is related to their understanding of reading and to their identity as a reader' (1996: 31). In this way, as young children develop, mathematics is just one of the many ways in which they discover who they are and develop ways of coping with the world in which they live (Devlin, 2000).

As children develop their symbolic activity and recognition it is more usually in these situations that more sophisticated numeric, reasoning and mathematical skills are required in order to solve a problem or to make a decision. Davis (1984: 1) views problem solving as having a fundamental role in work, social and private lives and he goes on to emphasise that learning about mathematics influences 'how one thinks through the analysis of mathematical problems'.

Although the use of numeric and mathematical skills to reason and solve problems will be for many individuals largely an unconscious process, it has a key role in everybody's life. Where good decisions are made, it follows that individuals are likely to do the right thing and be happier or more content with the outcomes from such decisions. For this reason children from a very early age need to make sense of numeracy and mathematics as they comprise an evolving life skill, almost like a language, that enables them to face both certain and uncertain situations with greater confidence. According to Nunes and Bryant (1996: 1), 'children need to learn about mathematics in order to understand the world around them'. Doing so helps them to explore, to become rational human beings, to take advantage of the opportunities that surround them and to develop their conceptual abilities to solve problems.

Developing problem solving skills

Perhaps the best starting point is to consider what numeric and reasoning skills involve in order to appreciate the extent to which each contributes to problem solving in everyday life. It is frequently felt that as a way of thinking or as a form of language 'mathematics encompasses a wide range of ideas and activities' (Cooke, 2007: 2). As you think about mathematic or numeric skills you probably find that many different thoughts materialise; for example, you may think of some of the more abstract mathematical concepts, such as equations, fractions, algebra, geometry, data handling or even trigonometry. Alternatively, at its very basic level, it is easy to associate numeric skills with counting, measuring, size, patterns, relationships, recognising different shapes or undertaking simple calculations. The EYFS curriculum states that children should recognise and use numbers, while it emphasises the relationships of mathematics to a context by using the notion of mathematics to solve practical problems (DCSF, 2008: Card 2.12). It also links mathematics to language so that children understand words such as 'more' and 'less' or 'greater' and 'smaller'. In doing so it emphasises the link between learning about mathematics and play within everyday life, and sees mathematics as an enabler that contributes to the wider learning and development of young children.

For some children mathematics can seem difficult. There are probably many different kinds of reasons for this. In several ways mathematics is very different to many other curriculum subjects: it has its own signs and symbols; it involves developing an understanding of concepts that require progression in preparation for absorbing other concepts. Even simply the word 'mathematics' has been identified as a barrier, as it can communicate negative perceptions for learners (Skemp, 1989). If children are not confident they may feel challenged by the activities that they face. They may simply get stuck and not be able to think about how to move forward. Such a situation may create anxiety, which makes it more difficult for the learners to become unstuck.

These situations are often where the role of the practitioner is so important in being able to identify and recognise that a difficulty exists and then support children, perhaps by providing them with more information or through simplifying or structuring the problem in a way that enables the situation to become a positive learning experience. The irony is that, according to Skemp (1989: 49), 'mathematical thinking is not essentially different from some of the ways in which we use our intelligence in everyday life'.

There is a strong link between how individuals think about mathematics and the pedagogy that might have provided the basis for their learning. For example, learning might take place by rote to include learning how to count from one to ten or by undertaking repetitious activities within the setting. Certainly, children might be able to undertake activities following processes of rote learning, while the real problem is that the learning simply assembles information and children may not really learn or comprehend what they are doing (Downs, 1998). Learning may simply transform a discipline into an area that depends upon memory rather than real understanding. By contrast, developing numeric and mathematical skills may be used as a way of solving problems so that children make clear connections between what they are learning and how they can use that information to reason, make decisions, or solve problems in everyday life (Cooke, 2007). It is, therefore, particularly pleasing that EYFS (DCSF, 2008) places the mathematical and numeric development of children under the title of 'Problem Solving, Reasoning and Numeracy', which creates a clear and intentionally expressed creative implication for the way in which the EYFS curriculum and content should be delivered.

Using the technique of problem solving as a basis for teaching mathematics is grounded in sound educational research. Hiebert et al. (1996: 12) argue that:

> [A]llowing [mathematics] to be problematic means allowing students to wonder what things are, to enquire, to search for solutions, and to resolve incongruities. It means that both curriculum and instruction should begin with problems, dilemmas and questions for students.

They argue that the curriculum should be designed so that instructions can 'problematise' the subject. This means that instead of children simply acquiring the skills and answering questions, they are resolving problems; this builds upon Dewey's (1938) notion of reflective enquiry.

Case Study

Gardening

Elliot (2 years and 7 months old) joined the gardening activity. He became responsible for planting some beans. The group responsible for the gardening had to record in a notebook the development of the beans by drawing daily what happened to the beans.

Elliot started the planting with his group, and the practitioner introduced the notebook. The group had to put a symbol for who watered the beans and when, and to draw how the beans developed. Elliot was responsible for counting every day how many beans had grown. Then, with the assistance of the practitioner, the children started to fill in the notebook according to their daily observations. Every day, Elliot's group was asked to spend about five minutes checking on the beans, and then to record their observations in the notebook.

Elliot learned to count from one to four, indicating how many beans had grown, to distinguish between small and big, and also to recognise 'more' or 'less' when he was watering the beans.

Developing mathematical knowledge

As young children grow and develop they need to develop strategies enabling them to interact with and make more sense of their own environment and setting. From 0–5 children's learning is a continuum of development whatever the setting they are in. Initially, through this interaction learning takes place before children start their formal schooling. For example, even as early as 6 months old babies are able visually to identify small sets. Babies are also able to identify repetitions and identify size differences. This implies that they have some kind of basis on which they can make quantitative judgements.

There is also an issue concerning the sort of mathematics that children should learn about. Clements et al. (2004: 366) states that 'basic mathematics for preschool children can be organised into two areas: (a) geometric and special skills and (b) numeric and quantitative ideas and skills'. Schaeffer et al. (1974) identified the first three number skills understood by children include 'more', their judgement of relative numbers (which involves recognition that one array has more than another) and their pattern recognition of small numbers.

Clearly, all of the early learning that takes place in the home environment has implications for the requirements of the curriculum once a child attends a nursery or goes to school. As Resnick emphasises:

[T]here is a constructivist assumption about how mathematics is learned. It is assumed that mathematical knowledge – like all knowledge – is not directly absorbed but is constructed by each individual. This constructivist view is consonant with the theory of Jean Piaget. (1989: 162)

As a result children bring into their first experience of education a depth of informal mathematical knowledge based upon the strategies that they have developed within their environment. Aubrey points out that:

> [Y]oung children construct their own knowledge and invent their own strategies in everyday situations and through their interactions with the environment. For connections to be made between this knowledge and the formal mathematical knowledge of school, however, analyses of children's strategies, including their errors, must be made, as well as detailed analyses of the mathematical content required to carry out these tasks. (1993: 29)

This has clear ramifications for the role of those who support learning for Early Years children. Furthermore, as Aubrey (1993) emphasises, the competencies brought by children into the classroom from their own backgrounds may 'pose some challenges to the conventional reception-class curriculum'. She highlights that reception teachers need to be aware of the mathematical levels and abilities that learners bring into the school, as well as the need to be able to assess the learning that has taken place. Through this understanding of learning, practitioners can build upon the ongoing development of mathematical concepts.

Mathematics as a social activity

As has been seen, mathematics is a living subject. It lives because of the need for individuals to deal with numeric issues all around us. As children make sense of the world they begin to understand patterns and seek solutions that help them to explore and deal with everyday issues. For example, Resnick (1989: 162) indicates that: 'infants of about six months can discriminate the numerosity of small sets when these are presented visually. What is more, they can match sets cross-modally, recognising the same quantity where it is presented visually or auditorily'.

According to Schoenfeld (1992: 3), 'mathematics is an inherently social activity'. He also emphasises that as children learn about mathematics the process becomes empowering for the learner. In fact, Vygotsky (1978) mentioned the importance of understanding the social context of learning. Nowhere is the social aspect of learning about mathematics better underlined than the ways in which young children learn through the process of play during their Early Years. According to Wood and Attfield (2005: 1), 'early childhood education is underpinned by a strong tradition which regards play as essential for learning and development'. Although not all play is purposeful, playing can contribute to the learning and development of children as they grow. It provides an opportunity for them to be creative and to experiment; such behaviours can have widespread implications for the development of each individual. Many of the activities in which children engage while they play can be used to develop and support learning. As Wood and Attfield emphasise (2005: 13), 'if playing and growing are synonymous with life itself, then lifelong playing can be seen as an important aspect of lifelong learning'.

As will be demonstrated, play is therefore a good opportunity purposefully to develop social interactions with children in a way that provides a context for learning opportunities within the area of mathematics. For example, well-structured and planned play may provide situations in which the practitioner can set up a challenging learning environment for the child; it may extend their language and improve their understanding of key areas such as numeracy and mathematics. In doing so, play also provides the opportunity to set up creative and imaginative learning experiences for the child. While these experiences may challenge individuals, they will also satisfy their curiosity and encourage them to ask questions or want to learn more. Play also provides a creative pedagogy through which problem solving can be used as a base for learning.

Contextualised learning opportunities

There are so many different activities and opportunities through which children can interact with adults to develop their mathematical skills that it is just not possible for this chapter to do them all justice. Instead, this section simply highlights a range of contextualised learning opportunities to provide a sample of the sorts of activities in which adults and children can engage.

The context for learning about mathematics may be provided by the home or other setting as well as the school. Research shows that both the home and the school have the capability of making key contributions to the development of academic skills at the age of 5 years (Dickinson and Tabors, 1991). As children are learning in two very different environments, a strong argument can be made that in order to create synergy and make the most of how children learn in such contrasting contexts, home and school should work closely together, so that school can take account of the learning experiences that children bring with them from home (Jones, 1998).

By exploring through interaction children intuitively learn about size and shapes (Price et al., 2003). At a very early stage, simply building a tower with blocks or making a house, having a range of toys with bright colours, or sorting sweets helps them to learn basic mathematical skills. Blocks are particularly useful in introducing children to shapes, sizes and colours. As infants become toddlers, there are many more social opportunities to interact with the child. For example, counting while handing objects over to a toddler, reciting songs that use numbers or using finger-play to reinforce numbers will help them to understand more about the notions of 'more' or 'less' such that they may start to compare numbers. It may also help children to say and use the names of numbers within an appropriate context, and encourage them to start counting objects independently.

Reading books with a mathematical bias help children to learn literacy skills alongside their development of mathematical terms and concepts in a context that they may enjoy.

Children are naturally curious, which stimulates them to ask many questions. For example, they might want to know how many cars are in the street, or how many people there are on a bus. By answering questions, it is possible to count with them or to provide them with some way of understanding greater, smaller, heavier or lighter. It may also provide an opportunity for them to understand the notion of shapes such as circles or squares or to be able to describe in their own words the shape of something. For example, when slicing up a cake or a pie it is possible to count each of the pieces out to the child. In a similar vein, when placing objects in front of the child, his or her understanding of adding and subtracting can be developed by adding objects to or taking objects from the pile. Measurement activities may also satisfy curiosity. If the child uses a sand pit or wants to play with water, measuring cups and spoons will enable him or her to understand which containers hold less.

'Story sacks' were initially developed by Neil Griffiths (1998). They provide a creative opportunity to develop materials to stimulate the interest of children and make their stories more 'real'. A story sack is a large cloth bag inside which is placed a children's book and other associated materials related in some way to the story. Items could be counted out, or may involve different shapes and sizes; they can be discussed in relation to the story, in order to make the story come alive. Story sacks provide a fresh approach to enjoying books, and also provide a learning opportunity for the reader and the child to interact using a range of tangible materials in a way that sustains their motivation to read. Materials provide an element of curiosity and at the same time make learning active. By providing materials focused upon numeracy, such as cards, games, activities or lines that promote mathematical development effectively, the story sacks become number sacks to be used to help children to learn key mathematical skills such as counting.

For Early Years children role-play is an imaginative way in which to learn. According to Staub:

> [C]hildren role-play extensively in their interaction with other children. By enacting a variety of roles and exchanging roles in interactive situations, children may learn to view events from a variety of points of view. (1971: 806)

Role-playing provides a situation where children can imitate behaviour and act out different situations. The home is a perfect setting for children to engage in role-play. The role of the facilitator is simply to adapt the setting and create a role-play area. For example, the child may help with some cooking and be involved in sorting ingredients; this helps them to learn about more or less, or how to compare the sizes or amount of ingredients. They may have a cooker as a toy or another item that can contribute to the role-playing situation. Role-play might include growing cress or sunflowers, counting plant pots, using money in a retailing role-play, sorting objects such as sweets or shells, weighing ingredients, or developing the notion of time.

Case Study

Role-play

A group of 2- to 3-year-old children, after reading the story of Little Red Riding Hood, decided to do a role-play in front the rest of the group of children. They made a list of the things they would need: a cake and a basket with some food in it. Finally, they decided they would have to choose roles in their play.

First, they chose to prepare the basket with the foods that Little Red Riding Hood was to offer to her grandmother. The children decided to make a cake. They searched for a recipe and they 'wrote the recipe' on a big poster so everyone could see. They had opportunities to explore concepts such as 'more' or 'less', 'big' or 'small' and 'adding'.

They had opportunities to measure the ingredients for the cake, to add or to take away; for example, when they added two glasses of sugar, one glass of water, the flour, and so on. The practitioner decided to focus only on these three concepts during the process of baking the cake and the subsequent activities.

Secondly, the children decided to pack the basket by adding different objects. Again, they had the opportunity to explore the concepts 'big' and 'small', 'more' and 'less', and add how many objects were going into the basket.

Finally, the role-play took place. The children, after preparing Little Red Riding Hood's basket, chose their roles: who would be Little Red Riding Hood, the wolf, the trees, the grandmother, the hunter and the mother. During this activity, derived from a fairy tale, the children had the chances to negotiate roles, responsibilities and plans, and to re-create roles and experiences. The whole project targeted children's problem solving and numeracy while other areas such as language and communication, social development and creativity were also developed.

The practitioner provided opportunities for the children that encouraged them to use the concepts of more/less, and big/small, as well as to count up to five. A number of different materials were used to conceptualise the different concepts and to help the children interact with different materials and objects in order for them to understand the concepts in different contexts. Time was provided for children to initiate discussions from shared experiences.

Puzzles are good for helping children to develop their spatial skills within a different environment that enables them to achieve a range of purposes (Siraj-Blatchford et al., 2002). As children work with puzzles, they are actually putting bits together and solving problems at first hand. Puzzles help with coordination; children begin to recognise that individual parts all contribute towards a whole. Puzzles help children to understand that by rotating pieces, they can find the way in which each piece fits.

Then, piece by piece, the puzzle becomes a whole. A wide range of puzzles designed for different ages of children are available today. They may be 3D puzzles, pegboards, bead threading, as well as puzzles linked to different sounds and made of different materials.

The indoor and outdoor environments

Young children require an interesting environment with the capability of stimulating their learning and development. The key features of such an environment must be the setting, the materials and the toys available, and any equipment required. While such an environment should prompt a child to explore in a challenging way, it needs to be safe and secure. According to Schroeder (1991: 129): 'the health and well-being of children, in comparison to adults, are often more severely affected by the quality of the physical environment'. An appropriate environment would offer children the opportunity to explore both outdoors and indoors. The children would also need to be supported and supervised by adults.

An indoor play area should be a place where children can be either active or quiet; it should be designed to support their active learning and development. The environment should contain resources and materials that enable children to play and to further their learning at their own pace. The nature of such resources or toys will depend upon the respective age of each child and, of course, their particular phase of development. The items should also be imaginative: natural materials such as shells and pine cones are as enjoyable and instructive as wooden spoons, containers and other simple household equipment; a brief glance at various commercial websites can identify toys such as teaching watches, cash tills with money, blocks and shapes, shopping games, puzzles, number games, electronic maths toys, match-it puzzles, jigsaws, thinking games, wooden toddler toys, manipulative toys and imaginative play sets. The list is almost endless. As Taylor et al. have written, 'toys can be used to promote children's cognitive, physical, motor, language, social and emotional development' (1997: 235).

Any outdoor space should offer children both shade and shelter, and within this area both natural and manufactured resources should be available for play. For example, items could help the child dig, swing, roll, move, stretch, or play with wheeled toys. The children can also play in a water area where concepts such as wet, dry, floating, skimming, similarities and differences can be explored. The practitioners, with the help of the children, can create a fish market where children can have opportunities to act such roles as seller or customer, to count money, to think how the fish will be stored, and to count the fish for sale.

In such an environment children need at their own pace to make choices about how to explore and learn. Natural materials such as sand, soil, garden snail shells, a slatted tray and cardboard boxes can be very helpful for children's participation in meaningful activities such as those which encourage children to sort, group and sequence play. Resources designed to help their mathematical development might help them to collect, measure, make patterns or build as they play. Swings, seesaws, slides, tents or a climbing house help to support such an environment. The outdoor environment is an enabler for children to be energetic and to exercise while enjoying some concrete experiences. There are a range of outdoor toys designed to help children with the development of their mathematical skills, such as number bean bags, giant inflatable numbers, a numeracy octopus, shape wands, what-is-it boxes and scatter boards, as well as giant puzzles.

Planning for progression

The EYFS (DCFS, 2008) identifies three areas that provide appropriate opportunities to support children in their learning and their development of problem solving, reasoning and numeracy skills. The first is that of positive relationships, which emphasises that children should be encouraged to develop mathematical concepts within the context of their own play, particularly in child-centred and -initiated activities. According to the Mathematical Association (1955: v, vi), 'children developing at their own individual rates, learn through their active response to the experiences that come to them through constructive play, experiment and discussion, [and] children become aware of relationships and develop mental structures which are mathematical in form'. EYFS emphasises the need to allow children to explore real life problems and to make patterns that match.

The second area emphasised by EYFS is that of creating an enabling environment for children. It includes both an outdoor environment in which a physical activity can be used in order to discover about distances, shapes and measurement, as well as an indoor area where children have the chance to learn to count and calculate. Resources are a key feature of both of these environments.

Finally, EYFS links both areas, positive relationships and enabling environments, to the learning and development of Early Years children. Mathematical development should be creative and include songs, games and imaginative play. Activities should enable mathematical learning and problem solving to take place; they need to be built into daily routines to provide a route for development and progression.

The importance of home–school links as part of the planning process

The learning and development of young children should be a shared experience among parents and carers as well as schools. Parents may be concerned about how their children are getting on within school while, at the same time, teachers may want to discuss with parents issues affecting learning. This may not always be easy, particularly for parents who might not be sure about how they could help the educational development of their children. According to Booth and Dunn (1996: 3), 'parents play a critical role in both their children's academic achievement and their children's socio-emotional development'. They identify in their text evidence that illustrates how such a relationship contributes to the success of children within a classroom setting over their period in school.

Parents or carers may feel that they require information to help them to complement the nature and type of activities engaged in by their child when at school. For some (particularly better-educated parents) this may be easier than for parents who were challenged by learning mathematics. The level and strength of participation may depend upon the resources available to parents, the strength of their belief in the need for participating with schools, and attitudes towards schooling and education in general.

   Key points to remember

- EYFS identifies three different areas that help to develop learning in the area of Problem Solving, Reasoning and Numeracy. These are: (a) positive relationships, involving the provision of time, space and opportunities for children to explore and develop their learning and understanding; (b) enabling environments, whether indoors or outdoors, that are well resourced to promote and develop learning; and (c) learning and development through play and activities based upon regular daily routines.
- Mathematics helps children to make sense of and better understand the world around them in their Early Years setting. It enables them simultaneously to develop their conceptual abilities and to solve problems. From the very earliest stage of development babies recognise patterns and make connections.
- Mathematics can seem difficult for some children because the area has its own language. It is important to develop strategies that help children to develop their mathematical knowledge and problem solving abilities. As this development is undertaken, it must be remembered that learning about mathematics is a social activity. There are a wide variety of ways in which mathematical knowledge can be developed, and this may be within the context of either indoor or outdoor play.

Points for discussion

- If children start school with a range of numeric and mathematical knowledge constructed from their individual backgrounds, what are the implications for how those working with them should organise their strategies for support?
- Based upon your experiences of working with Early Years children, identify concrete experiences or evidence of situations in which you have observed babies and children constructing mathematical knowledge.
- Think of concrete examples of where the learning of mathematics by children can be set up as a socially mediated activity. How does the social aspect of learning influence the richness of the learning activity? Are there any problems or issues that might arise as part of this social interaction?

Further reading

Cooke, H. (2007) *Mathematics for Primary and Early Years: Developing Subject Knowledge*. 2nd edn. London: Sage.

Hughes, A.M. (2009) *Problem Solving, Reasoning and Numeracy in the Early Years Foundation Stage*. London: David Fulton.

Pound, L. (2006) *Supporting Mathematical Development in the Early Years*. Maidenhead: Open University Press.

Useful websites

Helium

www.helium.com/items/1117913

Helium is a site that provides a range of topical and first-hand content about diverse issues for readers, submitted by a wide variety of contributors. This particular part of the site is entitled 'How to help your young child to develop maths skills at home'. With more than 40 papers from parents and practitioners to read and review on the site, as well as plenty of advice, there is a plethora of suggested activities.

Edhelper

http://edhelper.com/

Although there are parts of this website that require a subscription, there are a number of free areas with a series of number, shape, colouring, counting and matching activities, attractively presented and really useful for mathematically developing Early Years children.

www.apples4theteacher.com/math.html#geometrygames

Apples for the Teacher describes itself as a 'fun educational website for teachers and kids'. The site links itself to other pages, and has a huge number of downloads and links to puzzles, games and problem solving activities. Activities range from measurement games and money games to those that help learners to make sense of the principles of number.

CHAPTER 12

KNOWLEDGE AND UNDERSTANDING OF THE WORLD

Gary Beauchamp

Chapter Aims

The fourth principle of the Early Years Foundation Stage is that children develop and learn in different ways and at different rates, with all areas of learning and development considered equally important and inter-connected. In this context, Knowledge and Understanding of the World (KUW) cannot when planning be considered in isolation from other areas of learning and development. Research has shown that 'the brain will learn from every experienced event, but because cognitive representations are distributed, cumulative learning is crucial. There will be stronger representation of what is common across experience ('prototypical') and weaker representation of what differs' (Goswami and Bryant, 2007: 4). In this context it is important in the Early Years environment for the Early Years workforce to plan to reinforce key ideas across different areas of learning. In planning these experiences, however, it is essential that key ideas and concepts are presented in a recognisable form in a variety of contexts and formats, so that children learn to recognise things which are common (for instance, the concept of a shape, e.g., of a ladybird, a 2D shape, and in patterns) when presented in different locations and materials, or even in life forms.

(Continued)

(Continued)

As Goswani and Bryant (2007: 4) conclude: 'there will be multiple representations of experience (for example in motor cortex and in sensory cortices). This supports multi-sensory approaches to education.' It is here that KUW can offer unique and distinctive multi-sensory opportunities both to *introduce* new ideas (which can be reinforced in other areas) and to *reinforce* ideas (as introduced in other areas of learning). The key issue lies in recognising the distinctive opportunities offered by KUW in a variety of learning contexts and interactions – including between children and teachers, among children themselves, and between children and their environment.

This chapter aims to help you:

- develop an understanding of the distinctive features of Knowledge and Understanding of the World within the context of the Early Years Foundation Stage (EYFS)

- develop an understanding of how these features integrate with, and enhance, other areas of learning

- enhance your awareness of the variety of learning perspectives offered by adopting a variety of curricular 'lenses'

- consider the role, and effective use, of other adults in a variety of learning situations

- develop an awareness of inclusive practice in the area of Knowledge and Understanding of the World in the classroom and in other settings.

The child: a unique actor in their own social world?

EYFS acknowledges that 'every child is a unique individual with their own characteristics and temperament' and that 'early relationships strongly influence how children develop'. Indeed, it is essential to remember that 'learning in young children is socially mediated. Families, peers and teachers are all important' (Goswami and Bryant, 2007: 20). In this context, although the child is often focused on his or her own world, the role of the Early Years workforce is to broaden this focus so as to help them to develop a variety of relationships. To do so, practitioners need to consider how to develop a range of partnerships both within and outside of the school or another setting. As well as providing opportunities to enhance social development, the partnerships should also be considered as vital parts of cognitive development as 'those settings which see cognitive and social development as complementary achieve the best profile in terms of child outcomes' (Siraj-Blatchford et al., 2002: 10). Indeed, there is evidence that enhancing cognitive development can be a catalyst to higher levels of parental involvement. A review of research concluded that 'parental involvement is strongly influenced by the child's level of attainment: the higher the level of attainment, the more parents get involved' (Desforges and Abouchaar, 2003: 4).

It is much easier to enhance partnerships within a school or other setting, as the Early Years workforce has direct access to other professionals. Conversely, it is much harder to develop partnerships with parents and carers, especially when students are on a teaching placement, where it may seem a higher priority to develop relationships with children. It is vital, however, that students should not neglect opportunities to develop relationships with families – even if this appears difficult on a time-limited placement. They should also take chances to understand the family background of the children whenever possible. Even simple steps such as being seen by, and making yourself available to talk to, parents at the beginning and the end of each day can be a starting point in achieving this.

EYFS acknowledges that:

- All families are important and should be welcomed and valued in all settings.
- Families are all different. Children may live with one or both parents, with other relatives or carers, with same-sex parents or in an extended family.
- Families may speak more than one language at home; they may be travellers, refugees or asylum seekers.

In trying to develop an understanding of what parents have to offer there should be 'a two-way flow of information, knowledge and expertise between parents and practitioners' (DCSF, 2008: Card 2.2). An essential first step is in seeing the knowledge and expertise of parents (and other members of their families) as an asset and as another resource that practitioners can use to enrich the learning experiences that they then offer to children. The involvement of parents should be viewed as the opportunity it is, rather than a challenge (as is emphasised in Chapters 6 and 7).

Although each aspect of KUW will be considered separately below, it is essential that a classroom practitioner be aware of how this fits holistically into a child's education. There is always a tension, when looking at KUW and indeed other areas of learning, between ensuring subject rigour (for instance, correct science-subject knowledge in exploration and investigation) and providing a broader topic-based or thematic curriculum (i.e., in covering a range of 'subjects'). Barnes (2007: 1) points out that 'our experience of the world is cross-curricular. Everything which surrounds us in the physical world can be seen and understood from multiple perspectives'. One of these perspectives may be that of a scientist, geographer or historian; here the challenge begins in framing learning experiences for young children. They will, soon enough, encounter a subject-based curriculum – although it is not suggested that this approach be used in the Early Years. What *will* be suggested below is that each subject gives a child a unique way of understanding the world and that viewing teaching ideas through, for example, a 'scientific lens', can offer new insights into how to develop effective learning opportunities. The children will not be aware of this, while classroom practitioners should consider what such a viewpoint has to offer. This does not mean teaching a 'subject', but adopting a methodology: for example, history (as a body of knowledge) may not be taught as a subject, although a historian's approach to learning may be adopted.

Exploration and investigation

In essence, exploration and investigation form the beginning of scientific enquiry:

> The child's exploration of the world is the springboard from which the next step is taken, that of more systematic enquiry. Systematic enquiry may be described as 'scientific investigation' in later years. Nevertheless, the first step in any scientific enquiry is exploration, or 'play'. (de Boo, 2000: 1)

This play is not time-scaled; children will often repeat the same activity time and time again. This is not time wasted, as it allows the child to reinforce their understanding of what is happening: for example, every time I tip water from the jug it goes down; every time I put water on the sand it seems to change colour; every time the sun comes out the puddles disappear. Young children need opportunities to explore materials and objects in many different contexts. For example, modelling clay can be squashed, made into shapes, joined together with more modelling clay of a different colour, and there are still many other properties to be explored: does it float?; can you paint it?; can it be used to stick things together?; will it mix with other materials? or does it go hard like pottery clay? A curious child will surely come up with many more enquiries. This example is about exploring just one material, let alone how it works with others. It is essential that the Early Years workforce provide opportunities to explore and have to hand the suitable resources (water, different coloured modelling clay, paint and so on) to do so. Some of these explorations can be anticipated and planned for, while others will be spontaneous and unexpected. Both should be welcomed and encouraged. Indeed, as has been emphasised in Chapter 4, the Early Years workforce learns much from observing the spontaneous explorations of children and considering the extent, if any, to which they are worth replicating in planning for another occasion. Careful observation is the key both to assessment and in considering whether practitioners can help develop children's understanding by building on, and adding progression to, these spontaneous events by providing other resources and settings. Overall, implementing curricula is about aiming to provide quality experiences that are meaningful and 'worthy of active involvement. If children are to continue their struggle to make sense of the world, then the world must be worth the struggle' (Fisher, 2002: 15).

One of the key features of active involvement is including children in planning. This is particularly true of exploration and investigation. Most topics can start with a 'brainstorming' by staff and children to ask the questions: 'What do you know already?' and 'What do you want to find out/would you like to learn?' The idea of children's having ownership of the direction of their learning is central, no matter how young the children. Obviously, Early Years practitioners need to retain an overview to ensure coverage of relevant skills, and to avoid repetition; the central message, though, is that practitioners do not always need to follow a pre-determined and detailed scheme of work. As one Early Years practitioner interviewed while this chapter was being written put it, with this sort of planning 'You can't just pick it up and run with it'. For some experienced practitioners this may remind them of a more open approach prior to the introduction of a National Curriculum, with the key difference being the need to match experiences (however open-ended) with purposeful assessment. In addition, ensuring suitable progression in these activities can present a huge challenge. The move away from schemes of work with predefined assessment tasks and progression criteria means that for each investigation and exploration teachers need to consider how they are going to assess the outcomes and ensure that adequate challenges are built in to extend children's learning. In considering assessment the importance of looking at situations through a 'scientific lens' is crucial, as the processes of exploration and investigation (including the so-called 'process skills', identified by Harlen (2003) as observing, raising questions, hypothesising, predicting, planning, interpreting and communicating) are in themselves outcomes and are just as important as the end product of the investigation.

To assist the Early Years workforce in both teaching and assessment in KUW, two skills are central: observation and questioning. Although there is guidance available on observation (for example, 'Observing Children' – see Further Reading below) one teacher interviewed for this chapter noted that there was still a need to 'mould things to what we need to do for our children and it will be different for every school'. The use of questions was a more generic issue and, although good questions can increase the interactivity of teaching, much depends on Early Years professionals' developing listening skills (hearing what children actually say, and not what you think children were going to say!). All members of the Early Years workforce should also develop 'a repertoire of strategies to manage critical moments' (Myhill et al., 2006: 117) when children ask questions or make a comment and practitioners need to decide on how best to respond.

Designing and making

Many of the issues covered above are also relevant to designing and making activities. During designing and making, children are laying the foundations for design and technology. This can be regarded as 'the holistic activity, involving thinking and doing, action and reflection', as well as providing opportunities to 'apply' any scientific principles already encountered (Davies, 2003: 4–5). As designing and making activities are essentially acts of creativity they should be regarded as a process, not an event. Central to this process is critical appraisal: by teachers, by children themselves, and their peers and parents. This appraisal can, however, be both a positive and a negative experience, as 'at the wrong point, criticism and the cold hand of realism can kill an emerging idea' (Barlex, 2004: 103). From a more positive perspective, designing and making activities provide ample opportunities for children to develop an awareness of the needs of others and in working together – both important features of personal and social development.

In designing and making, opportunities are again found to reinforce work from other areas and to provide original starting points. In these activities, play is very important as children use their imagination to explore, and possibly even re-create, their ideas. It has already been considered (above) how children begin exploring the properties of different materials, and this can naturally lead to exploring what they can do with them. This has been classified as moving from 'specific exploration' (the kind of play which explores what a material is and what it can do) to 'diversive exploration' (the kind of play where a child explores what they *personally* can do with it) (Moyles, 1989 cited in Davies and Ward, 2003). An example provided by Davies and Ward (2003) is where a child might explore the properties of playdough (a scientific enquiry) and then move onto making an animal from it (beginning to design and make).

Information Communication Technology (ICT)

It is very likely that young children have some understanding of ICT and a degree of 'tacit knowledge' (Hayes, 2006) of computers and electronic toys. They live in an age where ICT is a part of everyday life and many homes have access to the Internet. In addition, children's toys are becoming ever-more sophisticated and children are 'surrounded by products of the information and communication age' (Feasy and Gallear, 2001: 5). Children will need to find out about a wide range of resources, including cameras, photocopiers, CD players, tape recorders and programmable toys, as well as learning how to use them. The EYFS Practice Guidance (DFCS, 2008) notes that even the school intercom and pelican crossing buttons are practical examples of ICT that could be used during and after a walk around the locality. On this trip children could also be encouraged to look for other uses of ICT as well as other physical features – which can be used when exploring 'place' later in this chapter. It may be best to consider ICT as:

> [A] new tool that could and should be incorporated into existing early-years practice in developmentally appropriate ways, supplementing, not replacing, other important first-hand experiences and interactions and accompanied by quality adult input to help children learn about and through the technology. (O'Hara, 2008: 30)

As children explore ICT resources, all members of the Early Years workforce, parents and children need to consider when it is appropriate to use ICT and when not. In general terms, the Early Years workforce make informed choices about how and when to use ICT (if at all) based on the pedagogic demands of a subject and the age of the children concerned (Beauchamp, 2006). With young children, the demands of subject teaching do not apply, but the age of the children is central. While teachers need to consider how to develop children's specific IT skills (such as moving a mouse), they are also concerned with how ICT can contribute to the learning environment: what it has to offer that other resources do not. The features of ICT will influence this:

- *Speed*: making processes happen more quickly than by other methods.
- *Automation*: making previously tedious or effortful processes happen automatically (other than changing the form of representation).
- *Capacity*: the storage and retrieval of large amounts of material.
- *Range*: access to materials in different forms and from a wider range of sources than otherwise possible.
- *Provisionality*: the facility to change content.
- *Interactivity*: the ability to respond to user input repeatedly.
  (Kennewell and Beauchamp, 2007)

Some of these features will be more relevant to Early Years practitioners as they plan and prepare work (such as the ability to store large amounts of pre-prepared resources); others may be more useful in engaging the children in learning experiences (such as the speed things appear and the range of resources available from, for instance, the Internet); others still may be a feature of the learning experience itself (such as interactivity). They are all, however, also open to children as they work with ICT devices. It is therefore necessary to consider the role of ICT in Early Years settings. Beauchamp and Kennewell (2008) suggest that the broad roles of ICT are:

- ICT as a *participant* in interaction – children playing with an electronic toy, or playing a game, quiz, or challenge ... (*ICT* usually provides the structure for interactions)
- ICT as the *object* of interaction – showing a video clip or pupil's work (the *teacher* usually provides the structure for interactions)
- ICT as a *tool* for interaction – children annotate on the interactive whiteboard, or send electronic messages (*learners* usually provide the structure for interactions).

In planning activities through an ICT 'lens' it may be appropriate to consider which of the above roles practitioners are intending ICT to play. The main consideration when using ICT is that children are required to 'find out about and learn how to use appropriate information technology ... that support their learning'. The key question should perhaps always be: is this use of ICT supporting learning, or is it just an end in itself? If it is the latter, don't use it!

Time

It is always difficult for young children to understand the past when they cannot conceive that it directly affects them. Cooper (2002:18) cites Marbeau's argument that 'history at first is the historicisation of a child's own existence' and contends that children "build continuity into their existence by reciting it to others (and to themselves)." This reflects a view of history which is based on evidence or an experience, and which is interpreted and then retold to others in a variety of forms (such as written or oral stories, photographs, through art or song) – both separately and combined. To do this effectively, the Early Years workforce needs to realise the interrelation between the learning goals within the EYFS. There is a necessity for a cross-fertilisation with other areas of the EYFS, as well as within KUW – such as activities in exploring and investigating, which may allow children to notice the effects of change over time (for example, when growing plants).

The key starting point for children is that they find out about past and present events relevant to *their own lives or those of their families*. There are many ways in which they can tell their own stories, and much can be learned about diversity and cultural milestones in the process, while the very fact that these stories are so personal must mean that they are handled with care.

When planning activities within this aspect of KUW, practitioners need to be aware of the historical processes of inquiry so that appropriate foundations are laid for subject work, as children grow older. Again, we are not considering teaching knowledge of the subject (historical 'facts', such as the year of a particular battle), but considering what skills need to be developed to allow children to become effective historians later in their school life. The following are suggested as processes of enquiry that are appropriate for historians:

- Searching for evidence
- Examining the evidence
- Recording of accounts
- Summarising historical narrative or argument.
  (Turner-Bisset, 2005)

It can be noticed that these have much in common with processes in other areas that have already been identified. In considering 'time' activities, the importance of skilful questioning becomes most apparent. It should be self-evident that to develop the enquiring skills above, teachers need to use open-ended questions that encourage children to seek their own answers to questions (both individually and with others), as well as focusing their attention on important details and processes. When planning learning activities, it is always helpful to consider how to develop the processes outlined above and how adequate progression in each can be ensured.

Some examples of relevant progression might be in:

- children's use of language (for example, 'yesterday', 'tomorrow' or 'next week' leading to 'past', 'now' and 'then') – "learning about the past involves learning vocabulary which is to some extent specific to the history" (Cooper, 2002: 16)
- moving from considering events that affect themselves to those that affect others
- the ability to sequence ever-longer and more complicated series of events.

Place and communities

Work in this area is fundamentally about developing concepts of 'space' and 'place' (Palmer and Birch, 2004). This development will be based on children's existing awareness of the world around them and their place in it; children are "young geographers with a world inside their head" (Smeaton, 2001:15). These worlds may, however, vary tremendously based on the experience, or lack of it, children have already had before they come into a nursery, school or other setting. In order both to broaden experience and to provide common ground (both literally and metaphorically) it is common for KUW themes to begin with a trip. This could be in the local area or further afield, and the stimulus provides a focus for planning subsequent work – using the brainstorming approach with children, as discussed above ('What do you know already? What do you want to know?'). A shared experience of a new place can provide the basis for an open discussion without any loyalties to street, town or even country influencing views. It also ensures that all children have the same level of exposure to the location – for example, in a study of 'On the farm' it is important to determine whether all of the children have indeed been to a farm and experienced the sights (and smells!). Remember, however, that equality of experience should not be taken for granted even in the area around your school, especially in view of the large catchment areas of some schools and nurseries (for more detail on using areas outside the classroom *see* Chapter 8).

One idea for using any area (including inside the school) is to consider how the Early Years workforce can make it 'strangely familiar' (Barnes and Shirley, 2007). This means encouraging the children to explore and express the uniqueness of the place by representing it though a range of curricular areas, specifically the arts such as poetry, painting and music. In this approach practitioners are again looking at the area of learning though a variety of 'lenses' (for instance, the musician, the film-maker or the dancer) to see how children can be engaged in their own learning, by being presented with alternative perspectives and new challenges. The role of the Early Years workforce as facilitator and control is passed to the children. In presenting their views of the local area (including their likes and dislikes) children can use sounds, shapes, materials collected from around the area, video images, still photos, stories, dances, songs, art shows and even sculpture. Such an approach also naturally leads on to, or, better still, incorporates, an exploration of the communities that make up the area. The end result can be shared with a variety of audiences using traditional means (paintings), ICT (slide shows and movies) and live performances (dances).

In exploring communities the knowledge of families, and key figures within the community, can also be very valuable, as these can often provide first-hand experience and life stories of growing up in, or moving into, the area and different communities. These stories may, however, be deeply personal and revealing, so it is important to allow time for discussion with visitors on what they will be saying before they meet with the children.

Inclusion

Another area where all Early Years practitioners must develop a shared understanding and common practice is inclusion. As many of the KUW activities discussed above involve skills – such as manipulation and coordination, and use of language and specific vocabulary – it is vital to consider how practitioners can ensure that all children can become involved, especially in view of the Every Child Matters (ECM) agenda. Among the key roles of the Early Years practitioner is that of retaining the ultimate responsibility for ensuring that an inclusive culture be developed and perpetuated. Nevertheless, 'LSAs [Learning Support Assistants] can play a pivotal role in the process of inclusion' (Jones, 2004: 110). The same could equally be said of other adults, such as language assistants and parents. In fact, anyone visiting a classroom must accept and continue the inclusive culture that has developed. The question arises: how will they know about it if it is their first visit? Newcomers can learn much from observing the way in which teachers and others interact with the children – in fact this may be the most powerful way of demonstrating commitment to inclusive practice. They may also have had some written guidance prior to their visit: does the school or setting have a policy and information leaflet that can be used? However the guidance is provided, it is essential that the practice be shared with others.

  Key points to remember

- Knowledge and Understanding of the World (KUW) is a learning area of EYFS where Early Years practitioners can help children develop a set of skills to help them explore the world around them and also in laying the foundation for later work in science, history, geography, or ICT.
- For young children to develop skills, learning should be viewed through a variety of subject 'lenses'; these each offer a unique insight into the world. The way these skills are developed depends on good practice such as the use of questioning and careful, systematic observation.

- KUW can become the area in Early Years settings where a number of different, creative activities can be hosted. KUW can be met within the Early Years setting – and outside of the setting as well. Activities can be designed to meet group or individual needs and capabilities so that every child is included.

Points for discussion

- Can you identify the unique features, opportunities and approaches provided by KUW that do not arise in other areas of learning? Is it ever appropriate to use ICT (such as an interactive whiteboard) in place of 'real' objects, such as plants and creatures? If so, when and why? If not, what do 'real' objects offer that ICT cannot?
- In exploring the world around children, in designing and making tools, both inside and outside the classroom, there will be times when you need to consider the safety of children as they discover things through using their senses. Can you identify any particular situations or types of activity you need to consider in order to keep children safe when planning for KUW?

Further reading

Athey, C. (2007) *Extending Thought in Young Children: A Parent–Teacher Partnership* 2nd edn. London: Paul Chapman Publishing.

Cooper, H. (ed.) (2004) *Exploring Time and Place through Play*. London: David Fulton Publishers.

Rodger, R. (2003) *Planning an Appropriate Curriculum for the Under-fives: A Guide for Students, Teachers and Assistants*, 2nd edn. London: David Fulton Publishers.

Useful website

KUW
www.standards.dfes.gov.uk/eyfs/site/4/4.htm
The KUW section of the EYFS website, as well as outlining requirements, provides links to research and videos that provide examples of relevant practice.

CHAPTER 13

PHYSICAL DEVELOPMENT

Ioanna Palaiologou

Chapter Aims

One of the most important characteristics in a child's early life is the physical activity that takes place during their early childhood. Bruner (1983: 121) emphasised the importance of physical activity in young children, and he claimed that the physical activities of a child are part of their 'culture of childhood'. A number of theorists that have been explored throughout this book have discussed in detail the importance of the physical aspects of a child's life. For example, Piaget states that children start their development from a sensory motor stage where they acquire sensory schemata. Currently, the importance of physical literacy is being discussed more than ever, as is the integration of physical activity into curricular approaches as an essential aspect of children's overall and therefore holistic development (Almond, 2000; Bailey, 1999; Parry, 1998; Talbot, 1999).

The Early Years Foundation Stage sets the physical development of children as one of the six learning goals. Aspects of physical development are stated as being (DCSF, 2008: Card 4.2):

- **Movement and Space** – how children learn to move with confidence, imagination and safety, and with an awareness of space, themselves and of others.

- **Health and Bodily Awareness** – how children learn the importance of keeping healthy and the factors that contribute to maintaining their health.

- **Using Equipment and Materials** – the ways in which children use a range of small and large equipment.

This chapter aims to help you to understand:

- the importance of the physical and biological development of children

- the impact of physical development on children's health and well-being

- how physical development can be enhanced in Early Years settings.

Physical and biological growth

When children are born, they display a number of skills crucial to their survival. In the first few months of infants' lives reflexes play an important role in physical development; they help infants to build social relationships, essential to all other aspects of their development. Infants' reflexes, such as breathing, sucking, swallowing and blinking, help babies and parents to establish interactions. When babies grasp a parent's fingers, for example, parents respond and encourage these behaviours, and this is the start of an intimate relationship.

Around the age of 6 months babies begin losing these reflexes. Gradually, as the brain matures, the reflexes become voluntary control behaviours. This is a complex developmental task. For example, initially babies suck the bottle or the mother's breast as an automatic reflex, yet at around the age of six months they are able to combine their vision with arm movement, and eventually reach for the bottle or the mother's breast by themselves.

One of the aspects in the physical development of children, as stated in EYFS, is that of movement. The motor development of children is divided between 'gross' and 'fine' motor development. 'Gross' motor development refers to all spatial movements used by children to manoeuvre around their environment, such as crawling, sitting, walking, and eventually running, jumping and climbing. 'Fine' motor development concerns all of the smaller and more intricate movements, such as grasping, building a tower with cubes, putting objects into boxes, drawing and writing.

During their Early Years stage children are undergoing rapid physical development. There are changes in the size and proportions of the body, and both skeletal and hormonal growth. During this period children display tireless physical activity, thus it is essential for children to be provided with the space in which to move freely and safely, as well as with activities to encourage their developing movements. Hale (1994), among other researchers (Almond, 2000; Bailey, 1999; Doherty and Bailey, 2003; Parry, 1998; Talbot, 1999), emphasises the importance of an enriched and stimulating environment that helps children to engage with physical activity, because an active, supportive environment makes children feel comfortable and leads to their learning.'

Children learn constantly by moving. They touch, feel, smell, move around, and have fun 'translating movements into spoken language' in a variety of contexts (Hopper et al., 2000: 1). Physical activity is the best way for children to experience the world around them, practising skills, gaining in confidence by achieving, and making explorations through motor play such as running, walking, jumping, climbing, catching or throwing.

Much of children's play is characterised by movement, and it is impossible to keep young children from running or force them to sit down for long periods of time. When children are given opportunities to move around freely at home or in Early Years settings they engage in constant motor play. Activities such as songs with movements, role-playing involving movement, climbing, jumping and balancing are among the favourite activities in Early Years settings. All of their play is characterised by constant movement.

Brain growth

Essential to physical development is the development of the brain. The brain regulates all areas of development. As has been shown in Chapter 3, neuroscientific evidence has an impact on pedagogy, and has helped us to understand the importance of brain growth in all aspects of children's learning and development.

The first years of a child's life are very important for brain development. A baby's brain develops at an astonishing rate in the first three years, such that by the age of 3 a child's brain is as complex as it will ever be (Shore, 1997). The brain is comprised of billions of nerve cells (neurons) designed to send and retrieve information across organs and muscles. An important process in the growth of the brain is the development of synapses. All of the billions of neurons are rapidly connected to each other in the first years of life.

As can be seen in Figure 13.1, opposite, during the first six years there is a rapid development of synapses in the human brain. However, the number of new synapses decreases as children enter adolescence and then adulthood. Babies acquire more synapses than they will need. After the age of 3 some connections are lost. For example, a typical 18-year-old has lost half of the synapses acquired in early childhood. Synapses in the brain that are unused disappear. It is inevitable that an individual wonders why we could do certain things when we were children that we cannot do now as adults. Shore (1997) argues that synapses are eliminated if they are not used, which has implications for the continuation of a stimulus environment. For example, if children fail to continue being physically active, they will become less interested in physical activity, and it is less likely to become part of their adult lives. Kimm et al. (2002) found that by the age of 15 one in five English girls exercises for no more than 60 minutes a week. In Western societies teenagers spend more than 5 hours a day watching television, at computer screens and playing video games (Hardman and Stensel, 2003).

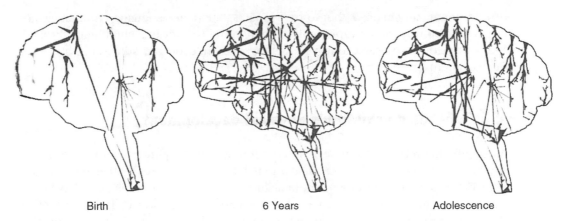

Birth   6 Years   Adolescence

Figure 13.1   The development of synapses in early childhood (after Chugani, 1997)

Growing up in urban apartment buildings, with fewer opportunities for physical development, movement and activity, may create a loss of those synapses responsible for physical activity. It is crucial that physical activity be promoted from a very early age; there is emphasis on continuing children's physical activity for their progression.

As illustrated in Figure 13.1, the first six years of a child's life are important for brain development. This period is considered as 'prime time' for neuron growth. Shore (1997: 26) suggests that the primary responsibility of parents and care providers is 'day to day care of young children's brains'. The care of the brain is accomplished through the creating of a stimulating environment. Early stimulation is important for helping children to achieve their developmental potential and for promoting infant brain growth. Providing a number of opportunities for physical and cognitive development will enhance the formation of synapses in the brain then the continuation of stimulation will prevent the loss of these synapses.

The study of brain growth has given insiders an understanding of many aspects of children's development. For example, Chapter 9 discussed the importance of 'attachment' during early childhood. It is known that infants under stress, or infants who suffer from anxiety, are more likely to produce a hormone called cortisol (Hertsgaard et al., 1995; Nachmias et al., 1996). When this hormone is produced, the brain is threatened and reduces the synapses, leaving neurones vulnerable to damage.

Gunnar (2001) found that when infants form secure relationships with their parents and their carers the levels of cortisol are kept low. A warm and secure environment with parents and with other caregivers – an environment where the children are playing happily with stimulation – helps positively towards the physical development of their brain.

Studies into the development of the brain have offered an extensive knowledge and understanding of children's development, not only as regards the physical development of children, but other aspects, such as language, numeracy and creativity. Knowing about rapid brain growth in the infancy of a child helps the Early Years workforce to create environments where children are stimulated and their development promoted.

Cultural influences on children's physical development

Although children's physical development follows similar patterns and stages across the world, cross-cultural research demonstrates how the respective environment contributes to motor development. In a study conducted by Dennis (1960), babies in Iranian orphanages were observed. These babies were deprived; Dennis observed that they were spending a lot of time lying in cots with no toys available to them. After several observations, he found that these babies delayed movement until they were 2 years of age. When they finally moved, the experience of constantly lying on their backs led them to remain in a sitting position rather than crawling as children normally do.

In a later study, Hopkins and Westra (1988) studied babies around the world and found that in some cultures there is an emphasis on children to start moving from an early stage. They found that in Western India, for example, the parents have a routine in which they exercise their babies daily. From the first months, parents exercise their babies by stretching each arm while suspending the baby, or holding the baby upside down by the ankles. However much these routines may surprise us, Hopkins and Westra found through interviewing the mothers that it is embedded in their culture for them to help their babies to grow physically strong, healthy and attractive.

In Kenya, Kipsigi parents deliberately teach children motor skills. In the first few months babies are rolled in blankets to keep them upright then seated in holes dug into the ground. Walking is promoted by frequently bouncing babies on their feet (Super, 1981). It was observed that these babies walk earlier than do babies in economically more developed societies.

Levels of physical activity vary by culture. A study of Puerto Rican and Euro-American mothers revealed that children's physical activities were rated more highly by Puerto Rican mothers, while the Euro-American mothers characterised physical activity as undesirable (Harwood et al., 1995).

When working with children from different cultural backgrounds, it is important to understand cultural differences. As it is important to work in partnership with parents, their values and beliefs need to be understood and channels of communication need to be developed, so they will feel comfortable with the level of their children's physical activity in the Early Years setting.

In the modern Western world there is a trend to emphasise academic development of children, whereas there is far less emphasis on physical activity. Children are supported and encouraged when they try to be physically active during early childhood, but this is limited later when formal schooling is starting and the focus on the children's academic progress is more intense.

It is noticed that there is a lack of physical activity among children when they grow older. The World Health Organisation (1999) states: 'in many developed countries, less than one third of young children and people are sufficiently active to benefit their present and future health'. It is a positive point that EYFS clearly views physical activity of children as being important for children's development, a foundation on which children can build confidence and acquire habits leading to a healthy lifestyle.

Health and well-being

Within EYFS, central to Physical Development is helping children to learn what healthy living is and to sustain attitudes towards healthy living. As discussed above, children are physically active during early childhood, but they do not sustain this level of activity as they grow older. Hardman and Stensel (2003) state that three modern trends – obesity, physical inactivity and an ageing population – are the main 'diseases' of the twenty-first century and highlight the importance of physical activity.

Obesity has increased rapidly over the past two decades. More and more children are overweight. There are a number of factors involved in the increase of obesity, such as eating habits, poor nutrition and lack of physical activity. However, a number of researchers (Baur, 2002; Kimm et al., 2002; Prentice and Jebb, 1995) link obesity with physical inactivity rather than with overeating. Given that most children are brought up in urban settings with a lack of space in which to move around, children tend to adopt alternative ways to play, such as with computer and video games. It is important to create opportunities for young children to be able to be physically active. The activities around Physical Development should appeal to children and be enjoyable for them. Contextualised activities, such as catching and throwing in games situations, or more complex activities like singing, dancing and swimming (where movements by children are required) promote their physical development.

Doherty and Bailey (2003) suggest that activities designed to promote physical development within educational settings should be characterised first and foremost by enjoyment. Children should want to take part in these activities and have fun. Such activities should be continued throughout the curriculum and not only during early childhood (EYFS). By promoting physical activities across all ages a 'firm foundation base of movement experience' (EYFS, 2008) is established from a very young age.

Doherty and Bailey also suggest that children should, on a daily basis, become involved in physical activities if the aim is to develop physical activity as a lifelong habit for health and well-being. Children should have the freedom to choose the activities and the materials, according to their personal interests and physical skills.

Children's physical development and brain growth are important in order to sustain good health and well-being in children's lives. Young children should acquire habits of healthy living from an early age. There are many factors influencing a child's health and well-being, such as nutrition, emotional health, the structure of the family, and the structure of their communities, which combine to contribute to children's physical, biological, mental and sexual health.

The physical activities of children help them to sustain a healthy lifestyle. In their study, Biddle et al. (1998: 4–5) highlight the benefits of physical activity. They claim that physical activity leads to psychological well-being, the increase of self-esteem, contributes to children's moral and social development, and prevents obesity, chronic disease and risk factors. Thus, it is essential that children in their daily routine are provided with opportunities to be physically active, that they have adults who are supportive and who facilitate children to move and, of course, most importantly, that children are given time to be physically active and to be able to play within the Early Years.

Whitehead (2000) extends this idea by introducing the concept of 'physically literate' children. He claims that children who are physically active, become physically literate:

> The characteristics of a physically literate individual are that the person moves with poise, economy and confidence, in a wide variety of physically challenging situations. In addition the individual is perceptive in 'reading' all aspects of the physical environment, anticipating movement needs or possibilities and responding appropriately to these with intelligence and imagination. Physical literacy requires a holistic engagement that encompasses physical capacities embedded in perception, experience, memory, anticipation and decision making. (2000: 10)

He emphasises the importance of a challenging environment where children are offered opportunities to move in a way that stimulates them and where, at the same time, they can experience enjoyment. He also suggests that physical activities are linked with other areas of development. For example, when children are having a dance activity or play in the water area, they are not only physically active but they are engaged in a number of cognitive activities such as language development (*'let's put our hands up'*, *'let's move around in a circle'*, *'let's move in a line'*) or problem solving activities (*'let's throw objects in the water that float or objects in the water that sink'*). Central to this is the creation of an environment that promotes physical activities.

The role of the environment

Before exploring the role of the environment in children's physical development it is important to understand what a 'healthy environment' means. Nutbeam (1998: 362) characterises a healthy environment as 'a place or social context in which people engage in daily activities, in which environmental, organizational and personal factors interact to affect health and well-being'.

A healthy environment has many forms and is influenced by cultural values and practices. For example, in some families the home environment is redesigned and furniture is moved so children can move freely and have space to play in; in other families children have rules about what they may touch and where they can go to play. It is not necessarily the case that one situation is 'wrong' and the other is 'right'. Physical activity and the space around children are related to the families' values. In the second situation it could be argued that in this way children learn about rules, learn about what is right and what is not, learn about safety from a very young age, and learn about their limitations.

A classic study conducted by Levine (1996) showed the diversity of strategies used in the world to provide healthy and safe environments for children. He observed different tribes and different cultures around the world and he offers a case from Kenya. In Kenya, babies and young children spent a lot of time outdoors as mothers are involved in their daily chores. Leaving young children outdoors without supervision seemed to hold many risks, as they could burn themselves in cooking fires, fall off cliffs or into lakes, or suffer snakebite. However, he found that the parents in this village protected their children by carrying them on their backs and allowed them to be outdoors without supervision only when they were old enough to understand rules and the dangers around them.

Cultural aspects have an impact on physical development in terms of choosing outdoor or indoor environments. In the following case studies from three different curricular approaches, it can be seen how the indoor and outdoor environments are used to promote children's physical development.

Case Study

Arts to promote physical development (example from Reggio Emilia)

In the Reggio approach, the artistic development of children is central. Gandini (1997) describes activities such as drawing, painting, sculpting and singing as fundamental methods for children's learning, at the same time as they enhance the physical development of children (i.e., gross motor development and fine motor development). Gandini describes the arts as essential not only to children's cognitive development, but as a major part of children's physical development.

The arts can help children more with their personal, social and creative development. Children, after a visit to a museum or gallery, can use materials to express themselves and experiment with water, painting, sculpting, etc., and all these activities require sophisticated and complex movements. Consequently, their physical development is shaped in a contextualised environment. Children's movements are viewed as creative; there are no constraints in time and space, and children can take as much time or space as they need in which to express themselves.

Case Study

Physical development in a Te Whāriki class

The Te Whāriki curriculum has been introduced in New Zealand's Early Years settings. Emphasising multiculturalism and allowing children the freedom to choose materials and activities, it promotes children's having ownership of their own learning. This curriculum approach views the child as: 'competent and confident learners and communicators, healthy in mind, body and spirit, secure in their sense of belonging and in the knowledge that they make a valued contribution to society' (New Zealand Ministry of Education, 1996).

A Te Whāriki class, similarly to the EYFS, is underpinned by five goals: well-being, belonging, contribution, communication and exploration. In a Te Whāriki class children move between freely indoors and outdoors, and choose which materials to play with. In the sand area they can make castles, whereas in another area they can make solid objects, such as chairs, using a number of tools that develop their fine motor skills.

Outdoors, children are offered opportunities to practise climbing, running, and jumping, either individually or in small groups. The Te Whāriki outdoors environment is rich in real objects and thus encourages and motivates children to engage in physical activity through play.

They create tunnels from car tyres for children to crawl through, swings and water points, where they can 'splash about'.

Inside the class, singing is accompanied by physical movement, such as children imitating waves by using their bodies and their hands. The children have the opportunity to move constantly and to use a number of materials. In a corner of the room there are several clothes for dressing up, and this way the children's motor skills are developed.

Physical exploration of different materials meets one of the main principles in the Te Whāriki approach: Kotahitanga ('holistic development'), where the child is viewed as a 'whole'. It is emphasised that the child learns in a holistic way by taking into consideration not only the child's physical, social, emotional and cognitive development, but also the cultural context and the spiritual aspects of the children's environment.

Case Study

The Forest School: Using the outdoor environment

In 1950 throughout the Scandinavian countries (especially in Sweden and Denmark) the concept of Forest Schools was developed. Central to Forest Schools is the idea to inspire children from a very young age to have positive experiences by interacting with nature. There is the ecological view that if children love nature from a very young age, they will grow up respecting nature and try to protect it from pollution. Moreover, the Forest Schools approach is based on the argument that when children spend time in nature, in the fresh air, they grow healthy, are at minimum risk from disease, and become stronger. It is also believed in the Forest School approach that children are helped with their social relationships, as this approach increases children's understanding and respect for others. Finally, in the Forest Schools children have opportunities to promote their physical development, and also to learn a number of skills, and to develop cognitively in a pleasant, natural, enjoyable and low-stress environment.

Increasing numbers of Early Years settings across the UK have adopted this innovative approach.

A typical Forest Schools project is to take a group of children to a woodland area or a forest. Children can stay in the woodlands or forest anything from one day up to a few days with adults, depending upon the ages of the children. During their time in the forest, children have the opportunities to play games, to create materials from wood by cutting timber, to build fires, to observe nature and record their observations, and to cook their own food. Prior to a visit children normally agree on a certain project that they will carry out when they are in the woods.

 Key points to remember

- This chapter discussed the importance of physical development for children's holistic development. Children's play is characterised by movement and it should be encouraged. The physical activity of children is important to all aspects of their learning.
- Brain growth in early childhood is rapid. The formation of synapses between neurons is happening far more rapidly in the first few years of a child's life than later. This has implications when an environment is created for young children.
- Children's concepts of healthy living and well-being are strongly related to the enjoyment of physical movement. If adults want children to acquire healthy living styles then physical activity has to become a life-long habit. Only when they are pleasurable will children wish to carry out physical activities.

Points for discussion

- Look at the plan in Figure 13.2. Consider that this is the room you have been given in which to work with 2-year-old children. How are you going to design the environment so that you can promote children's physical development? In your new design you need to consider whether there is sufficient space for children to move around in, what equipment you will have, and how you will redesign and resource your room.

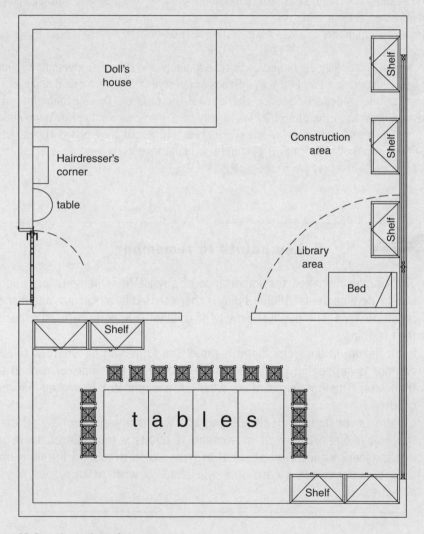

Figure 13.2 Floor plan of a nursery

- Bilton (2003: 38) suggests that when organising work in the outdoor environment the following should be considered: layout of the environment, the amount of space available, the use of fixed equipment, the weather element and the need for storage. Can you think of any other aspects when you organise activity in the outdoor environment? What activities can you plan to offer appropriate physical challenges to children?
- Compare a Reggio Emilia, a Te Whāriki and an EYFS class. Where do they differ and where are they similar in promoting the physical movement of children?

Further reading

Doherty, J. and Bailey, R. (2003) *Supporting Physical Development and Physical Education in the Early Years*. Buckingham: Open University Press.

Hardman, A. and Stensel, D. (2003) *Physical Activity and Health*. London: Routledge.

Nurse, A. (2009) *Physical Development in the Early Years Foundation Stage*. London: David Fulton.

Useful websites

Forest Schools:
www.forestschools.com/index.php

Institute of Outdoor Learning (IOL):
www.outdoor-learning.org/

Outdoor play in Europe:
www.eoe-network.org/

This is the official website of the European Institute of Outdoor Adventure Education and Experiential Learning (EOE).

CHAPTER 14

CREATIVE DEVELOPMENT

Nick Owen

Chapter Aims

This chapter aims to show that 'being creative' in Early Years settings is a richer, more extensive and far more common form of human expression and experience than these limited equations suggest, through an exploration of how we can promote creative practice in the Early Years. This chapter will stress the value of serendipity, chance and accident as being uncontrollable contextual factors that can enhance, rather than confound, emerging creative practices.

However, it will be drawing upon activities usually deemed creative (such as the arts, music, dance and drama) to highlight the necessary mindset and skills required in order to ensure that all planning involves creative thought and expression in its widest interpretation. This will involve some discussion of the challenges involved in supporting the developing creative child, particularly for practitioners who feel their own early experiences of creative expression were neither enabling nor positive.

Consequently, the activities that will be discussed will reflect the principle that creative practice is not a domain exclusive to arts practice. Examples of activities will demonstrate not only effective planning but also efficacious risk taking, and will give insight into the creative thought processes involved when working with a range of variously experienced practitioners. An example of a creative collaboration questionnaire will be offered for you to use, in order to understand what skills, attitudes and attributes you bring to a creative collaboration.

The notion of collaboration here is critical, for it is suggested that instead of interpreting creativity solely as an attribute of individuals, it arises from the gravitational pull of relationships; it is thus a situational and contextual phenomenon, as opposed to an individual or psychological one. Collaboration will therefore be stressing the need for the co-intentional imaginations of adults and children to embrace, together, attitudes of improvisation, keeping an eye open for the off-chance, taking the occasional, unassessed risk, and accepting the generation of and pleasure in 'mess'.

This chapter aims to help you to:

- understand that creative practice can be developed in all areas of Early Years settings and is not exclusive to arts practice

- undertake activities which form the basis in an Early Years setting of an action research project, which aims to address a 'Creativity Challenge' in that setting

- appreciate the contextual factors that have informed the development of contemporary creative practice in Early Years settings

- understand the qualities you bring to a creative collaboration.

Developing creative practice: What's all the fuss about?

The notion of developing children's creativity has never been far off the political agenda in recent years. The educational establishment has frequently been jolted by politicians to come up with more and better methods to make sure not only that children are more creative but that creativity is part of the daily routine, especially within the Early Years environment.

More jobs, more wealth, more growth, more prosperity: the drive towards creative nirvana is fuelled by the political expediency of economic growth, an element clearly identified in the 1999 NACCCE Report on Creativity and Cultural Education, *All Our Futures*. That report produced an almost canonical definition of creativity – 'imaginative activity fashioned so as to produce outcomes that are both original and of value' (Robinson, 1999: 30) – which on the surface allows little room for manoeuvre as regards thinking about and planning for creativity in Early Years settings.

It is no wonder that parents and practitioners are frequently asking themselves, 'How *can* I get young children to be more creative? What can I do to – in the words of the QCA – to *find it, promote it*, without then stifling it into the bargain?'

Creativity: Find it, promote it – stifle it

Many educationalists have applied themselves in recent years to thinking how to get more creative bang for the always-limited educational buck. Do we achieve it by amending learning outcomes, rewriting the Foundation Stage curriculum, training practitioners to be more creative, and by building new Children's Centres? Or do we do it by being completely child-centred in our outlook? An outlook that privileges the ideas of the children over the ideas of adults, one that interprets all children's views and attitudes as the sacrosanct voice of the pure, unadulterated human being and witnesses the holy grail of creativity in the play and expression of very young children, for whom the world is a perpetual mystery? How can we promote creative development without stifling it?

Ironically, there are two easy routes to stifling creativity in young children.

- Route 1: Say 'no' to everything they suggest, muse on, play with and are curious about. Be sure to block initiative, stifle unacceptable behaviour and generate fear about the consequences of their actions. Worry them about their appearance, their status in other people's eyes, and what their attitudes and behaviour might rather say about *you* than it might about *them*.
- Route 2: Say 'yes' to everything they suggest, muse on, play with and are curious about. Be sure they understand there are no such things as boundaries of any sort, that all kinds of behaviour in any circumstances are completely acceptable. Encourage them to think that all of their ideas are perfect and require no further modification from any other source at all. Offer free, unconditional, unending praise for any kind of behaviour and have an unending supply of house points for every time they do something you deem creative.

However, creativity development in Early Years settings – if it is to encourage and challenge children's experiences of creativity – needs to inhabit an uncomfortable place somewhere in between the extremes set out by the structural approach and the child-centred approach. That place is likely to be found if we understand what the nature of the creative process is all about: something else that is frequently perceived as one of two extremes.

For some, the creative process is either the result of an unbridled process of self-expression and the unending generation of artefacts, all of which have equal merit and value, and which are generally deemed 'artistic', or are the results of a self-punishing process (in which an individual is caught up in an almost permanent psychotic episode of self-criticism and self-loathing, out of which is wrought their 'masterpiece').

The process is, however, more complex than these two extremes offer and yet is understandable and observable: furthermore, steps can be taken to ensure that a child stands the best possible chance of undertaking and completing the creative development journey. Making a child 'more creative' is not as tangible as letting their hair grow longer or passing an examination; it is about offering time and space to understand and experience the processes involved – which need personal qualities of application, struggle and testing, alongside the social qualities of cooperation, collaboration and mutual criticism. To accomplish all of that needs the presence of an element far more important than a paintbrush, a guitar or a pair of ballet shoes: it needs *you* – another human being.

Creative Relationships in the Early Years

Understanding creativity has been introduced into many Early Years settings in recent years by organisations such as Creative Partnerships, through Anna Cutler's work on the Four-Phase Stepped Progression model of creative learning. This model has, as its name implies, four phases, which suggest what we might look for when it comes to encouraging our children's creativity and approaches to learning. These are simply entitled 'Input', 'Doing', 'Showing' and 'Reflecting' (see Figure 14.1).

Cutler (2005) lists seven features of creativity required for creative learning within the 'Doing' phase of the model: the ability to identify and/or to make problems, the ability to think divergently (opening the mind to new, surprising, unusual and perhaps uncomfortable ideas), attributes such as being open to experiences of fascination and curiosity, the ability to take risks, to play with and to suggest. These would occur in a climate marked by an absence of fear and in which children find pleasure in their endeavours for their own sake, as opposed to an anxious educational agenda that might be hovering over their shoulders. Briefly, the key questions characterising these seven features can be summarised as follows:

- **Identifying problems** – Does this project seek to challenge any issues? What kinds of problems might the project bring up, and will these be an important part of the experience for everyone? How will such issues be handled?
- **Divergent thinking** – How does the project offer different and original ways of thinking, different perspectives and opportunities for the novel use of the imagination? What unusual elements or ideas can be put together, and how can people try them out?
- **Co-learning** – How do practitioners work with children and staff in a situation where all participants are learning something new together, or where teachers are learning with the pupils from the practitioners?

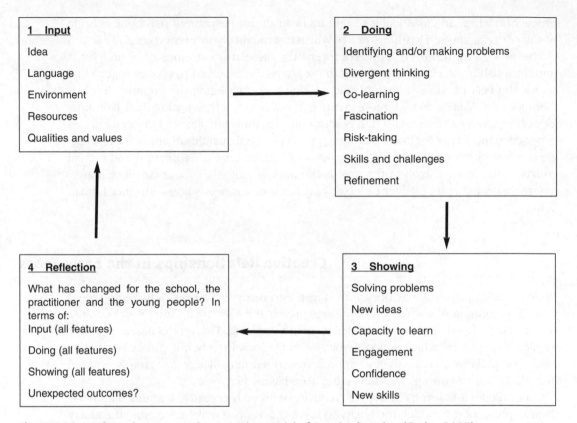

1 Input

Idea

Language

Environment

Resources

Qualities and values

2 Doing

Identifying and/or making problems

Divergent thinking

Co-learning

Fascination

Risk-taking

Skills and challenges

Refinement

4 Reflection

What has changed for the school, the practitioner and the young people? In terms of:

Input (all features)

Doing (all features)

Showing (all features)

Unexpected outcomes?

3 Showing

Solving problems

New ideas

Capacity to learn

Engagement

Confidence

New skills

Figure 14.1   A four-phase stepped progression model of creative learning (Cutler, 2005)

- **Fascination** – How is this generated by the activity? Is it sustained beyond the project hours?
- **Risk-taking** – Is the project able to offer something beyond the comfort zone of the individuals concerned? Is the project offering opportunities for risk-taking in practice?
- **Skills and challenges** – Does the programme or project effectively use the skills of those involved and stretch them? Or are they kept within what they can do (and so risk boredom) or thrown in the deep end without the resources to get themselves out (and so risk fear)?
- **Refinement** – How does the activity allow for practice, repetition and fine-tuning?

While this is a significant description of the climate needed to bring forth creative practice, Cutler's work also makes it clear that creativity is not solely a feature of individuals alone: it is a shared, constructed and collaborative experience. It makes more sense to talk of 'our' creativity than 'my' or 'your' creativity, for instance, so when it comes to our own thoughts about how we make our own children more creative, and how to prevent their creativity being stifled … then starting with ourselves – and how we are creative with our children (not *on* them or *to* them or *at* them) – is indeed an excellent place to start.

Towards creative relationships: constructing pedagogies for creative practice

Craft (2002) envisages creative practice as something of which all individuals are capable: a function such as breathing or digestion, which we carry out unconsciously and automatically in order to get us through our daily lives. Creativity is not the exclusive preserve of the rich, famous, artistic genius; it is a phenomenon we all share, irrespective of age, class, gender, race, ability or impairment. It is a frighteningly democratic and democratising process and thus might, one would think, be an easy enough matter to identify when 'little-c creativity' *or* 'possibility thinking' (as Craft, 2002, refers to it) is present:

> Little-c creativity … focuses on the resourcefulness and agency of ordinary people … it refers to an ability to route find, successfully charting new courses through everyday challenges … It involves being imaginative, being original/innovative, stepping at times outside of convention, going beyond the obvious, being self-aware of all of this in taking active, conscious, and intentional action in the world. It is not, necessarily, linked to a product outcome. (Craft, 2002: 56)

However, were it such a simple matter to identify the subconscious, automatic – and perhaps invisible – nature of creativity, there would be no need for chapters like this or the myriad of texts attempting to explain how creativity can be encouraged in schools or in the workforce.

What is offered here is a framework of how to look for creative practice within Early Years settings: to try to make the invisible creative force partially and temporarily visible so that we can understand its actions better, plan to encourage its emergence, and work towards a more satisfying educational experience for children, practitioners and parents.

It is argued that the framework provides the means to develop pedagogies of practitioners and children working together in Early Years settings. This framework is described in terms of zones: as Zones for Scrap, Disguise, Infectivity, Intimacy, Surprise and Grace. They are intended as means of identifying and discussing emergent properties of a setting or a relationship, not as a means of observational scrutiny, and are certainly not to be reduced to a performative, tick-box crib sheet.

Creativity was here: the role of the six Zones of Creative Development

The metaphor of the zone is a recurring element of educational discourses in which space and time is bounded in such a way as to generate a learning space whose properties are thought to magnify, extend, or transform a particular aspect of learning activities. Vygotsky's 'Zone of Proximal Development' theory (Vygotsky, 1978: 86) is acknowledged by many as being a means of understanding the process through which children learn, with the support of significant others. Siraj-Blatchford et al. (2003) suggest that this kind of zone has a transformational effect on children's skills by the practitioner:

> [D]rawing the child from their position of present understanding into the area or zone just beyond what the child could achieve alone. This zone is called the 'zone of proximal development' and is where the child, when supported by others, can make the most rapid progress. (Siraj-Blatchford et al., 2003: 2)

A Zone of Scrap

In discussing mess theory in Western fiction and painting, Wright relates to both the significance of 'mess':

> Baudelaire, who described the metamorphosis of raw reality into crafted artifact as the transformation of mud into gold … [and] Samuel Beckett's use of the term, in his 1961 interview with Tom Driver, when he spoke of seeking in art 'a form that accommodates the mess'. (Wright 2001–02: 179)

Similarly, in Sternberg's Propulsion Model of Creative Leadership (Sternberg, 2004) scrap materials are like initiatives, powerless and yet powerful in their potential for catalysing change within a system. Scrap's lack of determinedness and specificity provides the agents who work with it the conceptual space to make decisions about it, and to determine its character and identity, rather than being confronted with a predetermined identity. This is corroborated by the Arts Council's policy document on Early Years, *Reflect and Review*, which proposes a number of specific recommendations about the aesthetic values that should be applied to building a *creative curriculum*. These are presented in the form of a checklist, and include the suggestion:

> Materials and artefacts should stimulate open-ended play and offer opportunities to develop children's imaginations, as opposed to limiting them. (Woolf and Belloli, 2005: 16–18)

From a rhetoric of creative education derived from agendas and desires of economic development ('imaginative activity fashioned so as to produce outcomes that are both original and of value' [Robinson, 1999: 30]), the proposition that humble scrap materials such as junk, detritus, the unworthy, the broken and the discarded can offer a starting point for an alternative rhetoric of creativity based on preservation, and conservation of human development, is an exciting one that needs particular support in Early Years settings.

A Zone of Disguise

The concept of a Zone of Disguise has arisen from the phenomenon of artists in particular, and outsiders in general, performing different identities as they begin to develop a relationship with participants who are inside a particular setting. As a consequence, both outsiders and insiders adopt different functional and cultural roles within the setting.

Case Study

The Chameleon (the visitor in the setting)

When someone from the outside is coming into the Early Years setting the first move the outsider needs to make in establishing his or her presence inside is to spend time initially establishing relationships with the children through conversing with them and getting to know them and showing interest in them instead of spending time on the task he or she is there to carry out. In that instance, the practitioner is the bridge between the class and the outsider visitor. The outsider visitor is *the honorary practitioner for the day*, thus giving him/herself the temporary, borrowed identity of insider.

The (Reverse Trojan) Horse

Liam and Maria run a design company in Hull. Sculptor Liam describes how the two of them work as a double act which plays with the inside/outside dynamic: *she can ask a question but has to be aware of people's feelings – and so I can ask the same question from a naïve position and perhaps ask it more challengingly.* He describes how, when she goes into the school as a visiting artist, she is sensitive to the dynamics of the setting, and in doing so 'recces' the site. As outsider, she collects sensitive insider knowledge by assuming temporary insider status: but then assumes a 'reverse Trojan horse role', taking that information back to an outsider, who then enters the school as a self-confessed *wicked uncle being slightly more provocative* to ask similar questions but without the need to be seen to be sensitive: and in doing so, disrupts the status quo on the basis of

(Continued)

(Continued)

that information which has been smuggled out to him: *it's useful you being on the outside – people inside 'place the rocks to run over': people outside take the rocks away.*

While on the one hand this may appear to be an over-elaborate process, it could be that without this subterfuge, direct questions from Maria to staff about sensitive issues may be spurned and her access to information about relaionships, agendas and other insights into school life data subsequently restricted.

'Disguise' can therefore take a number of forms. Artists sometimes choose to play the identity of 'the wild one', yet other choices are available to other types of outsider: meta-author, sorcerer, chef, commissioner, parent or teacher. The presence of an alternative persona – a dramatic reconstruction of a person – in the setting assists participants to wipe the slate clean and dismantle any preconceptions they may have about those other participants in the common learning space.

Inhabiting a Zone of Disguise also allows protagonists to become 'invisible' – a process in which attention on the outsider, for example, is refocused on the products of the outsider's work. Musicians might, for example, ask children participants in their sessions to 'just use your ears', suggesting children listen to the music they are playing rather than to the words they are speaking. This can be extended by asking participants to watch, regard, or listen to other artefacts, such as the nurse's uniform, the music or other products (that is, do anything other than pay attention to the outsider who has introduced these artefacts to the group).

The outsider, in disguising his/her identity through becoming 'invisible', places the artefacts as significant tools that mediate learning, a concept familiar in the work of Vygotsky (Daniels, 2001) and of Trevarthen on intersubjectivity (Stern, 1985; Trevarthen, 1993). By becoming invisible and heightening the status of the artefact in the learning space, the outsider introduces possibilities for modifying power relationships in the learning space, as participants are presented with possibilities of relating to each other in relationships that can confound the everyday manifestation of the common power relationship within a classroom.

A Zone of Infectivity

Infectivity is proposed as a concept describing how efficacious an outsider is in affecting the values, techniques, ideas and knowledge of the insider. Infectivity is brought about by the outsider's capability to rupture cultural membranes, and thus leading to the flow across the membrane in the directions of knowledge, information, culture and skills.

Many arts practitioners describe the different techniques they use, to which they attribute the effectiveness of their work and which contribute to the rupturing of the membrane between insiders and outsiders. These techniques relate to the transformative power of scrap materials, pedagogical values of respect and access, the place for multisensory engagement and the judicious balance between the production of unique events or artefacts with the replication and distribution of those artefacts.

Examples

Abe the musician: Scrap as infectious agents

Abe explains his drumming technique as having a number of components: either he establishes a set of rhythms to a group of children within a class and then juxtaposes that against another set of rhythms played by another group in the class; or he establishes an aural 'chaos' in the class, listens for hints from the chaos and then points to members of the group to be aware of certain aspects of the chaos which he repeats; he advises members to *play what you want but not too much ... to play simple patterns ... to copy others if you like something you hear ...* which he claims *guarantees something magical will happen. So I let that go on for a few minutes and then if I, if I want, if I think, if I catch some eye contact I will probably play something that I know somebody will copy then when I can feel something happening I will kind of light up my face and say 'can you hear it, can you hear it' and they all go 'yeah, yeah' ...*

Christine the puppeteer: Transformation as infectious agents

Transformation is described by Christine, a puppeteer, who claims that the power of puppetry lies in its ability to transform, through personalisation, inanimate low-status objects (which might be in a story), to becoming high-status subjects (which may shape the story).

Julie the textile artist: Respect and access – the values that promote infectivity

Julie articulates the pedagogical values she employs in the setting: *respecting the children and assuming that they can do it, treating them as adults ... I'm doing a fun thing and if you listen to me and mostly to what I say then you'll have a fun time too ... I expect them to stay the course, I expect them to keep doing as I ask.*

Nigel, theatre director: Accessibility

Nigel describes a technique based on the importance of employing all five senses in the artist educator engagement. This approach stems from his theatre company's work with

(Continued)

(Continued)

children with special educational needs and aims to ensure that every participant, irrespective of any sensory limitation they may have, can in some manner engage with the company's work. This approach relies on participants' not merely using their eyes or ears to learn, to develop knowledge, to have an emotion and to develop understanding: it is about employing the other senses of taste, touch, smell to find routes to experience the work, to develop both affectively and cognitively and hence learn and develop a higher state of understanding.

In summary, the techniques articulated by artists, ones that break the rules of engagement and thus rupture the membrane between 'outside' and 'inside', involve the use of low status, incomplete and fragmented resources: 'chaos', or scrap; the engagement of all participants' senses with appropriate, accessible languages; the need to balance the application of a variety of technologies in the production of both individual, unique and authentic artefacts as well as the replication and dissemination of mass-produced artefacts.

A Zone for Intimacy

This Zone is proposed to host the development of a pedagogical relationship, termed here a 'Creative Relationship', between two protagonists, A and B. While the case is intended to describe a relationship between two people, it is not inconceivable that one of the protagonists might be something more abstract – whether this be a project, a procedure or even an initiative. The model – in which A is symbolised by the white block and B by the grey block – is summarised thus in Figure 14.2:

The phases of the Creative Relationship model are characterised as follows:

Phase 1:   *Non-alignment*. The phase in which A and B are in no relationship with each other and are unaware of each other's presence, needs, interests or desires. For example, A can be an Early Years practitioner and B can be a parent who is an actor.

Phase 2:   *Alignment*. The phase in which A and B have been brought together by the presence of a third party – a catalyst (which may be a project, initiative or challenge) that acts to bind the responder and stimulus. The practitioner and the children after reading a story have decided to create a pantomime, and the manager thinks this is a great idea and asks the Early Years practitioner and the parents/actor if they would like work together to create a pantomime with the children of the setting.

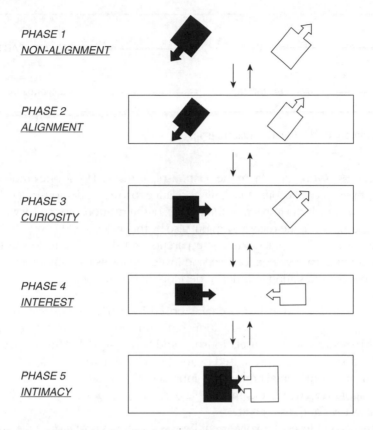

Figure 14.2   A simple model of the Creative Relationship

Phase 3:   *Curiosity*. The phase in which either one of the two agents exhibits curiosity about the other; if both parties become mutually curious then the relationship response demonstrates a mutually reinforcing amplifying feedback loop, the response becomes more intense, and the relationship shifts to the next phase. The Early Years practitioner and the parents are discussing their ideas and they have found a number of common interests and ideas to help the children with the project.

Phase 4:   *Interest*. The phase in which curiosity has been superseded by a more intense attraction to each other's presence, needs, interests or desires. The two agents come closer together, whether this be physically or emotionally. As with the phase preceding it, if this interest is reciprocated then another mutually amplifying positive feedback loop is established, and the relationship then shifts to the next phase. The practitioner and the parent work together with the children, they rehearse, feed back, listen to the children, and explore new ideas based on children's interests.

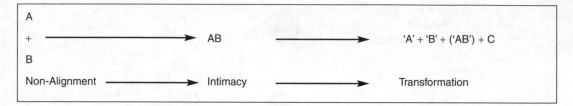

Figure 14.3   Summary of the Creative Relationship

Phase 5:   *Intimacy*. Where the relationship is marked by strong emotional, intellectual or physical connections, and feelings relating to love are demonstrated. This may be the point at which the impact, or the results, of the relationship can be witnessed not only by the agents in the relationship but also by the wider world in which those two agents are situated. The practitioner, the parents and the children decide to perform this pantomime to a wider audience, and invite the locals to communicate and raise some money for the setting in order to develop their outdoor area.

The Creative Relationship is characterised by a number of features. First, the two agents start in a state of 'no-relationship' and 'no-bond', and progress through five phases to a state of 'strong-relationship' and 'strong-bond'. Mutually reinforcing amplifying feedback loops, represented by the 'equilibrium arrows' ($\rightleftharpoons$) drive the relationship from non-alignment to intimacy. This model also suggests how relationships might break down to a final phase of repulsion, through phases that might include dismissiveness and disinterest.

An increasing level of involvement between the two protagonists, A and B, marks the movement through the five phases of a relationship response. This model proposes that once the fifth phase of the relationship is reached, this leads to a process of catalysis, after which the close juxtaposition of the two agents (A and B) leads to the production of new states of A and B ('A' and 'B'), and the production of 'third significant others' (3SOs), 'significant' in this context referring to the members of the relationship or the wider field in which the two respondents are placed.

Creativity thus becomes the phenomenon in which two individual protagonists (A and B) participate in a relationship, characterised by a shift from non-alignment to intimacy, which catalyses processes of transformations and the subsequent production of new states of 'A' and 'B' – a new relationship of AB – and the production of third significant other(s) (C). This is summarised in Figure 14.3.

Creative products in these terms can therefore be understood as a change of the individual states of A and B (mental, physical, emotional, spiritual, identity); a change of relationship between A and B (understanding, configuration, alignment, purpose, function, direction, partnership); and the generation of third significant others (methods, attributes, attitudes or artefacts).

Transformation in this model does not imply any moral position: change is not necessarily 'for the best'. This is a model of value-free creativity, and values are placed upon it by its protagonists and by the fields in which the protagonists operate.

A Zone of Surprise

The Zone of Surprise is so named due to the frequency with which practitioners and other 'insiders' express surprise at the capabilities of the children they teach, which come to the fore whilst working with outsiders. Surprise arises from the interplay among previous zones of disguise, infectivity and intimacy, and involves a number of interrelated components concerned with altering the rules of engagement among protagonists. For example, this may involve changing the rules by which practitioners and teachers address children, or changing the rules that determined the dress code within the setting. It can involve the redefining of the spaces in which learning occurs; encounters can be presented as 'workshops' instead of as classes and can be presented as separate from the prescribed, everyday curriculum.

A Zone of Surprise is also engendered when a lack of prescription about the outcome of a session is acceptable, and when there are fewer preconceived plans by adults of what they want from an encounter. Involving children in setting their own goals and making explicit their own desires and wants (exemplified in some schools by the reintroduction of the space of 'choosing time') can also encourage the potential for surprise. This process requires resistance to the development of schemata – or schemes of work – that can be used to analyse and judge encounters in advance.

Encounters that arise from Zones of Surprise also rely on appropriate framing to ensure that an audience's experiences of the encounters are understood. Framing is a process that qualifies, justifies and contextualises the journey, and will steer interpretations of results away from discourses about 'end products' and towards an understanding that intermediate results of encounters are emergent, transitional artefacts which still have further potential for development, growth or even deterioration. A Zone of Surprise also requires time to be set aside to ensure the full effect of the creative relationship can be experienced. This requires a view of time as festal instead of pragmatic:

> [A]s feast art replaces the 'normal' pragmatic experience of time – the experience of time as 'time for something'. This is the time of which one disposes, which one fills with some kind of activity. Instead of this, the arts feature a different type of time: fulfilled time. When the feast starts, the present is being fulfilled by the celebration. It is not that someone has had to fill in empty time but, conversely, time has become festal when the time of the feast has arrived. The calculating way in which one disposes of one's time is brought to a standstill in the act of feasting. (Gadamer, 1970: 55–6)

A Zone of Grace

> When one is most absorbed in the act of creation one almost feels that one is wandering in the great corridors of all minds. Creativity makes us part of it all. There is no genuine creative or human problem that cannot be solved if you are serene enough, humble enough, hardworking enough, and if you have learnt the gentle arts of concentration, visualization, and meditation. For me, tranquillity is the sign of the invisible presence of grace. (Okri, 1997: 28)

The journey to grace is the process in which the Creative Relationship is marked by a sense of communion between its protagonists: a state of higher understanding that might simply be a moment of expressed, articulated, demonstrated shared belief, or knowledge learned, with witness borne to it. The journey to grace produces understanding that is composed of (exponentially more than the sum of its) individual parts of skill, technique, learning and intellectual and affective knowledge.

The visiting artists in a nursery, for example, in the journey towards grace achieve a state of 'meta-authorship', a super-author of authors, who listens to the multiple voices of the participants in their learning spaces and simultaneously models this capability to their apprentice authors. They demonstrate the ability to listen to a multiplicity of conflicting and competing voices and points of view, and synthesise from those voices a common, shared state of understanding and authenticity.

It is through the concept of authenticity that the relationship between insider and outsider is bridged: both roles needing to take responsibility for their actions in the context in which they work; both roles responding to the deepest needs of the situation; both roles involving the change of perspective of the world, and both roles transforming the world and being transformed by it.

Case Study

Applying the six Zones – The Black and White Project

The use of the six Zones of Creative Development has been successfully developed within a case study project in Clubmoor Children's Centre in Liverpool in 2007/2008 through a 'Crèche Artist' project entitled 'Through the Eyes of a Child', which aimed to develop Early Years practitioners' understandings of child-centredness and creative practice, through the identification of a research question (the *creative challenge*) that practitioners wished to address in their respective settings.

'Through the Eyes of a Child' was delivered through a series of seminars, workshops and mentoring support. It was based at Clubmoor Children's Centre and its three associated Early Years settings: a private provider, a group of childminders and a local primary school. Twelve Early Years practitioners participated in the programme, a mix of qualified practitioners and volunteers studying towards their NVQ2 in Child Care.

The basis of the programme was the introduction to those practitioners of the six Zones of Creative Development, and to the use of the framework as a means of articulating and discussing a particular creative challenge faced by those practitioners. It introduced this by reviewing how children looked in classrooms, i.e., what they could see, how they might be seen, how the space contributed to or hindered these viewings, and then established a short observational project in which practitioners went into neighbouring classrooms in pairs to observe children's creative behaviour and to identify hindrances to that behaviour.

Participants had a wealth of experience working in the Early Years, but were still enthusiastic to find out how to bring a more creative practice into their settings. They saw the programme as offering them the opportunity to learn something else and saw enhancing their creativity as means to becoming more rounded teachers. Some were particularly interested in learning new practical/creative activities they could implement in their own practice, and to find more ideas to develop and inspire their practice in the Early Years Foundation Stage.

The observational exercise prompted much interest and surprise from the practitioners in what they saw when looking at the setting through particular children's eyes. They related many interesting stories about children's relationships with their peers, teachers and parents, which led them to question how their setting could be enhanced to develop more effective creative practice. Themes that emerged included the need to simplify storage in the setting by letting children see clearly artefacts in the classroom; the desire to develop a 'creativity tool kit' for parents, which would have a wider range of resources in it than the usual play-pack would allow; and a project that wanted to explore the effect of black and white on children between 2 and 7 years old. This project – the Black and White Project – has been extended by the childminders who developed it (Jo and Tim) into a fully fledged project, which they are now piloting in their setting.

The Black and White Project: the six Zones in action

Jo and Tim developed the project by transforming their baby room for one week, by emptying out everything, including all conventional toys, except the furniture (which they covered in black cloth). They then introduced only black and white objects into the space (*the random stuff*, as they described it – equivalent to the Junk or Scrap Zone) – striped mats, a striped door cover, black and white jigsaw floor tiles, white candles, a black fisherman's net, white gloves, white net curtains, a black and white blow-up dog, ping-pong balls, a white drain pipe, black bowls, white shells, etc.

(Continued)

(Continued)

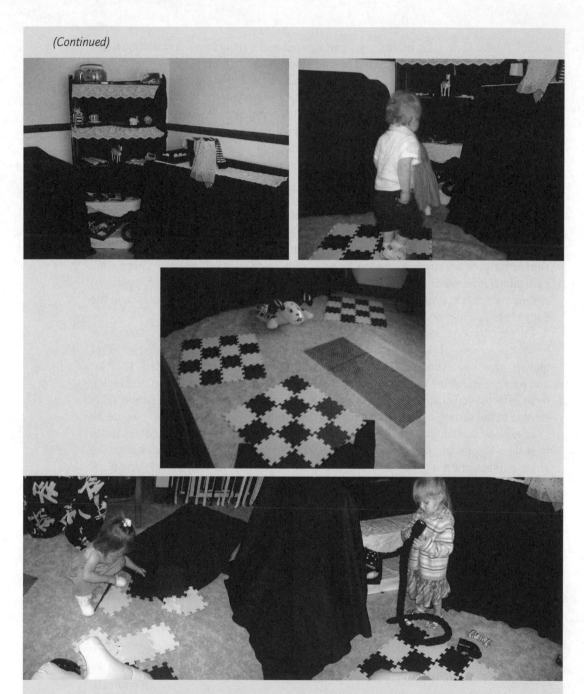

Figure 14. 4   The Black and White Project

Joe and Tim reported that the children would pick up different objects and ask 'What does this do?' While they supported the children in finding out what the children thought it did or what it was for, they were clear that the roles they took were about *not being involved but almost becoming disengaged ... invisible* – another form of disguise, as suggested by the Zonal model.

Jo and Tim's Zone of Infectivity was generated by their use of scrap materials and their disguise of detachment. This resulted in children's playing with the materials in new ways, designing three-dimensional pictures (instead of the usual two-dimensional drawing they were accustomed to) and being able to share ideas with each other, and some older children who were curious about how the space worked. They have some lovely photographic evidence of the children in the space: one little girl exploring the fisherman's net with her hand – noticing the texture and the changes in its appearance.

Jo and Tim also talk about how the relationships between them and the children changed and how this led to many surprises. They had set up a drainpipe with the ping-pong balls, and were surprised when the children played in a completely different way to the manner they had been expected to. One 2-year-old girl they looked after could not otherwise put jigsaw pieces together, but she managed to do so on the black and white jigsaw floor tiles. Jo felt that the definition of the black and white helped the girl to see the pieces joining together.

Jo talked of the children's responding very positively to 'The Space', and all the children wanting to go into the space: when referred to as 'the baby room', the older children would not choose to go into that room at all – but its transformation offered the possibility for new relationships to be formed. One of the parents had come to pick up her child during the week of 'The Space' and commented on how creative the transformations were. Jo was delighted that a parent had recognised and valued this, one who also appreciated that her intention of making the space more creative had been acknowledged. A state of grace – of higher understanding, knowledge and skill – had been achieved not just for the children, but for their parents and childminders, too.

Jo and Tim both found that it had been beneficial to change the look of the environment into which the children come, and are planning to have other days when they transform the space using other colour schemes and see what the children's reactions are to these. Tim is particularly interested still in finding out the impact the black and white scheme could have on young babies. They are planning to share their bag of black and white goodies with other childminders through their network group.

In the short space of a few days, Jo and Tim's imaginative approach to making new toys from scrap items had led to a change of identity for themselves; infectious fun-filled activities for children; new relationships between children, surprises of engagement and learning and higher states of understanding and appreciation among all partners engaged in the nurturing and development of their children's creative capabilities. The gravitational pull of relationships between children and adults had, again, demonstrated how creative practice can be encouraged, developed and celebrated.

Key points to remember

- This chapter has attempted to address the complexities of trying to approach creativity. Our views about creativity are often influenced by our personal experiences and attitudes towards creative practice.
- A theoretical understanding of creativity is important when we plan activities to promote creative activities in Early Years settings.
- Creativity can be a solitary activity yet a social activity at one and the same time, and it is argued that when creativity is seen as a social activity with play as a tool then children are able to produce outcomes that are beyond adults' expectations.

 Points for discussion

- What are your personal experiences and perceptions of and attitudes towards creativity? Considering the example of Cutler's work, can you remember whether you were given opportunities to explore creativity in a shared, constructed and collaborative way?
- Within the Early Years Foundation Stage creativity is characterised as an 'exploration of thoughts, ideas and feelings through a variety of art, music, dance, imaginative and role-play activities, mathematics, and design technology'. Considering the six Zones of Creative Development, can you devise any appropriate activities for young children?
- In a visit to an Early Years setting try out 'looking at children through their own eyes':

  making something from nothing: e.g., role-playing and 'hot seating'
  making something from nothing: the use of different visual stimuli and textures
  making something from nothing: percussion and group music-making
  making something from nothing: automatic writing, and writing for monologue, dialogue and story structure.

Reflect on these activities with young children and identify how creativity was promoted.

Further reading

Abbott, L. and Nutbrown, C. (2001) *Experiencing Reggio Emilia: Implications for Pre-School Provision.* Buckingham: Open University Press.

Bruce, T. (2004) *Cultivating Creativity in Babies, Toddlers and Young Children.* London: Hodder and Stoughton.

Rinaldi, C. (2005) *In Dialogue with Reggio Emilia: Listening, Researching and Learning.* London: Routledge.

Useful websites

Creative Partnerships
www.creative-partnerships.com/
The national creative learning programme

QCA *Creativity: Find it, Promote it.*
www.qca.org.uk/1158_14928.html.

Sightlines
www.sightlines-initiative.com
The national agency for Reggio Emilia schools

REFERENCES

Chapter 1   Policy Context in England and the Implementation of the Early Years Foundation Stage

Alexander, R., Rose, J. and Woodhead, C. (eds) (1992) *Curriculum Organization and Classroom Practice in Primary Schools: A Discussion Paper*. London: DES.

Anning, A. (2009) 'The co-construction of an early childhood curriculum', in A. Anning, J. Cullen and M. Fleer (eds), *Early Childhood Education: Society and Culture*. London: Sage. pp. 67–79.

Anning, A. and Ball, M. (eds) (2008) *Improving Services for Children and Young People*. London: Sage.

Anning, A. and Edwards, A. (eds) (2006) *Promoting Children's Learning from Birth to Five: Developing the New Early Years Professional*. Milton Keynes: Open University Press.

Athey, C. (1990) *Extending Thought in Young Children*. London: Paul Chapman Publishing.

Aubrey, C. (2007) *Leading and Managing in the Early Years*. London: Sage.

Baldock, P., Fitzgerald, D. and Kay, J. (2009) *Understanding Early Years Policy*, 2nd edn. London: Paul Chapman Publishing.

Bertman, P. and Pascal, C. (2002) Early Years Education: An International Perspective. www.inca.org.uk (accessed September 2008).

Blair, T. (1998) *The Third Way: New Politics for the New Century*. London: The Fabian Society.

Bloom, A. (2006) 'Fears new nursery staff will squeeze teachers', *Times Educational Supplement*, 1 December 2006. www.tes.co.uk (accessed September 2008).

Cohen, B., Moss, P., Petrie, P. and Wallace, J. (2004) *A New Deal for Children? Reforming Education and Care in England, Scotland and Sweden*. Bristol: The Policy Press.

CWDC (2007) *Guidance to the Standards for the Award of Early Professional Status*. Leeds: CWDC.

David, T. (1993) 'Educating children under 5 in the U.K.', in T. David (ed.), *Educational Provision for Our Youngest Children, European Perspectives*. London: Paul Chapman Publishing.

DCSF (Department for Children, Schools and Families) (2007) *The Children's Plan: Building Brighter Futures*. London: HMSO.

DCSF (Department for Children, Schools and Families) (2008) *The Early Years Foundation Stage: Setting the Standards for Learning, Development and Care for Children from Birth to Five*. Nottingham: DCSF Publications. (Comprises the *Statutory Framework, Practice Guidance*, Cards and other resources.)

Devereux, J. and Miller, L. (eds) (2003) *Working with Children in the Early Years*. London: David Fulton.

DfEE (Department for Education and Employment) (1997) *Excellence in Schools*. London: DfEE.

DfEE (Department for Education and Employment) (1998) *Meeting the Childcare Strategy*. London: DfEE.

DfES (Department for Education and Skills) (2001) *Children's Day Care and Facilities at 31 March*. London: DfES.

DfES (Department for Education and Skills) (2003) *Every Child Matters*. Nottingham: DfES Publications.

DfES (Department for Education and Skills) (2004a) *Every Child Matters: Change for Children,* Nottingham: DfES Publications.

DfES (Department for Education and Skills) (2004b) *Choice for Parents, The Best Start for Children: A Ten Year Strategy for Childcare*. London: HMSO.

DfES (Department for Education and Skills) (2007) *Practice Guidance for the Early Years Foundation Stage: Setting the Standards for Learning, Development, and Care for Children from Birth to Five*. Nottingham: DfES Publications.

Glass, N. (1999) 'Sure Start: the development of an early intervention programme for young children in the United Kingdom', *Children and Society*, 13: 257–64.

Goldschmied, E. and Jackson, S. (1994) *People Under Three: Young Children in Day Care*. London: Routledge.

Hennessy, E., Martin, S., Moss, P. and Melhuish, P. (1992) *Children and Day Care: Lessons from Research*. London: Paul Chapman Publishing.

Her Majesty's Government (1989) *Children Act 1989*. London: HMSO.

Her Majesty's Government (2004) *Children Act 2004*. London: HMSO.

Her Majesty's Government (2006) *Childcare Act 2006*. London: HMSO.

Mortimore, P., Sammons, P., Stoll, L., Lewis, D. and Ecob, R. (eds) (1998) *School Matters*. London: Open Books.

Moss, P. (2000) 'Foreign services', *Nursery World*, 3733: 10–13.

Moss, P. (2001) 'Britain in Europe: finger or heart?', in G. Pugh (ed.), *Contemporary Issues in the Early Years*, 3rd edn. London: Paul Chapman Publishing. pp. 25–39.

Moss, P. and Pence, A. (eds) (1994) *Valuing Quality in Early Childhood Services: New Approaches to Defining Quality*. London: Paul Chapman Publishing.

Moyles, J.R. (1989) *Just Playing? The Role and Status of Play in Early Childhood Education*. Milton Keynes: Open University Press.

Moyles, J. (ed.) (2007) *Early Years Foundations: Meeting the Challenge*. Maidenhead: Open University Press.

Moyles, J., Adams, S., and Musgrove, A. (2001) *The Study of Pedagogical Effectiveness: A Confidential Report to the DfES*. Chelmsford: Anglia Polytechnic University.

National Statistics (2007) Teacher Numbers, in www.statistics.gov./uk/cci/nugget.asp?id=1765> (accessed September 2008).

Nutbrown, C. (1999) *Threads of Thinking*. London: Paul Chapman Publishing.

Ofsted (2008) Early Years Foundation Stage (EYFS). www.ofsted.gov.uk (accessed September 2008).

Penn, H. (1997) *Comparing Nurseries: Staff and Children in Italy, Spain and the UK*. London: Paul Chapman Publishing.

Penn, H. (2000) *Early Childhood Services: Theory, Policy and Practice*. Oxford: Oxford University Press.

Penn, H. (2008) *Understanding Early Childhood: Issues and Controversies*, Maidenhead: Open University Press.

Pugh, G., (ed.) (1996) *Contemporary Issues in the Early Years: Working Collaboratively for Children*, 2nd edn. London: Paul Chapman Publishing.

QCA/DfEE (Qualifications and Curriculum Authority/Department for Education and Employment) (2000) *Curriculum Guidance for the Foundation Stage*. London: QCA.

Smith, C. and Vernon, J. (1994) *Day Nurseries at the Crossroads: Meeting the Childcare Challenges*. London: National Children's Bureau.

Sure Start Unit (2002) *Birth to Three Matters: A Framework to Support Children in Their Earliest Years*. Nottingham: DfES Publications.

Sylva, K., Melhuish, E., Sammons, P. and Siraj-Blatchford, I. (2001) *The Effective Provision of Pre-School Education (EPPE) Project*. The EPPE Symposium at the British Educational Research Association Annual Conference, University of Leeds, September 2001.

United Nations (1989) *The Convention on the Rights of the Child*. Geneva: Defence International and the United Nations Children's Fund.

Chapter 2   The National Picture

Carmichael, E. and Hancock, J. (2007) 'Scotland', in M. Clark and T. Waller (eds) (2007) *Early Childhood Education and Care: Policy and Practice*. London: Sage.

CCEA (Council for the Curriculum Examinations and Assessment) (2007) *The Northern Ireland Curriculum: Primary*. Belfast: CCEA.

Centre for Early Childhood Development and Education (2006) *Síolta: The National Quality Framework for Early Childhood Education*. Dublin, Ireland: CECDE.

Children's Commissioner for Wales (2008) United Nations Committee on the Rights of the Child Report. www.childcomwales.org.uk.

Cohen, B., Moss, P., Petrie, P. and Wallace, J. (2004) *A New Deal for Children? Re-forming Education and Care in England, Scotland and Sweden*. Bristol: The Policy Press.

Curriculum Framework (1997) www.hmie.gov.uk/documents/publication/sqpse-05.htm.

DCSF (Department for Children, Schools and Families) (2008) *The Early Years Foundation Stage: Setting the Standards for Learning, Development and Care for Children from Birth to Five*. Nottingham: DCSF Publications. (Comprises the *Statutory Framework*, *Practice Guidance*, Cards and other resources.)

DENI (1996) *The Northern Ireland Curriculum. Key Stages 1 and 2*. Belfast: HMSO.

DENI (2004) *Review of Preschool Education in Northern Ireland*. Belfast: DENI.

DENI (2006) *Outcomes from the Review of Preschool Education in Northern Ireland*. Belfast: DENI.

DENI and DHSS (1998) *Investing in Early Learning: Preschool Education in Northern Ireland*. Belfast: The Stationery Office.

DENI, TEA and DHSS (1999) *Children First: The Northern Ireland Childcare Strategy*. Belfast: DHSS, TEA and DENI.

DHSS, CCEA and DENI (1997) *Curricular Guidance for Preschool Education*. Belfast: CCEA.

DHSS PS, CCEA and DENI (2006) *Curricular Guidance for Preschool Education*. Belfast: CCEA.

Government of Ireland (1991) *Child Care Act*. Dublin, Ireland: The Stationery Office.

Government of Ireland (1998) *Education Act*. Dublin, Ireland: The Stationery Office.

Government of Ireland (1999a) *Ready to Learn: White Paper on Early Childhood Education*. Dublin, Ireland: The Stationery Office.

Government of Ireland (1999b) *Primary School Curriculum: Introduction*. Dublin, Ireland: The Stationery Office.

Government of Ireland (2000) *National Children's Strategy, "Our Children: Their Lives"*. Dublin: The Stationery Office.

Government of Ireland (2004) *Education of Persons with Special Educational Needs Act*. Dublin, Ireland: The Stationery Office.

Government of Ireland (2006a) *National Childcare Strategy 2006–2010*. Dublin, Ireland: The Stationery Office.

Government of Ireland (2006b) *Child Care (Pre-School Services) (No. 2) Regulations 2006 and Explanatory Guide to Requirements and Procedures for Notification and Inspection*. Dublin, Ireland: The Stationery Office.

Great Britain (1989) *Education Reform (Northern Ireland) Order*. Belfast: HMSO.

Laevers, F. (2005) Deep-level-learning and the experiential approach in early childhood and primary education. www.ltscotland.org.uk-/earlyyears/professionaldevelopment/events/LTSseminars/involvementseminar/index.asp (accessed 23 July 2008).

National Economic and Social Forum (2005) *Early Childhood Care and Education: Report 31*. Dublin, Ireland: National Economic and Aid Forum.

OFMDFM (Office of the First Minister and Deputy First Minister) (2006) *Our Children and Young People – Our Pledge: A Ten-Year Strategy for Children and Young People in Northern Ireland 2006–2016*. Belfast: OFMDFM.

Organisation for Economic Co-operation and Development (OECD) (2004) *OECD Thematic Review of Early Childhood Education and Care Policy in Ireland*. Dublin, Ireland: The Stationery Office.

Pinkerton, D. (1990) 'Four year olds in primary schools in Northern Ireland', *Oideas*, 36: 42–7.

Rinaldi, C. (2005) *In Dialogue with Reggio-Emilia: Contextualising, Interpreting and Evaluating Early Childhood Education*. London: Routledge.

Scottish Executive (2000) *The Child at the Centre*. Edinburgh: Scottish Executive.

Scottish Executive (2002) *The National Care Standards: Early Education and Childcare up to the Age of 16*. Edinburgh: Scottish Executive.

Scottish Executive (2005) *A Curriculum for Excellence*. Edinburgh: Scottish Executive.

Scottish Executive (2005) *Birth to Three: Supporting Our Youngest Children*. Edinburgh: Scottish Executive/Learning and Teaching Scotland.

Scottish Executive (2006a) *National Review of the Early Years and Childcare Workforce*. Edinburgh: Scottish Executive.

Scottish Executive (2006b) *National Review of the Early Years and Childcare Workforce: Scottish Executive Response: Investigating in Children's Futures*. Edinburgh: Scottish Executive.

Scottish Office (1997) *National Guidance: A Curriculum Framework for Children 3 to 5 years*. Edinburgh: Scottish Office.

Sheehy, N., Trew, K., Rafferty, H., McShane, E., Quiery, N. and Curran, S. (2000) *The Greater Shankill Early Years Project: Evaluation Report*. Belfast: The Greater Shankill Project and CCEA.

UNCRC (1992) UK ratification of the Convention of the Rights of the Child. www.direct.gov.uk/en/Parent/ParentsRights/DG_4003313 (accessed 12 July 2008).

Walsh, G. (2007) 'Northern Ireland', in M. Clark and T. Waller (eds), *Early Childhood Education and Care*. London: Sage.

Walsh, G., Sproule, L., McGuinness, C., Trew, K., Rafferty, H. and Sheehy, N. (2006) 'An appropriate curriculum for 4–5 year old children in Northern Ireland: comparing play-based and formal approaches', *Early Years*, 26 (2): 201–21.

WAG (2001) *The Learning Country*. Cardiff: Welsh Assembly Government.

WAG (2002a) *The Learning Country: Vision into Action*. Cardiff: Welsh Assembly Government.

WAG (2002b) *Children and Young People: Rights to Action*. Cardiff: Welsh Assembly Government.

WAG (2007) *Building Effective Learning Communities Together: A National School Effectiveness Framework for Wales*. Cardiff: Welsh Assembly Government.

WAG (2008a) *The Foundation Phase, 3–7*. Cardiff: Welsh Assembly Government.

WAG (2008b) *Skills Framework, 3–19*. Cardiff: Welsh Assembly Government.

WAG (2008c) *Play/Active Learning: Overview for 3–7 Year Olds*. Cardiff: Welsh Assembly Government.

WAG (2008d) *Observing Children*. Cardiff: Welsh Assembly Government.

Wood, E. and Attfield, J. (2005) *Play, Learning and the Early Childhood Curriculum*, 2nd edn. London: Paul Chapman Publishing.

Chapter 3   Pedagogy in Context

Adey, P., Shayer, M. and Yates, C. (1995) *Thinking Science: Student and Teachers Materials for CASE Intervention*, 2nd edn. London: Nelson Thornes.

Benson, N.C. (2003) *Introducing Psychology*. Cambridge: Icon Books.

Burman, E. (1994) *Deconstructing Developmental Psychology*. London: Routledge.

Bronfenbrenner, U. (1977) *The Ecology of Human Development*. Cambridge, MA: Harvard University Press.

Bruner, J.S. (1996) *In Search of Pedagogy. Volume II: The Selected Works of Jerome S. Bruner*. Oxford: Oxford University Press.

Claxton, G. (2008) 'Too formal too soon'. Speech at an Early Years conference in Northern Ireland (2008).

David, T. (1990) *Under Five, Under-Educated?* Milton Keynes: Open University Press.

DCSF (Department for Children, Schools and Families) (2008) *The Early Years Foundation Stage: Setting the Standards for Learning, Development and Care for Children from Birth to Five*. Nottingham: DCSF Publications. (Comprises the *Statutory Framework, Practice Guidance*, Cards and other resources.)

Donaldson, M. (2006) *Children's Minds*, 3rd edn. London: HarperCollins (1st edn. 1978).

Gardner, H. (1993) *Multiple Intelligences: Theory in Practice*. New York: HarperCollins.

Gardner, H. (1999) *Intelligence Reframed. Multiple Intelligences for the 21st Century*. New York: Basic Books.

Gardner, H. (2007) *Five Minds for the Future*. Boston, MA: Harvard Business School.

Harrison, C., and Howard, S. (2008) *Inside the Primary Black Box*. UK: GL Assessment.

Howard, S. (2006) *Let's Speak Out*. 3rd edition. S E H Associates DE738DG Derbyshire

Maslow, A. H. (1987) *Motivation and Personality*. New York and Cambridge, MA: Harper and Collins.

Palaiologou, I. (2008) *Childhood Observation, Achieving EYPS*. Exeter: Learning Matters.

Pennington, D. (ed.) (2002) *Introducing Psychology. Approaches, topics and methods*. London: Hodder & Stoughton.

Piaget, J. (1950) *The Psychology of Intelligence*. (First published in French, 1947; first English translation, 1950.) London: Routledge Classics Edition, 2001.

Robertson, A. (2005) *Let's Think! Early Years Developing Thinking with Four- and Five-Year-Olds*. London: GL Assessment.

Rogers,C.R. (1970) 'Towards a theory of creativity', in P.E. Vernon (ed.) *Creativity*. Harmondsworth: Penguin.

Siraj-Blatchford, I., Sylva, K., Muttock, S., Gilden, R. and Bell, D. (2004) *Researching Effective Pedagogy in the Early Years (EPPE)*. Research Report 356. London: DfES/ The Stationery Office.

Shayer, M., and Adey, P. (2002) *Learning Intelligence: Cognitive Acceleration Across the Curriculum 5 to 15 years*. Milton Keynes: Open University Press.

Vygotsky, L.S. (1978) *Mind in Society. The Development of Higher Psychological Processes*. Cambridge, MA: Harvard University Press.

Chapter 4   Assessment in the Early Years Foundation Stage

Carr, M. (1998) *Assessing Children's Learning in Early Childhood Settings: A Development Programme for Discussion and Reflection*. Wellington: New Zealand Council for Educational Research.

Carr, M. (1999) *Learning and Teaching Stories: New Approaches to Assessment and Evaluation*. www.aare.edu.au/99pap/pod99298.htm (accessed December 2007).

Carr, M. (2001) *Assessment in Early Childhood Settings*. London: Paul Chapman Publishing.

Clark, A. and Moss, P. (2001) *Listening to Young Children: The Mosaic Approach*. London: National Children's Bureau.

DCSF (Department for Children, Schools and Families) (2008) *The Early Years Foundation Stage: Setting the Standards for Learning, Development and Care for Children from Birth to Five*, Nottingham: DCSF Publications. (Comprises the *Statutory Framework, Practice Guidance*, Cards and other resources.)

Draper, L. and Duffy, B. (2001) 'Working with parents', in G. Pugh (ed.), *Contemporary Issues in Early Years: Working Collaboratively for Children,* 3rd edn. London: Paul Chapman Publishing.

Driscoll, V. and Rudge, C. (2005) 'Channels for listening to young children and parents', in A. Clark, A.T. Kjorholt and P. Moss (eds), *Beyond Listening*. Bristol: The Policy Press. pp. 91–110.

Drummond, M.J. (2003) *Assessing Children's Learning*, 2nd edn. London: David Fulton.

Elfer, P. (2005) 'Observation matters', in L. Abbott and A. Langston (eds), *Birth-to-Three-Matters*. Maidenhead: Open University Press.

Laevers, F. (ed.) (2005) *Well-Being and Involvement in Care Settings: A Process-Oriented Evaluation Instrument* Brussels: Kind and Gezint/Research Centre for Experiential Education.

McClennan, D. and Katz, L. (1992) 'Young children's social development: a checklist adapted from assessing the social development of young children: a checklist of social attitudes', *Dimensions of Early Childhood*, pp. 9–10.

Palaiologou, I. (2008) *Achieving EYPS: Childhood Observations*. Exeter: Learning Matters.

QCA (Qualifications and Curriculum Authority) (2008) *Profile Handbook for the Early Years Foundation Stage*. London: QCA.

Rinaldi, C. (2005) 'Documentation and assessment: what is the relationship?', in A. Clark, P. Moss and A.T. Kjorholt (eds), *Beyond Listening to Children: Children's Perspectives on Early Childhood Services*. Bristol: The Policy Press. pp. 17–28.

Smidt, S. (2005) *Observing, Assessing and Planning for Children in the Early Years*. London: Routledge.

Chapter 5   Using Learning Stories in the Early Years Foundation Stage

Anning, A. and Edwards, A. (2006) 2nd edn. *Promoting Children's Learning from Birth to Five*. Milton Keynes: Open University Press.

Anning, A., Cullen, J. and Fleer, M. (eds) (2004) *Early Childhood Education*. London: Sage.

Baczala, K. (2003) *Guidance on Gifted and Talented (Very Able) Children in Foundation Stage*. Medway: Medway Council.

Bennett, N., Wood, L. and Rogers, S. (1997) *Teaching and Learning Through Play*. Buckingham:Open University Press.

Broadhead, P. (2001) 'Investigating sociability and cooperation in four and five year olds in reception class settings,' *International Journal of Early Years Education,* 9 (1): 23–35.

Bruner, J. (1960) *The Process of Education*. Cambridge, MA: Harvard University Press.

Bruner, J.S. (1983) 'Child's talk: learning to use language', cited in S. Smidt (2006) *The Developing Child in the 21st Century*. London: Routledge.

Carr, M. (2001) *Assessment in Early Childhood Settings: Learning Stories*. London: Paul Chapman Publishing.

CCEA (Council for the Curriculum, Examinations and Assessment), NES (NES Arnold) and BELB (Belfast Education and Library Board) (2002) *Enriched Curriculum: The Beginning*. Belfast: CCEA.

Clark, B. (1997) *Growing Up Gifted*. New York: Macmillan.

Clark, B. (2007) 'Understanding Intelligence and the Gifted Brain'. Paper presented at the 17th Biennial Conference of the World Council for Gifted and Talented Children, University of Warwick.

Coates, D., Thompson, W. and Shimmin, A. (2008) 'Using learning journeys to develop a challenging curriculum for gifted children in nursery (kindergarten) settings', *Gifted and Talented International,* 23 (1): 94–101.

DCSF (Department for Children, Schools and Families) (2008) *The Early Years Foundation Stage: Setting the Standards for Learning Development and Care for Children from Birth to Five*. Nottingham: DCSF Publications. (Comprises the *Statutory Framework*, *Practice Guidance*, Cards and other resources.)

DfES (Department for Education and Skills) (2002) *Schools Achieving Success*. www.dfes. gov.uk/achievingsuccess (accessed 4 February 2008).

DfES (Department for Education and Skills) (2006a) GTEU Early Years Bulletin, February 2006, Issue 1. www.learningwithsouthglos.org/GiftedandTalented/acrobat/ misc/EYsGT Bull206.pdf (accessed 5 November 2008).

DfES (Department for Education and Skills) (2006b) *Improving Outcomes for Children in the Foundation Stage in Maintained Schools*. Nottingham: DfES Publications.

Eyre, D. (1997) *Able Children in Ordinary Schools*. London: David Fulton.

Eyre, D. (2007) *What Really Works in Gifted and Talented Education*. www.brightonline. org.uk/what_really_works.pdf (accessed 7 November 2008).

Howard, J. (2002) 'Eliciting children's perceptions of play using the Activity Apperception Story Procedure', *Early Child Development and Care*, 172 (5): 489–502.

Howard, J., Jenvey, V. and Hill, C. (2006) 'Children's categorisation of play and learning based on social context', *Early Child Development and Care*, 176 (3&4): 379–93.

Leyden, S. (1998) *Supporting the Child of Exceptional Ability*. London: David Fulton.

Members of the British Educational Research Association Early Years Special Interest Group (2003) *Early Years Research: Pedagogy, Curriculum and Adult Roles, Training and Professionalism*. www.bera.ac.uk/pdfs/BERAEarlyYearsReview31May03.pdf (accessed 4 February 2008).

Moss, P. (2004) *Dedicated to Loris Malaguzzi, The Town of Reggio Emilia and its Schools*. www.sightlines-initiative.com/fileadmin/users/files/ReFocus/library/articles/PDFs/town ofrepmoss.pdf (accessed 4 February 2008).

Moyles, J. (1989) *Just Playing: The Role and Status of Play in Early Childhood Education*. Milton Keynes: Open University Press.

Moyles, J. (ed.) (2005) *The Excellence of Play*. Miadenhead: Open University Press.

Porter, L. (1999) *Gifted Young Children*. Buckingham: Open University Press.

QCA/DfEE (Qualifications and Curriculam Authority/Department for Education and Employment) (2000) *Curriculum Guidance for the Foundation Stage,* London: QCA.

Rich, D. (2002) 'Catching children's stories', *Early Education* 36.

Seifert, K.L. (2006) 'The cognitive development and the education of young children', in B. Spodek and O.N. Sarecho (ed.), *Handbook of Research On the Education of Young Children*. Hillsdale, NJ: Lawrence Erlbaum Associates.

Siraj-Blatchford, I. and Sylva, K. (2004) *The Effective Pedagogy in the Early Years Project: A Confidential Report to the DfES*. London: London University Institute of Education.

Smidt, S. (2006) *The Developing Child in the 21st Century*. London: Routledge.

Smutny, J.F. (2001) 'Teaching young gifted children in the regular classroom'. *ERIC Digest* www.ericdigests.org/2001-2/gifted.html (accessed 7 November 2007).

Vygotsky, L.S. (1978) *Mind in Society: The Development of Higher Psychological Processes*. Cambridge, MA: Harvard University Press.

Walsh, G., Sproule, L., McGuinness, C., Trew, K., Rafferty, H. and Sheehy, N. (2006) An appropriate curriculum for 4–5-year-old children in Northern Ireland: comparing play-based and formal approaches. *Early Years*, 26 (2): 201–21.

Westcott, M. and Howard, J. (2007) 'Creating a playful environment: evaluating young children's perceptions of their daily classroom activities using the Activity Apperception Story Procedure', *The Psychology of Education Review*, 31 (1): 27–33.

Wiltz, N. and Klein, E. (2001) 'What do you care? Children's perceptions of high and low quality classrooms', *Early Childhood Research Quarterly*, 16 (2001): 2009–236.

Wood, E. and Attfield, J. (1996) 'Play, learning and the early childhood curriculum', cited in N. Yelland (ed) (2005) *Critical Issues in Early Childhood Education*, Maidenhead: Open University Press.

Wood, E. and Bennett, N. (2000) 'Changing theories, changing practice: early childhood teachers' professional learning', *Teaching and Teacher Education*, 16 (5): 635–47.

Chapter 6   Working in Partnership

Afrey, C. (ed.) (2003) *Understanding Children's Learning*. London: David Fulton.

CWDC (Children's Workforce Development Council) (2007) *Early Years Professional Standards*. Available at www.cwdcounci.org.uk/assets/0000/0612/EYPS_Guidance_to Standards_Jan07.pdf (accessed 6 June 2008).

DCSF (Department for Children, Schools and Families) (2008) *The Early Years Foundation Stage: Setting the Standards for Learning, Development and Care for Children from Birth to Five*. Nottingham: DCSF Publications. (Comprises the *Statutory Framework*, *Practice Guidance*, Cards and other resources.)

DfES (Department for Education and Skills) (2003) *Every Child Matters*. Nottingham: DfES Publications.

DfES (Department for Education and Skills) (2005) *Common Core of Skills and Knowledge for the Children's Workforce*. London: DfES.

Fitzgerald, D. and Kay, J. (2008) *Working Together in Children's Services*. London: Routledge.

Freire, P. (1972) *Cultural Actions for Freedom*. Harmondsworth: Penguin.

Miller, L. and Cable, C. (eds) (2008) *Professionalism in the Early Years*. London: Hodder Education.

NCDS (1958) National Child Development Study. Available at www.ioe.ac.uk/eppe (accessed 9 June 2008).

QCA/DfEE (Qualifications and Curriculum Authority/Department for Education and Employment) (2000) *Curriculum Guidance for the Foundation Stage*. London: QCA.

Ryan, S. and Brofenbrenner, U. (eds) (1974) *A Report on Longitudinal Evaluations of Preschool Programs, Vols 1 and 2: Longitudinal Evaluations and Is Early Intervention Effective?* Washington, DC: US Department of Health, Education and Welfare.

Sylva, K., Melhuish, E., Sammons, P., Siraj-Blatchford, I., Taggart, B. and Elliot, K. (2003) *The Effective Provision of Pre-school Education (EPPE) Project: Findings from the Pre-school Period; Summary of Findings*. London: Institute of Education/Sure Start.

Training and Development Agency (2008) *QTS Standards Guidance*. Available at www.tda. gov.uk/partners/ittstandards/guidance08/qts.aspx (accessed 3 June 2008).

Vygotsky, L. (1978) *Mind in Society: The Development of Higher Psychological Processes*. Cambridge, MA: Harvard University Press.

Chapter 7   Effective Transitions into and out of the Early Years Foundation Stage

Bowlby, J. (1969) *Attachment and Loss. Volume 2: Separation and Anxiety and Anger*. New York: Basic Books.

Bronfenbrenner, U. (1979) *The Ecology of Human Development*. Cambridge, MA: Harvard University Press.

Brooker, L. (2008) *Supporting Transitions in the Early Years*. Maidenhead: Open University Press.

DCSF (Department for Children, Schools and Families) (2008) *The Early Years Foundation Stage: Setting the Standards for Learning, Development and Care for Children from Birth to Five*. Nottingham: DCSF Publications. (Comprises the *Statutory Framework, Practice Guidance*, Cards and other resources.)

Dunlop, A. W. and Fabian, H. (eds) (2007) *Informing Transitions in the Early Years: Research, Policy and Practice*. Maidenhead: Open University Press.

Vondra, J.I. and Barnett, D. (1999) 'Atypical attachment in infancy and early childhood among children at developmental risk', in *Monographs of the Society for Research in Child Development*, 64 (Series No. 258).

Chapter 8   Meeting EYFS Outcomes outside of the Early Years setting

CWDC (Children's Workforce and Development Council) (2006) *Early Years Professional National Standards*. Available at www.cwdcouncil.org.uk resources/ handbooks (accessed 2 June 2009).

DCSF (Department for Children, Schools and Families) (2007) *The Children's Plan: Building Brighter Futures*. Norwich: HMSO.

DCSF (Department for Children, Schools and Families) (2008) *The Early Years Foundation Stage: Setting the Standards for Learning, Development and Care for Children from Birth to Five*. Nottingham: DCSF Publications. (Comprises the *Statutory Framework, Practice Guidance*, Cards and other resources.)

DfES (Department for Education and Skills) (2005) *The Common Core of Skills and Knowledge*. Nottingham: DfES Publications.

Katz, L.G. (1998) 'Introduction: What is basic for young children' in S. Smidt (ed.), *The Early Years: A Reader*. London: Routledge. Also in S. Smidt (2006) *The Developing Child in the 21st Century*. London: Routledge.

Loveless, A. (2005) 'Thinking about creativity: developing ideas, making things happen'. Chapter 2 in A. Wilson (ed.), *Creativity in Primary Education*. Exeter: Learning Matters.

MLA (Museums, Libraries and Archives Council) www.mla.gov.uk (accessed 26 May 2008).

QCA (Qualifications and Curriculum Authority) www.qca.org.uk (accessed 3 June 2008).

Riley, J. (2007) *Learning in the Early Years*, 2nd edn. London: Sage.

Runco, M. (2006) 'The development of children's creativity', in B. Spodek and O.N. Saracho (eds), *Handbook of Research on the Education of Young Children* Hillsdale, NJ: Lawrence Erlbaum Associates. pp. 121–31.

Salaman, A. and Tutchell, S. (2005) *Planning for Educational Visits for the Early Years*. London: Paul Chapman Publishing.

Siraj-Blatchford, I., Sylva, K., Muttocks, S., Gilden, R. and Bell, D. (2002) *Researching Effective Pedagogy in the Early Years*. DfES Research Brief N. 356. London: DfES.

Smidt, S. (2005) *Observing, Assessing and Planning for Children in the Early Years*. London: Routledge.

Smidt, S. (2006) *The Developing Child in the 21st Century*. London: Routledge.

Sylva, K., Melhuish, E., Sammons, P., Siraj-Blatchford, I., Taggart, B. and Elliott, K. (2003) *The Effective Provision of Pre-School Education (EPPE) Project: Findings from the Pre-School Period*. Research Brief No. RBX15-03. London: Department for Education and Skills. Available at www.ioe.ac.uk/projects/eppe (accessed 24 June 2008).

TDA (Training and Development Agency) Qualified Teacher Standards and ITT Requirements. Available at www.tda.gov.uk (accessed 26 May 2008).

TRS (Teaching Resource Site) www.teachernet.gov.uk (accessed 3 June 2008).

UNCRC (1992) UK Ratification of the Convention on the Rights of the Child. Available at www.direct.gov.uk/en/Parents/ParentsRights/DG_4003313 (accessed 18 June 2008).

Walsh, G. and Gardner, J. (2005) 'Assessing the quality of early years learning environments', *Early Childhood Research and Practice,* 7 (1). http://ecrp.uiuc.edu/v7n1/walsh.html (accessed 2 June 2009).

Zwozdiak-Myers, P. (ed.) (2007) *Childhood and Youth Studies*. Exeter: Learning Matters.

www.artscouncil.org.uk

www.farmsforschools.org.uk

www.inspiringlearningforall.gov.uk

www.kew.org

www.nationalparks.gov.uk

Chapter 9   Personal, Social and Emotional Development

Ainsworth, M.D.S. (1969) 'Object relations, dependency, and attachment: a theoretical review of the infant–mother relationship'. *Child Development*, 40: 969–1025.

Ainsworth, M.D.S. (1979) 'Attachment as related to mother–infant interaction', *Advances in the Study of Behaviour*, 9: 2–52.

Ainsworth, M.D.S. (1985) 'Attachments across the life span', *Bulletin of the New York Academy of Medicine*, 61: 792–812.

Ainsworth, M.D.S. (1989) 'Attachment beyond infancy', *American Psychologist*, 44: 709–16.

Ainsworth, M.D.S. and Bell, S.M. (1970) 'Attachment, exploration, and separation: iIllustrated by the behaviour of one-year-olds in a strange situation', *Child Development*, 41: 49–67.

Ainsworth, M.D.S. and Bowlby, J. (1991) 'An ethological approach to personality development', *American Psychologist*, 46: 333–41.

Ainsworth, M.D.S., Bell, S.M. and Stayton, D.J. (1971a) 'Individual differences in the strange situation behaviour of one-year-olds', in H.R. Schaffer (ed.), *The Origins of Human Social Relations*. New York: Academic Press. pp. 15–71.

Ainsworth, M.D.S., Bell, S.M., Blehar, M.C. and Main, M. (1971b) 'Physical contact: a study of infant responsiveness and its relation to maternal handling'. Paper presented at the biennial meeting of the Society for Research in Child Development, Minneapolis, MN.

Ainsworth, M.D.S., Blehar, M.C., Waters, E. and Wall, S. (1978) *Patterns of Attachment: A Study of the Strange Situation*. Hillsdale, NJ: Erlbaum Associates.

Barnes, K.E. (1971) 'Preschool play norms: a replication', *Developmental Psychology*, 5: 99–103.

Bell, S.M. and Ainsworth, M.D.S. (1972) 'Infant crying and maternal responsiveness', *Child Development*, 43: 1171–90.

Black, B. and Logan, A. (1995) 'Links between communication patterns in mother child, father child, and child peer interactions and children's social status', in *Child Development*, 66: 951–65.

Bowlby, J. (1951) *Child Care and the Growth of Love*. Harmondsworth: Penguin.

Bowlby, J. (1960) 'Grief and mourning in infancy and early childhood', *The Psychoanalytic Study of the Child*, 15: 9–52.

Bowlby, J. (1969) *Attachment. Attachment and Loss*, Vol. I. London: Hogarth.

Bowlby, J. (1973) *Separation: Anxiety and Anger. Attachment and Loss*, Vol. 2. (International Psycho-analytical Library No. 95). London: Hogarth Press.

Bowlby, J. (1980) *Loss: Sadness and Depression. Attachment and Loss*, Vol. 3. (International Psycho-analytical Library No. 109). London: Hogarth Press.

Bowlby, J. (1986) 'Citation Classic: Maternal Care and Mental Health', Available at www.garfield.library.upenn.edu/classics1986/A1986F063100001.pdf (accessed November 2008).

Bowlby, J. (2005) *The Making and Breaking of Affectional Bonds*. London: Routledge Classics.

Damon, W. (1988) *The Moral Child*. New York: Free Press.

De Vries, L.M. (1969) 'Social identity and development', in E.M. Hetherington (ed.), *Handbook of Child Psychology*, Vol. 4: *Socialisation, Personality, and Social Development*, 4th edn. New York: Wiley. pp. 693–744.

DeRosier, M.E., Gillessen, A.H., Coie, J.D. and Dodge, K.A. (1994) 'Group social context and children's aggressive behavior', *Child Development*, 65: 1068–80.

Dunn, J. (1993) *Young Children's Close Relationships: Beyond Attachment*. London: Sage.

Elfer, P., Goldschmied, E. and Selleck, D. (2002) *Key Persons in Nurseries, Building Relationships for Quality Provision*. London: National Early Years Network.

Howes, C. (1990) 'Can the age of entry into child care and the quality of child care predict adjustment in kindergarten?', *Developmental Psychology* 26: 292–303.

Howes, C. (1992) *The Collaborative Construction of Pretend*. Albany, NY: SUNY Press.

Howes, C. and Matherson, C.C. (1992) 'Sequences in the development of competent play with peers: social and social pretended play', *Developmental Psychology*, 28: 961–74.

Hymel, S. (1983) 'Preschool children's peer relations: issues in sociometric assessment', *Merrill-Palmer Quarterly* 19: 237–60.

Hymel, S., Rubin, K., Rowden, L. and LeMare, L. (1990) 'Children's peer relationships: Longiditudinal prediction of internalizing and externalizing problems from middle to late childhood', *Child Development*, 61: 2004–21.

Nikolopoulou, A. (1993) 'Play, cognitive development, and the social world: Piaget, Vygotsky and beyond', *Human Development*, 36: 1–23.

Piaget, J.J. (1951) *Play, dreams and imitation in Childhood*. London: Routledge and Kegan Paul.

Rubin, K.H. (1982) 'Non social play in preschoolers: necessarily evil?', *Child Development*, 53: 651–7.

Rubin, K.H., Fein, G.G. and Vendenberg, B. (1983) 'Play', in E.M. Hetherington (ed.), *Handbook of Child Psychology*, Vol. 4: *Socialisation, Personality, and Social Development*, 4th edn. New York: Wiley. pp. 693–744.

Selleck, D. (2001) Attachment and the key person. Paper in http://209.85.229.132/search?q=cache: 445ZfJLdxsUJ:www.standards.dcsf.gov.uk/eyfsresources/downloads/p0000199. pdf+Selleck+2001&cd=1&hl=en&ct=clnk&gl=uk (accessed November 2008).

Singer, J.L. and Singer, D.C. (1990) *The House of Make Believe*. Cambridge, MA: Harvard University Press.

Smith, P.K. (1997) *Play Fighting and Fighting: How Do They Relate?* Lisbon: ICCP.

Sylva, K., Melhuish, E., Sammons, P., Siraj-Blatchford, I., Taggart, B. and Elliot, K. (2003) *The Effective Provision of Pre-school Education (EPPE) Project: Findings from the Pre-school Period; Summary of Findings*. London: Institute of Education/Sure Start.

Vygotsky, L. (1986) *Thought and Language*. London: The MIT Press.

Winnicot, D.W. (1986) *Holding and Interpretation: Fragment of an Analysis*. New York: Hogarth Press.

Winnicot, D.W. (1987) *The Child, the Family, and the Outside World*. New York: Addison-Wesley.

Winnicot, D.W. (1995) *Maturational Processes and the Facilitating Environment: Studies in the Theory of Emotional Development*. New York: Stylus.

Winnicot, D.W. (2005) *Playing and Reality*. London: Routledge.

Chapter 10   Communication, Language and Literacy

Adams, M.J. (1990) *Beginning to Read: Thinking and Learning about Print*. Cambridge, MA: MIT Press.

Athey, C. (1990) *Extending thought in Young Children*. London: Paul Chapman Publishing.

Bjorklund, D.F. (1995) *Chidren's Thinking: Developmental Functions and Individual Differences*. Pacific Grove, CA: Brooks/Cole.

Bloom, L. (1993) *The Transformation from Infancy to Language: Acquiring the Power of Expression*. Cambridge: Cambridge University Press.

Bloom, L., Lifter, K. and Broughton, J. (1985) 'The convergence of early cognition and language in the second year of life: problems in conceptualization and measurement', in M. Barret (ed.), *Children's Single-Word Speech*. New York: John Wiley.

Brown, R. (1987) *A First Language: The Early Stages*. Cambridge: MA: Harvard University Press.

Bruner, J. (1983) *Child's Talk: Learning to Use Language*. Oxford: Oxford University Press.

Clay, M. (1975) *What Did I Write?* London: Heinemann Educational Books.

Chomsky, N. (1957) *Syntactic Structures*. The Hague: Mouton.

Chomsky, N. (1959) 'Review of B.F. Skinner's *Verbal Behaviour*', *Language,* 35: 26–129.

Chomsky, N. (1976) *Reflections on Language*. London: Temple Smith.

Comber, B. and Cormack, P. (1997) 'Looking beyond "skills" and "processes": literacy as social and cultural practices in classrooms', *Reading*, 31 (1): 22–9.

Cooper, R.P. and Aslin, R.N. (1994) 'Developmental differences in infant attention to the spectical properties of infant directed speech', *Child Development*, 65: 1663–7.

Fernald, A. (1993) 'Approval and disapproval: infant responsiveness to vocal affect in familiar and unfamiliar languages', *Child Development*, 64: 637–56.

Fernald, A. and Simon, T. (1984) 'Expanded imitation contours in mother's speech to newborns', *Developmental Psychology*, 20: 104–13.

Ferreiro, E. and Teberosky, A. (1983) *Literacy Begins before Schooling*. London: Heinemann Educational Books.

Flavell, J.H. (1999) 'Cognitive development: children's knowledge about the mind'. *Annual Review of Psychology*, 50: 21–45.

Gardon, A.F. (1992) *Social Interaction and the Development of Language and Cognition*. Hove: Lawrence Erlbaum Associates.

Garton, A. and Pratt, C. (1998) *Learning to be Literate: The Development of Spoken and Written Language,* 2nd edn. Oxford: Blackwell.

Gelmen, S.A. and Williams, E.M. (1997) 'Enabling constraints for cognitive development and learning: domain-specificity and epigenesis', in D.D. Kuhn and R.S. Siegler (eds), *Cognition, Perception and Language*. Volume 2. New York: John Wiley. pp. 396–414.

Goodman, V.E. (1994) *Reading Is More than Phonics: A Parent's Guide for Reading with Beginning or Discouraged Readers*. Calgary, Alberta: Reading Wings.

Goodman, Y. (1980) 'The roots of literacy', in M.P. Douglas (ed.), *Reading: A Humanising Experience*. Claremont: Claremont Graduate School. pp. 42–68.

Hall, N. (1999) 'Play, literacy and the role of teacher', in J.R. Moyles (ed.), *The Excellence of Play*, Buckingham: Open University Press.

Hall, N. (2000) 'Play, literacy and the role of teacher', in J.R. Moyles (ed.), *The Excellence of play*. 2nd edn. Buckingham: Open University Press.

Hall, N. (1991) 'Play and the emergence of literacy', in J. Christie (ed.), *Play and Early Literacy Development*. New York: State University of New York Press.

Harste, J., Woodward, V.A. and Burke, C.L. (1984) *Language Stories and Literacy Lessons*. Portsmouth, NH: Heinemann Educational Books.

Heath, S.B. (1983) *Ways with Words*. Cambridge: Cambridge University Press.

Hillerich, R. (1976) 'Towards an assessable definition of literacy', *English Journal*, Feb: 50–5.

Holdaway, D. (1979) *The Foundations of Literacy*. Portsmouth, NH: Heineman Educational Books.

Luquet, G.H. (1959) *Le Dessin enfantin*, 2nd edn. Paris: Alcan.

Martinez, M. and Teale, W. (1988) 'Reading in a kindergarten classroom library', *The Reading Teacher*, 41: 568–72.

Minns, H. (1997) *Read It to Me Now! Learning at Home and at School*. Philadelphia: Open University Press.

Morrow, L.M. (1992) *Family Literacy: Connections in Schools and Communities*. Newark, DE: International Reading Association.

Neuman, S.B. (1992) 'Is learning from media distinctive? Examining children's inferencing strategies', *American Educational Research Journal*, 29 (1): 119–40.

Neuman, S.B. (1996) 'Children engaging in storybook reading: the influence of access to print resources: opportunities, and parental interaction', *Early Childhood Research Quarterly*, 11: 495–513.

Neuman, S.B. (1997) 'Guiding young children's participation in early literacy development: a family literacy programme for adolescent mothers', *Early Child Development and Care*, 32: 127–8.

Neuman, S.B. (1999) 'Books make a difference: a study of access to literacy', *Reading Research Quarterly*, 34 (3): 286–311.

Neuman, S.B. and Roskos, K. (1990a) 'Peers as literacy informants: a description of young children's literacy conversations in play'. Paper presented in IRA, supplied by the EDS/MFO1.

Neuman, S.B. and Roskos, K. (1990b) 'Play, print and purpose: enriching play environments for literacy development', *The Reading Teacher*, 44: 214–21.

Neuman, S.B. and Roskos, K. (1992) 'Literacy objects as cultural tools: effects on children's literacy development in play', *Reading Research Quarterly*, 27: 203–25.

Neuman, S.B. and Roskos, K. (1993) 'Descriptive observations of adult's facilitation of literacy in young children's play', *Early Childhood Research Quarterly*, 8: 77–97.

Neuman, S.B. and Roskos, K. (1994) 'Of scribbles, schemas, and storybooks: using literacy albums to document young children's literacy growth', *Young Children*, 49: 78–85.

Neuman, S.B. and Roskos, K. (1997) 'Literacy knowledge in practice: contexts of participation for young writers and readers', *Reading Research Quarterly*, 32 (1): 10–32.

Neuman, S.B. and Roskos, K. (1998) *Children Achieving: Best Practices in Early Literacy*. Newark, DE: International Reading Association.

Nutbrown, C. (2008) *Threads of Thinking: Young Children Learning and the Role of Early Education*, 2nd edn. London: Paul Chapman Publishing.

Piaget, J. (1952) *The Origins of Intelligence in Children*. New York: International Universities.

Piaget, J.J. (1948) *The Language and Thought of the Child*. London: Routledge and Kegan Paul.

Piaget, J.J. (1962) *Play, Dreams and Imitation in Childhood*. London: Routledge and Kegan Paul.

Piaget, J.J. and Inhelder, B. (1966) *La Psychologie de l'enfant*. Paris: Universitaires de France.

Sampson, M.R., Van Allen, R. and Sampson, M.B. (1991) *Pathways to Literacy: A Meaning-Centred Perspective*. London: Holt, Rinehart and Winston.

Searfoss, L. and Readence, J. (1994) *Helping Children to Read*. Boston, MA: Allyn & Bacon.

Shatz, M. and Gelman, R. (1973) 'The development of communication skills: modification in the speech of young children as a function of listener', *Monographs of Society for Research in Child Development*, 38 (5 Serial No. 152).

Sinclair-de-Zwart, H. (1967) *Acquisition du langage et developpement de la pensée*. Paris: Dunod.

Snow, C.E. (1972) 'Mother's speech to children learning language', *Child Development*, 43: 549–65.

Snow, C.E. (1983) 'Literacy and language: relationships during the pre-school years', *Harvard Educational Review*, 53 (2): 165–89.

Sulzby, E. (1985) 'Kindergarteners as writers and readers', in M. Farr (ed.), *Children's Early Writing Development*. Norwood, NJ: Ablex. pp. 82–126.

Sulzby, E. (1989) 'Forms of writing and rereading example list', in J. Mason (ed.), *Reading and Writing Connections*. Boston, MA: Allyn & Bacon. pp. 51–63.

Sulzby, E. (1992) 'Research directions: transitions from emergent to conventional writing', *Language Arts*, 69: 290–7.

Sulzby, E. and Teale, W.H. (1991) 'Emergent literacy', in R. Barr, M.L. Kamil, P. Mosenthal and D. Pearson (eds), *Handbook of Reading Research*, *vol. 2*. White Plains, NY: Longman. pp. 727–58.

Teale, W.H. (1986) 'Home background and young children's literacy development', in W.H. Teale and E. Sulzby (eds), *Emergent Literacy: Writing and Reading*. Norwood, NJ: Ablex. pp. 173–206.

Teale, W.H. and Sulzby, E. (1989) 'Literacy acquisition in early childhood: the roles of access and accommodation in storybook reading', in D.A. Wagner (ed.), *The Future of Literacy in a Changing World*. Oxford: Pergamon. pp. 111–30.

Voizot, B. (1975) *Le Developpement de l'intelligence chez l'enfant*. Paris: Armand Colin.

Vygotsky, L. (1962) *Thought and Language*. Cambridge, MA: MIT Press.

Vygotsky, L. (1978) *Mind and Society: The Development of Higher Mental Processes*. Cambridge, MA: Harvard University Press.

Vygotsky, L. (1986) *Thought and Language*. Cambridge, MA: MIT Press.

Wells, C.G. (1981) *Learning through Interaction: The Study of Language Development*. Cambridge: Cambridge University Press.

Wells, C.G. (1985) *Language Development in Pre-School Years*. Cambridge: Cambridge University Press.

Wells, C.G. (1986) *The Meaning-Makers: Children Learning Language and Using Language to Learn*. Portsmouth, NH: Heinemann Educational.

Whitehurst, G. (1998) 'Relative efficacy of parent and teacher involvement in a shared-reading intervention for pre-school children from low income backgrounds', *Early Childhood Research Quarterly*, 13 (2): 263–90.

Wolf, A.S. and Heath, S.B. (1992) *The Braid of Literature: Children's Words of Reading*, London: Harvard University Press.

Chapter 11   Problem Solving, Reasoning and Numeracy

Aubrey, C. (1993) 'An investigation of the mathematical knowledge and competencies which young children bring into school', *British Educational Research Journal*, 19 (1): 27–41.

Booth, A. and Dunn, J. (1996) *Family–School Links: How Do They Affect Educational Outcomes?* Philadelphia: Lawrence Erlbaum Associates.

Clements, D.H., Sarama, J. and DiBiase, A. (2004) *Engaging Young Children in Mathematics*. Philadelphia: Lawrence Erlbaum Associates.

Cooke, H. (2007) *Mathematics for Primary and Early Years: Developing Subject Knowledge*, 2nd edn. London: Sage.

Davis, R.B. (1984) *Learning Mathematics: The Cognitive Science Approach to Mathematical Education*. Norwood, NJ: Greenwood.

Department for Children, Schools and Families (DCSF) (2008) *Early Years Foundation Stage: Setting the Standards for Learning Development and Care for Children from Birth to Five*. Nottingham: DCSF Publications. (Comprises the *Statutory Framework, Practice Guidance*, Cards and other resources.)

Devlin, K.J. (2000) *The Language of Mathematics*. New York: Henry Holt.

Dewey, J. (1938) *Logic: the theory of enquiry*, New York: Henry Holt.

Dickinson, D.K. and Tabors, P.O. (1991) 'Early literacy: linkages between home, school and literacy achievement at age five', *Journal of Research in Childhood Education*, 6 (1): 30–46.

Downs, S. (1998) 'Technological change and education and training', *Education and Training*, 40 (1): 18–19.

Griffiths, N. (1998) *Story Sacks* Video. Bury: Story Sacks Ltd.

Hiebert, H., Carpenter, T.P., Fennema, E., Fuson, K., Human, P., Murray, H., Olivier, A. and Wearne, D. (1996) 'Problem solving as a basis for reform in curriculum and instruction: the case of mathematics', *Educational Researcher*, 25 (4): 12–21.

Jones, L. (1998) 'Home and school numeracy experiences for young Somali pupils in Britain', *European Early Childhood Education Research Journal*, 6 (1): 63–72.

Mathematical Association (1955) *The Teaching of Mathematics in Primary Schools*. London: Mathematical Association.

Munn, P. (1996a) 'Progression in literacy and numeracy in preschool', in M. Hughes (ed.), *Progression in Learning*. Bristol: Multilingual Matters.

Munn, P. (1996b) 'Assessment of literacy and numeracy acquired before school', in R. Duggan and C.J. Pole (eds), *Reshaping Education in the 1990s: Perspectives on Primary Schooling*. London: Routledge.

Nunes, T. and Bryant, P. (1996) *Children Doing Mathematics*. London: Blackwell.

Price, S., Rogers, Y., Scaife, M., Stanton, D. and Neale, H. (2003) 'Using tangibles to promote novel forms of playful learning', *Interacting with Computers*, 15: 169–85.

Resnick, L.B. (1989) 'Developing mathematical knowledge', *American Psychologist*, 44 (2): 162–9.

Schaeffer, B., Eggleston V.H. and Scott, J.L. (1974) 'Number development in young children', *Cognitive Development*, 5: 357–9.

Schoenfeld, A.H. (1992) 'Learning to think mathematically: problem solving, metacognition, and sense-making in mathematics', in *Handbook for Research on Mathematics Teaching and Learning*. New York: Macmillan.

Schroeder, H.E. (1991) *New Directions in Health Psychology*. Oxford: Taylor & Francis.

Siraj-Blatchford, I., Sylva, K., Muttock, S., Gilden, R. and Bell, D. (2002) *Researching Effective Pedagogy in Early Years*. London: HMSO.

Skemp, R.R. (1989) *Mathematics in the Primary School*. London: Routledge.

Staub, E. (1971) 'The use of role playing and induction in children's learning of helping and sharing behaviour', *Child Development*, 42 (3): 805–16.

Taylor, S.I., Morris, V.G. and Rogers, C.S. (1997) 'Toy safety and selection', *Early Childhood Education Journal*, 24 (4): 235–8.

Vygotsky, I. (1978) *Mind in Society: The Development of Higher Psychological Processes*. Cambridge, MA: Harvard University Press.

Wood, E. and Attfield, J. (2005) *Play, Learning and the Early Childhood Curriculum*. London: Sage.

Worthington, M. and Carruthers, E. (2003) *Children's Mathematics: Making Marks, Making Meaning*. London: Sage.

Chapter 12   Knowledge and Understanding of the World

Barlex, D. (2004) 'Creative design and technology', in R. Fisher and M. Williams (eds), *Unlocking Creativity: Teaching Across the Curriculum*. London: David Fulton.

Barnes, J. (2007) *Cross-curricular Learning 3–14*. London: Paul Chapman Publishing.

Barnes, J. and Shirley, I. (2007) 'Strangely familiar: cross-curricular and creative thinking in teacher education' *Improving Schools* 10 (2): 162–79.

Beauchamp, G. (2006) 'New technologies and "New teaching": a process of evolution?', in R. Webb (ed.), *Changing Teaching and Learning in the Primary School*. Maidenhead: Open University Press. pp. 81–91.

Beauchamp, G. and Kennewell, S. (2008) 'The influence of ICT on the interactivity of teaching', *Education and Information Technologies*, 13 (4): 305–15.

Cooper, H. (2002) *History in the Early Years,* 2nd edn. London: Routledge Falmer.

Davies, D. (2003) 'Introduction', in D. Davies and A. Howe (eds), *Teaching Science and Design and Technology in the Early Years*. London: David Fulton.

Davies, D. and Ward, S. (2003) 'Young children as scientists, designers and technologists', in D. Davies and A. Howe (eds), *Teaching Science and Design and Technology in the Early Years*. London: David Fulton. pp. 10–24.

DCSF (Department for Children, Schools and Families) (2008) *The Early Years Foundation Stage: Setting the standards for Learning, Development and Care for Children from Birth to Five,* Nottingham: DCSF Publications. (Comprises the *Statutory Framework, Practice Guidance*, Cards and other resources.)

De Boo, M. (2000) Science 3–6: *Laying the Foundations in the Early Years*. Hatfield: ASE.

Desforges, C. and Abouchaar, A. (2003) *The Impact of Parental Involvement, Parental Support and Family Education on Pupil Achievement and Adjustment: A Literature Review*. Research Report No. RR 433. Norwich: HMSO.

DfES (Department for Education and Skills) (2005) *The Common Core of Skills and Knowledge*. Nottingham: DfES Publications.

DFES (Department for Education and Skills) (2007) *The Early Years Foundation Stage*. Nottingham: DfES Publications.

Feasey, R. and Gallear, B. (2001) *Primary Science and ICT*. Hatfield: ASE.

Fisher, J. (2002) *Starting from the Child: Teaching and Learning from 3 to 8,* 2nd edn. Maidenhead: Open University Press.

Goswami, U. and Bryant, P. (2007) *Children's Cognitive Development and Learning* (Primary Review Research Survey 2/1a). Cambridge: University of Cambridge Faculty of Education.

Harlen, W. (2003) *The Teaching of Science in Primary School*, 3rd edn. London: David Fulton.

Hayes, M. (2006) 'What do the children have to say?', in M. Hayes and D. Whitebread (eds), *ICT in the Early Years*. Maidenhead: Open University Press.

Jones, C. (2004) *Supporting Inclusion in the Early Years*. Maidenhead: Open University Press.

Kennewell, S. and Beauchamp, G. (2007) 'The features of interactive whiteboards and their influence on learning', *Learning, Media and Technology,* 32 (3): 227–41.

Moyles, J. (1989) *Just Playing? The Role and Status of Play in Early Childhood Education*. Milton Keynes: Open University Press.

Myhill, D., Jones, S. and Hopper, R. (2006) *Talking, Listening, Learning: Effective Talk in the Primary Classroom*. Maidenhead: Open University Press.

O'Hara, M. (2008) 'Young children, learning and ICT: a case study in the UK maintained sector', *Technology, Pedagogy and Education,* 17 (1): 29–40.

Palmer, J. and Birch, J. (2004) *Geography in the Early Years,* 2nd edn. London: Routledge Falmer.

Siraj-Blatchford, I., Sylva, K., Muttock, S., Gilden, R. and Bell, D. (2002) *Researching Effective Pedagogy in the Early Years*. Research Report No. RR 356. Norwich: HMSO.

Smeaton, M. (2001) 'Questioning geography', in R. Carter (ed.), *Handbook of Primary Geography*. Sheffield: Geographical Association. pp. 15–17.

Turner-Bisset, R. (2005) *Creative Teaching: History in the Primary Classroom*. London: David Fulton.

Chapter 13   Physical Development

Almond, L. (2000) 'Physical education and primary schools', in P.R. Bailey and T.M. Macfadyen (eds), *Teaching Physical Education 5–11*. London: Continuum.

Bailey, P.R. (1999) 'Play, health and physical development', in T. David (ed.), *Young Children Learning*. London: Paul Chapman Publishing.

Baur, L.A. (2002) 'Child and adolescent obesity in the 21st century: an Australian perspective', *Asia Pacific Journal of Clinical Nutrition*, 11: 524–8.

Biddle, S., Cavill, N. and Sallis, J. (1998) 'Policy framework for young people and health-enhancing physical activity', in S. Biddle, J. Sallis and N. Cavill (eds), *Young and Active? Young People and Health Enhancing Physical Activity: Evidence and Implications*. London: Health Education Authority.

Bilton, H. (2003) *Outdoor Play in the Early Years*, 2nd edn. London: David Fulton.

Bruner, J. (1983) *Child's Talk: Learning to Use Language*. Oxford: Oxford University Press.

Chugani, H.T. (1997) Neuroimaging of developmental nonlinearity and developmental pathologies, in R.W. Thatcher, G.R. Lyon, R. Rumsey and N. Krasnegor (eds), *Developmental Neuroimaging: Mapping the Development of Brain and Behaviour*, San Diego, CA: Academic Press.

Dennis, W. (1960) 'The effects of cradling practices upon the onset of walking in Hopi children', in *Journal of Genetic Psychology*, 56, 77–86.

DCSF (Department for Children, Schools and Families) (2008) *The Early Years Foundation Stage*: *Setting the Standards for Learning, Development and Care for Children from Birth to Five*. Nottingham: DCSF Publications. (Comprises the *Statutory Framework, Practice Guidance*, Cards and other resources)

Doherty, J. and Bailey, R. (2003) *Supporting Physical Development and Physical Education in the Early Years*, Buckingham: Open University Press.

Gandini, L. (1997) 'The Reggio Emilia story: history and organization', in J. Hendrick (ed.), *First Steps Towards Teaching the Reggio Emilia Way*. Englewood Cliffs, NJ: Merrill/Prentice Hill.

Gunnar, M.R. (2001) *Quality of Care and Buffering Stress Psychology: Its Potential for Protecting the Developing Human Brain*. Minneapolis: University of Minnesota Institute of Child Development.

Hale, J. (1994) *Unbank the Fire: Visions for the Education of African American Children*. Baltimore: Johns Hopkins University Press.

Hardman, A. and Stensel, D. (2003) *Physical Activity and Health*, London: Routledge

Harwood, R.L., Miller, J.G. and Irizarry, N.L. (1995) *Culture and Attachment: Perceptions of the Child in Context*, New York: Gilford Press.

Hertsgaard, L., Gunnar, M., Erickson, M.F. and Nachmias, M. (1995) 'Adrenocortical responses to the strange situation in infants with disorganized, disoriented attachment relationships', in *Child Development*, 66, 1100–6.

Hopkins, B. and Westra, T. (1998) 'Maternal handling and motor development: an intra-cultural study', in *Genetic, Social and General Psychology Monographs*, 14, 377–420.

Hopper, B., Grey, J. and Maude, T. (2000) *Teaching Physical Education in the Primary School*, London: Routledge Falmer.

Kimm, S.Y.S., Glynn, N.W, Barton, B.A., Kronsberg, S.S., Daniels, S.R., Crawford, P.B., Sabry, Z.I. and Liu, K. (2002) 'Decline in physical activity in black girls and white girls during adolescence', in *New England Journal of Medicine*, 347: 709–15.

Levine, R.A. (1996) *Child Care and Culture Lessons from Africa*, Cambridge: Cambridge University Press.

Ministry of Education (1996) *Te Whāriki. He Whāriki Matauranga mo nga Mokopuna O Aotearoa. Early Childhood Education*, Learning Media, http://www.minedu.govt.nz/web/downloadable/dl3567_v1/whariki.pdf (accessed December 08)

Nachmias, M., Gunnar, M., Mangelsdorf, S., Parritz, R.H. and Buss, K. (1996) 'Behavioral inhabitation and stress reactivity: the moderating role of attachment security', in *Child Development*, 67, 508–22.

Nutbeam, D. (1998) 'Evaluating health promotion – progress, problems and solutions', *Health Promotion International*, 13, 27–43.

Parry, J. (1998) 'The justification for physical education', in K. Green and K. Hardman (eds) *Physical Education: a reader*, Aachen: Meyer and Meyer.

Prentice, A.M. and Jebb, S.A. (1995) 'Obesity in Britain: gluttony or sloth?' in *British Medical Journal*, 311, 437–9.

Shore, N. (1997) *Rethinking the Brain: New Insights into Early Development*, New York: Families and Work Institute.

Super, C.M. (1981) 'Behavioural development in infancy', in R.H., Monroe, R.L., Monroe and B.B., Whiting (eds) *Handbook of Cross Cultural Human Development*, New York: Garland.

Talbot, M. (1999) 'The case for physical education.' Paper presented at the world Summit on Physical Education, Berlin: November 1999.

Whitehead, M. (2000) 'The concept of physical literacy'. Paper presented to The HEI Conference, 'Meeting Standards and Achieving Excellence. Teaching PE in the 21 Century' Liverpool John Moores University, 11 June 2000.

World Health Organisation (1999) Health Promotion, Active Living: The Challenge Ahead, www.who.int (accessed September 2008)

Chapter 14   Creative Development

Craft, A. (2002) *Creativity and Early Years Education: A Lifewide Foundation*. London and New York: Continuum.

Cutler, A. (2005) *Signposting Creative Learning*. Kent: Creative Partnerships Kent.

Daniels, H. (2001) *Vygotsky and Pedagogy*. London: RoutledgeFalmer.

Gadamer, H.G. (1975) *Truth and Method*. New York: Seabury.

Okri, B. (1997) 'Newton's Child', in *A Way of Being Free*. London: Phoenix.

Robinson, K. (1999) *All Our Futures: Creativity, Culture and Education*. London: National Advisory Committee on Creative and Cultural Education.

Siraj-Blatchford, I., Muttock, S., Sylva, K., Gilden, R. and Bell, D. (2003) *Researching Effective Pedagogy in the Early Years*. Research Report No. RR356. Norwich: HMSO.

Stern, D. (1985) *The Interpersonal World of the Infant*. New York: Basic Books.

Sternberg, R.J., Kaufman, J.C. and Pretz, J.E. (2004) 'A propulsion model of creative leadership', *Creativity and Innovation Management*, 13 (3): 145–53.

Trevarthen, C. (1993) 'The self born in intersubjectivity: the psychology of an infant communicating', in U. Neisser (ed.), *The Perceived Self*. Cambridge: Cambridge University Press.

Vygotsky, L.S. (1978) *Mind in Society: The Development of Higher Psychological Processes*. Cambridge, MA: Harvard University Press.

Woolf, F. and Belloli, J. (2005) *Reflect and Review: The Arts and Creativity in Early Years*. London: Arts Council of England.

Wright, B. (2001–02) 'Review of D. Trotter, *Cooking with Mud: The Idea of Mess in Nineteenth-Century Art and Fiction*. Oxford: Oxford University Press [2000]'. *Nineteenth-Century French Studies*, 30 (1 & 2): 179–82.

INDEX

Note: the letter 'f' after a page number refers to a figure; the letter 't' refers to a table.